'This is a thoughtful and very well balanced monograph in the area of accountability and legitimacy in the European Union. Overall, the book provides a timely evaluation and offers a much needed conceptual understanding with regards to the ongoing debate of the EU's accountability deficit.'

Professor Steve Peers, University of Essex

The Accountability Gap in EU Law

Almost two decades ago, the fall of the Santer Commission against a background of allegations of maladministration and nepotism had the effect of placing accountability on the political agenda of the EU institutions. More recently, the non-ratification of the Constitutional Treaty, the difficulties in the ratification of the Lisbon Treaty and the current financial crisis have increased the calls for accountability in the EU.

This book investigates whether any progress towards more accountability and transparency has been made in the post-Lisbon era by taking a holistic approach to the subject. Marios Costa argues that currently the EU institutions and the Member States are not in a position to hold the so-called independent agencies as well as the various committees and expert groups accountable. Despite recent progress, the EU still needs to put forward an acceptable constitutional framework which will truly secure accountability at the EU level of governance.

Marios Costa is a Senior lecturer at City, University of London, UK.

Routledge Research in Constitutional Law

This series features thought-provoking and original scholarship on constitutional law and theory. Books explore key topics, themes and questions in the field with a particular emphasis on comparative studies. Where relevant, titles will engage with political and social theory, philosophy and history in order to offer a rounded analysis of constitutions and constitutional law.

Series Editor: David Marrani

Available titles in this series include:

Constitutionalism in the Global Realm
A Sociological Approach
Poul F. Kjaer

The Legal Philosophy and Influence of Jeremy Bentham
Essays on 'Of the Limits of the Penal Branch of Jurisprudence'
Edited by Guillaume Tusseau

The Internet and Constitutional Law
The Protection of Fundamental Rights and Constitutional Adjudication in Europe
Edited by Oreste Pollicino and Graziella Romeo

Forthcoming titles in this series include:

Equal Citizenship, Civil Rights, and the Constitution
The Original Sense of the Privileges or Immunities Clause
Christopher R. Green

Constitution-making and Human Rights in the Sudans
Edited by Mohamed Abdelsalam and Lutz Oette

The Accountability Gap in EU Law

Marios Costa

Routledge
Taylor & Francis Group
LONDON AND NEW YORK

First published 2017 by Routledge

2 Park Square, Milton Park, Abingdon, Oxfordshire OX14 4RN
52 Vanderbilt Avenue, New York, NY 10017

Routledge is an imprint of the Taylor & Francis Group, an informa business

First issued in paperback 2020

British Library Cataloguing in Publication Data
A catalogue record for this book is available from the British Library

Library of Congress Cataloging in Publication Data
Names: Costa, Marios, author.
Title: The accountability gap in EU law/Marios Costa.
Description: Abingdon, Oxon; New York, NY: Routledge, 2017. |
Series: Routledge research in constitutional law | Includes bibliographical references and index.
Identifiers: LCCN 2016012050| ISBN 9781138939318 (hbk) |
ISBN 9781315675077 (ebk)
Subjects: LCSH: Administrative law—European Union countries. |
Transparency in government—Law and legislation—European Union countries. | Government accountability—European Union countries. |
Judicial review of administrative acts—European Union countries.
Classification: LCC KJE5602.C67 2017 | DDC 342.24/06—dc23
LC record available at http://lccn.loc.gov/2016012050

ISBN: 978-1-138-93931-8 (hbk)
ISBN: 978-0-367-59594-4 (pbk)

Typeset in Galliard
by Swales & Willis, Exeter, Devon, UK

Contents

List of abbreviations

ABM	Activity-Based Management
ACER	Agency for the Cooperation of Energy Regulators
BEREC	Body of European Regulators for Electronic Communications
CdT	Translation Centre for the Bodies of the European Union
CEDEFOP	European Centre for the Development of Vocational Training
CEPOL	European Police College
CFCA	Community Fisheries Control Agency
CFI	Court of First Instance
CFSP	Common Foreign and Security Policy
CIE	Committee of Independent Experts
CJEU	Court of Justice of the European Union
CPVO	Community Plant Variety Office
DG	Directorate-General
EAR	European Agency for Reconstruction
EASA	European Aviation Safety Agency
EASO	European Asylum Support Office
EBA	European Banking Authority
EC	European Community
ECDC	European Centre for Disease Prevention and Control
ECHA	European Chemicals Agency
ECHR	European Convention on Human Rights
ECSC	European Coal and Steal Community
EDA	European Defence Agency
EEA	European Environment Agency
EEC	European Economic Community
EFSA	European Food Safety Authority
EFT	European Training Foundation
EIGE	European Institute for Gender Equality
EIOPA	European Insurance and Occupational Pensions Authority
EMCDDA	European Monitoring Centre for Drugs and Drug Addiction
EMA	European Medicines Agency
EMSA	European Maritime Safety Agency
ENISA	European Network and Information Security

EP	European Parliament
ERA	European Railway Agency
ESAs	European Supervisory Authorities
ESMA	European Securities and Markets Authority
ETF	European Training Foundation
ETI	European Transparency Initiative
EU	European Union
EU-LISA	Agency for the operational management of large-scale IT systems in the area of freedom, security and justice
EUMC	European Monitoring Centre for Racism and Xenophobia
EU-OSHA	European Agency for Safety and Health at Work
EUROFOUND	European Foundation for the Improvement of Living and Working Conditions
EUROJUST	European Union's Judicial Cooperation Unit
EUROPOL	European Police Office
EUSC	European Union Satellite Centre
FRA	European Union Agency for Fundamental Rights
FRONTEX	European Agency for the Management of Operational Cooperation at the External Frontiers
GC	General Court
GSA	European GNSS Supervisory Authority
ISS	European Union Institute for Security Studies
JHA	Justice and Home Affairs
JRC	Joint Research Centre
MEPs	Members of the European Parliament
NGO	Non-governmental Organisation
OHIM	Office for Harmonization in the Internal Market
OJ	Official Journal of the European Union
OLAF	European Anti-fraud Office
OMC	Open Method of Coordination
RPS	Regulatory Procedure with Scrutiny
TEU	Treaty on the European Union
TFEU	Treaty on the Functioning of the European Union

Table of cases

The number in brackets following the page number refers to the note number.

European Ombudsman

Court of Justice/General Court

Case C-506/08 P, *Sweden* v. *Commission and MyTravel Group plc. (MyTravel)* [2011] ECR I-6237 56(n195), 59(n209)
Case C-52/05 P, *Sweden and Turco* v. *Council* [2008] ECR I-4723, Opinion of Advocate-General Leger 59(n211)
Case C-550/07 P, *Akzo Nobel Chemicals and Akcros Chemicals* v. *Commission and Others* [2008] ECR I-2649 59(208)
Case C-58/94, *Netherlands* v. *Council* [1996] ECR I-2169 28(n33)
Case C-583/11 P, *Inuit Tapiriit Kanatami and Others* v. *European Parliament and Council of the European Union* [2013] ECLI:EU:C:2013:625 105(n36)
Case C-64/05 P, *Sweden* v. *Commission* [2007] ECR I-11389 49(n146), 50(n151), 53(n170, 176 and 179), 54(n180)
Case C-64/05 P, *Kingdom of Sweden* v. *Commission of the European Communities and Others* [2007] ECR I-11389, Opinion of Advocate-General Maduro 26(n14), 43(n117), 53(n172)
Case T-105/95, *World Wildlife Fund (WWF)* v. *Commission* [1997] ECR II-313 28(n27 and 31), 29(n38), 30(n40 and 45), 31(n51)
Case T-111/00, *British American Tobacco* v. *Commission* [2001] ECR II-2997 84(n48)
Case T-121/05, *Borax* v. *Commission* [2009] ECR II-27 36(n80), 39(n91), 58(n206), 85(n50)
Case T-123/00, *Dr Karl Thomae GmbH* v. *Commission* [2002] ECR II-5193 69(n49)
Case T-124/96, *Interporc (I)* v. *Commission* [1998] ECR II-231 30(n45 and 46)
Case T-13/99, *Pfizer Animal Health SA* v. *Council* [2002] ECR-II 3303 71(n61)
Case T-135/96, *UEAPME* v. *Council* [1998] ECR II-2335 103(n25), 107(n45)
Case T-14/98, *Hautala* v. *Council* [1999] ECR II-2489 31(n49),32(n54), 36(n79), 38(n84), 39(n90),40(n94 and 95),
Case T-144/05, *Muniz* v. *Commission* [2008] ECR II-335 85(n49)
Case T-168/02, *IFAW Internationaler Tierschutz-Fonts Gmbh* v. *Commission* [2004] ECR II-4135 50(n148), 52(n164, 166 and 168), 53(n178)
Case T-174/95, *Svenska Journalistforbundet* v. *Council* [1998] ECR II-2289 30(n39 and 45), 31(n51), 34(n64)
Case T-177/01, *Jégo-Quéré et Cie SA* v. *Commission* [2001] ECR II-2365 97(n2), 104(n28), 105(n33)
Case T-18/10, *Inuit Tapiriit Kanatami and Others* v. *European Parliament and Council of the European Union* [2011] ECR II-5599 97(n1), 100(n7), 105(n33 and 38), 108(n49), 110(n63 and 65)
Case T-187/03, *Isabella Scippacercola* v. *Commission* [2005] ECR II-1029 50(n147 and 148), 51(n156,157 and 160), 52(n165)
Case T-187/99, *Agrana Zucker und Stärke* v. *Commission* [2001] ECR II-1587 26(n15)
Case T-188/12, *Patrick Breyer* v. *Commission* [2015] ECLI:EU:T:2015:124 56(n196)
Case T-188/97, *Rothmans* v. *Commission* [1999] ECR II-2463 33(n59 and 60), 84(n45)
Case T-188/98, *Kuijer* v. *Council* [2000] ECR II-1959 31(n49), 32(n54)

Table of European Union documents

Acknowledgments

There are many people who, directly or indirectly, have contributed to this research. Without their mostly enthusiastic support, the writing of this book would not have been possible. In particular, I would like to thank Professor Steve Peers from the School of Law, University of Essex for the inspiration as well as the guidance given to me while I was researching for my doctorate degree under his supervision. Steve's limitless ability to read the draft chapters of this book and provide me with constructive and effective comments throughout the journey that led to the publication of this monograph, is much appreciated. I simply cannot thank Steve enough.

I would also like to thank my current employer, City, University of London, and all my colleagues at the City Law School for their understanding during the composition of this monograph. Part of this book was written during my visiting fellowship at the Centre for European Legal Studies (CELS), University of Cambridge in autumn 2014. Therefore, special thanks go to CELS for the feedback, hospitality and support. Finally, warmest thanks go to my partner, Omiros, for always being by my side as well as for his invaluable encouragement. This book is dedicated to him.

Introduction

Accountability in the European Union (EU) is a massive subject that touches upon our daily lives. We have all, as ordinary citizens, experienced the fall of the Santer Commission in 1999 against a background of allegations of fraud, maladministration and chronic mismanagement as well as the effect of that legitimacy crisis upon the political agenda of the EU institutions. We have all, also, witnessed the background of the difficulties with regards to the ratification of the Maastricht and Nice Treaties. More recently, the non-ratification of the Constitutional Treaty and the number of difficulties in relation to the ratification of the Lisbon Treaty have reopened Pandora's Box and re-emphasised the level of dissatisfaction in the EU. In essence, the ratification problems that we have encountered through the years highlight rather consistently that EU citizens are deeply concerned about the status of accountability and legitimacy in the EU, which comes across as too technical and complex, and no more so than at present. Currently, the financial crisis and the way the EU is responding to it are raising the level of euro-scepticism unprecedentedly. In effect, the imposition of austerity measures to a number of EU countries questions the *raison d'être* of the EU to increase economic prosperity. In this regard, the Italian Prime Minister, Matteo Renzi, compared the current status of the EU with the orchestra playing continuously during the sinking of the Titanic.

With these considerations in mind, I aim with this monograph to contribute to the on-going debate about accountability and legitimacy in the EU. In doing so, I explore further the concept of accountability and the way it affects our lives. Therefore, in the introductory chapter, I explain the meaning or rather the non-single meaning of accountability by collating the various contributions that have been made in the legal as well as political literatures. The purpose of this exercise is threefold: to identify its origins, to understand fully the concept of accountability and third, to focus upon the core meaning of accountability. Providing a common understanding and demonstrating what accountability means are rather crucial stages that will help to identify whether the Union suffers from any accountability deficits. This exercise in definition is not as straightforward as it seems and is in fact more problematic than might at first be supposed. Hence, an explanation is given in order to understand what is, and what is not, meant by the concept of accountability while attempting to build an appropriate foundation which will be used as the essential tool for the analysis in the following chapters.

Chapter 2 focuses on the status of accountability within the European Commission. The European Commission has long been criticised for its administrative inadequacies and for the structural deficiencies in the Union's system of accountability. There have been a number of reports depicting the Commission as an institution suffering from structural and political irregularities. In the well-known *Cresson* judgment, the Court of Justice examined the legal aspect of the *en bloc* resignation of the Santer Commission. It was held that Mrs. E. Cresson had acted in breach of her Treaty obligations as a European Commissioner. The long-lasting constitutional implications of this ruling are examined since the finding of breach was seen by the Court as a sufficient penalty and no further sanction was imposed. The Commissioners' responsibility in the light of this judgment and the Commission's resignation are examined to assess whether the Commissioners retain a high level of accountability. The chapter concludes that the Court of Justice lost a unique opportunity to clarify which obligations are incumbent on members of the Commission within the meaning of ex Article 213(2) of the European Community Treaty, post Lisbon Article 245 of the Treaty on the Functioning of the European Union (TFEU).

Chapter 2 also focuses on the *Dalli* case: the latest case of the General Court (GC), currently under appeal before the Court of Justice, which is closely related to the topic of accountability within the Commission. *Dalli* shows that the resignation of the Santer Commission in 1999 against a background of allegations of fraud, maladministration and chronic mismanagement is still topical, almost two decades on. On 11 May 2015, the GC gave a significant judgment on a legal challenge brought by the former EU Health Commissioner, Mr John Dalli, against the Commission. Dalli argued that he was forced to resign, by the then President of the Commission, Jose Manuel Barroso, without being given enough time to consider his legal rights. Rather paradoxically, the GC ruled that Mr Dalli resigned voluntarily and dismissed the action as inadmissible.

Nevertheless, the *Dalli* judgment raises broader constitutional implications. With all due respect, the ruling comes as a surprise and fails to clarify issues in relation to the powers that can be lawfully exercised by the President of the Commission when he loses confidence in any of the members of his Commission. The final part of Chapter 2 examines the appropriateness of the recent ruling and concludes that the GC lost for a second time a rather rare opportunity to rule on significant aspects of the Treaty powers granted upon the President of the Commission to sack the individual Commissioners and as a result also fails to remedy the accountability deficits of the Commission.

Chapter 3 examines the regime of freedom of information and access to documents in the EU. We shall see that an essential prerequisite of the accountability relationship is to have the relevant information available so that the accountability *forum* can hold the *actor* to account. Therefore, I aim to explore a significant but simultaneously very difficult question regarding openness and transparency in the EU: How far and open can the Union's decision-making be? The chapter starts with the innovations introduced by the Maastricht Treaty, focusing on the major developments which attempted to establish a right of the general public to request and have access to information. The Code of conduct of access to EU documents, introduced in 1993, is also examined. In addition, the developments introduced by Regulation 1049/2001 on access to documents of the European Parliament (EP), the Council and the Commission are explained. A significant part of the analysis is to investigate the way in which the jurisprudence of the EU Courts has been developed over the years to ensure, as the Courts claim, openness, accountability and legitimacy of the EU's institutions and to contribute to the development of a Union which supposedly belongs, pursuant to the founding Treaties, to EU citizens.

A detailed investigation of all the above-mentioned developments reveals that access to documents in the EU has been increased to a considerable extent, especially when one compares the current situation to the pre-1992 position, when secrecy was the norm. The chapter concludes by focusing on how the alternative system should be in order to ensure accountability in the EU.

The analysis on accountability deficits within the EU would not have been comprehensive without examining the case of agencies established and active at the EU level of governance. Thus, Chapter 4 is entrusted with the task of assessing legally the accountability regime within which agencies operate. With this in mind, the chapter first seeks to set out the agencies' regime and its inherent problems while, second, attempting to explore whether the Union's key institutions and main delegators, the Commission, the Council and the EP, supervise agencies' acts, exercise sufficient control and ultimately accept accountability for the implementation of tasks entrusted to the agencies. It will be seen that EU agencies suffer from fundamental accountability problems.

Chapter 5 assesses the accountability regime of delegated and Implementing Acts, pre-Lisbon, known as the comitology regime. This chapter investigates whether the newly introduced procedures by the Lisbon Treaty are sufficient to remedy accountability deficits as regards Implementing Acts. More specifically, as far as accountability to the Council and the Member States is concerned, the chapter examines whether the Implementing Acts process enhances their accountability and concludes that control powers of the Council and the Member States have not been extended, but remain the same.

In addition, the new delegated acts procedure introduced by the Treaty of Lisbon grants the EP more control powers, which effectively increases democratic control over this new category of non-legislative measures. From the EP's perspective, the new delegated acts procedure enhances accountability of EU decision-making as a whole, when compared to the situation prior to the Treaty of Lisbon. However, the chapter concludes that this political gain of the EP has not been accompanied, as one would have expected, by an increase in accountability to the public by imposing firmer obligations on the Commission to enhance the previous transparency standards.

Finally, Chapter 6 deals with the various deficits in the field of access to justice, another form of accountability and an aspect of the rule of law, which I term 'legal accountability'. In the light of the Court of Justice's restrictive jurisprudence on the rules on the standing of private parties seeking judicial review, this chapter seeks to examine the appropriateness of the preliminary reference procedure as an alternative route for private parties seeking to challenge the validity of EU measures. Although the position of private parties is better than the one usually presented by the relevant literature, there are still gaps in judicial protection. It is argued that post Lisbon, some of these gaps in judicial protection have now been mitigated. In particular, the insertion of the term 'regulatory act' as a third possibility of bringing proceedings has the potential to mitigate the gaps in relation to the *locus standi* of private plaintiffs, subject to acceptable interpretation by the judiciary. Unfortunately, the latest tendency of the Court does not mitigate the gaps with regards to private litigants trying to have access to the Court of Justice of the European Union (CJEU).

Overall, it can be safely argued that the current state of play in relation to the issue of accountability in the EU, though necessarily confined to the issues examined, is that progress has been made. Having said that, it is essential that the EU institutions address the current level of dissatisfaction from which the EU is now widely believed to suffer. In the eyes of the citizens, the EU will be accountable and legitimate when the level of dissatisfaction is significantly reduced and equally when the financial crisis is over. Similarly, the average citizen will consider that the EU is less complex and opaque when the level of economic prosperity is raised again and when the austerity measures are over.

The law is stated as at 30 December 2015.

1 Introduction and preliminary remarks

European Union accountability

This book examines the accountability regime of the EU from a constitutional perspective. In this context, the need for accountability is augmented by the 'democratic deficit': members of the EU institutions, offices, bodies and agencies – with the notable exception of the European Parliament (EP) – are not elected directly by the people and can be removed from their positions only in the most extreme circumstances. While accountability within the EU context is a principle of innovative governance, the question that needs to be answered here is whether the EU is accountable.

Assessing the current state of accountability within the EU, along with examining alternatives on how to mitigate any potential deficit(s), presupposes a clear understanding of the meaning of accountability. This chapter, therefore, examines the various contributions that have been made in relation to the meaning of accountability. The aim is to provide a common understanding and/or definition. This exercise in definition is not as straightforward as it seems and is in fact more problematical than might at first be supposed. Hence, an explanation is given in order to understand what is, and what is not, meant by the concept of accountability, while attempting to build the appropriate foundation which will be used as an essential tool for the analysis in the following chapters. The chapter begins by explaining the meaning or rather the non-meaning of the term. Second, it analyses the reasons why more accountability is being called for in the EU. Finally, the chapter examines the requirements of accountability with particular reference to the present level of accountability and transparency in the EU.

Defining accountability: explanation of the term

Accountability is an important yet elusive concept that has different meanings, and its characteristics differ depending upon the context. It is a broad concept that reflects a variety of understandings rather than a single paradigm[1] and, in fact, in the literature there seem to be as many definitions of accountability as

1 D Curtin and A Nollkaemper, 'Conceptualizing accountability in international and European law' (2005) 3 *Netherlands Yearbook of International Law*, p. 36.

there are scholars.[2] From a legal point of view, there is no core statutory definition. Consequently, anyone studying accountability will soon discover that this is a term that no one can be against; this is because it can mean different things to different people, and as such, the meaning of accountability can change to cover a variety of processes and purposes. The relevant literature identifies distinct types of accountability such as legal, democratic, financial, political, administrative and electoral.[3] Also, commentators suggest that accountability can be internal, external, horizontal or vertical, formal or informal.[4] Overall, the emphasis herein is on the origins as well as the core meaning of accountability.

Accountability is a term frequently used in EU documents: 'we live in the age of accountability, wherever one looks there is a discussion and debate over accountability';[5] the word 'crops up everywhere, performing all manner of analytical and rhetorical tasks and carrying most of the burdens of democratic 'governance'.[6] The importance of accountability is highlighted in relation to almost every issue, from the provision of public services[7] and criminal justice[8] to transnational governance regimes.[9] Indeed, accountability is now considered to be an essential feature, if not the most important feature, of any system of governance in which the exercise of public power has been extended beyond the boundaries of the nation state, because of the desire to ensure the legitimacy of such modes of governance. The reason for this is the existence of 'a common assumption that accountability is an autonomous and neutral feature of any governing system, national or transnational'.[10]

In the context of the EU, the need for accountability is augmented by the obvious 'democratic deficit', as it has been argued that the EU suffers from serious accountability deficits:[11] as already stated above, members of the EU institutions, offices, bodies and agencies are not elected by the people[12] and can be thrown

2 G Brandsma, 'Accountability deficits in European "comitology"' (2011) Decision-making 11 European Integration Online Papers.

3 D Oliver, *Government in the United Kingdom: The Search for Accountability, Effectiveness and Citizenship* (Open University Press 1991).

4 C Scott, 'Accountability in the regulatory state' (2000) 27 *Journal of Legal Studies*, p. 38.

5 E Fisher, 'The EU in the age of accountability' (2004) 24 *Oxford of Journal Legal Studies*, p. 495.

6 R Mulgan, 'Accountability: An ever-expanding concept?' (2000) 78 *Public Administration*, p. 555.

7 A Davies, *Accountability: A Public Law Analysis of Government by Contract* (Oxford University Press 2001).

8 D Roche, *Accountability in Restorative Justice* (Oxford University Press 2003).

9 AM Slaughter, 'The accountability of government networks' (2001) 8 *Indiana Journal of Global Legal Studies*, p. 347.

10 *See* Fisher, op. cit. n 5 *supra*, p. 496.

11 M Bovens, D Curtin and P Hart, *The Real World of EU Accountability, What Deficit?* (Oxford University Press 2010); *See also* A Arnull, *Introduction: The EU's Accountability and Legitimacy Deficit* (Oxford University Press 2002).

12 Although Members of the Council and the European Council have a national democratic mandate, they lack democratic legitimacy because they are seen as very complex to the ordinary citizen who cannot hold them accountable because of their opaque method of operating.

out only in the most extreme circumstances. While accountability within the EU context is often characterised as the principle for an era of innovative governance, a common statement by many commentators is that the EU is not accountable enough and that accountability deficits are said to exist and are even growing, compromising the legitimacy of the EU.[13] EU institutions, bodies, offices and agencies are perceived to not be subjected to adequate accountability processes, and this threatens the EU's legitimacy. The obvious solution to this is to create mechanisms for accountability that hold decision-makers to account and thus contribute to the robustness of the EU governance system. Others of course may very well disagree with this statement. Indeed, there is this argument that the debate about the EU's democratic deficit is exaggerated due to the fact that the general public is not very concerned about the activities of the EU and, second, because of the fact that even if the EU had not been invented, the Member States themselves would have engaged in international agreements which by definition would be less transparent and less accountable rather than the current state of play in the EU.[14] On the other hand, these arguments are not very persuasive if one takes into account the core meaning of accountability, which requires that the public knows how it is governed.[15] At the same time, there is a strong need for the public to find out about how public money is spent and to receive assurances that it has been well spent.[16] All of this sounds quite straightforward. The executive of any public organisation has in its possession the taxpayers' money; it has the right and the obligation to use it wisely. It must be held accountable for doing so, otherwise it must face the consequences.[17]

But where did accountability come from?

Historically, accountability is closely related to 'to account' in its literal sense of bookkeeping.[18] Its origins can be found in an English idea emerging in the decades following the 1066 Norman Conquest and more specifically from William I's efforts to establish and legitimise his rule over England through the end of Henry II's reign (1189).[19] All property holders at the time were required to 'render a count' of what they possessed in the terms set out by the King's agents. This term, however, has arrived in the literature, and particularly

13 *See* Arnull, op. cit. n 11 *supra*, p. 1.

14 P Craig, 'Integration, democracy and legitimacy', in P Craig and G De Burca (eds), *The Evolution of EU Law* (2nd edn, Oxford University Press 2011).

15 D Osborne and T Gaebler, *Reinventing Government: How the Entrepreneurial Spirit is Transforming the Public Sector* (Plume 1992).

16 M Power, *The Audit Society, Rituals of Verification* (Oxford University Press 1997).

17 R Behn, *Rethinking Democratic Accountability* (Brooking Institution Press 2001).

18 E Normanton, *The Accountability and Audit of Governments: A Comparative Study* (Manchester University Press 1996).

19 M Dubnick, 'Seeking salvation for accountability' (2002), Paper presented at the annual meeting of the American Political Science Association, Boston Marriott Copley Place, Sheraton Boston & Hynes Convention Centre, Boston, MA.

into the legal research, quite recently and was not in common use outside the financial contexts of accountancy and auditing.[20] The reason for this appears to be that 'accountability is not a term for art for lawyers',[21] something which is also exaggerated by the fact that there is no core statutory definition. Rather, lawyers rely on the classical vocabulary of the rule of law, liberty, democracy and respect for fundamental rights and freedoms. Indeed, it is the rule of law that forms part of the constitutional law vocabulary, not the concept of accountability per se.

The legal aspect of accountability

In the contemporary literature, the term 'has come to stand as a general term of any mechanism that makes powerful institutions responsive to their particular publics'.[22] While citizens delegate power to their representatives, they have reasons to hold them accountable. '[A]ccountability is a factor in legitimacy and one that begins to run neck and neck with representation'.[23] Accountability is meant to keep a democratic check upon the actions of those exercising public power to ensure that the preferences of the voters are translated into policy. It also ensures that the terms on which political power is authorised are duly observed. It refers to the fact that decision-makers do not enjoy unlimited autonomy, but have to explain and justify their actions.[24] There is, therefore, 'an unquestionable thirst for accountability that cuts across the political spectrum'.[25] Where public policy does not correspond to the ultimate preferences of the people, accountability mechanisms come into effect.

In a concrete sense, there is a strong need for the public to know how public money is spent and to receive assurances that it has been well spent.[26] This relates to the public interest in knowing how it is governed.[27] The executive of any public organisation has in its possession the taxpayers' money. With the right to use that money on behalf of the public comes the obligation to use it wisely. The executive must therefore be held accountable for doing so, and face the consequences if it does not.[28]

20 *See* Davies, op. cit. n 7 *supra*.

21 C Harlow, 'European governance and accountability', in N Bamforth and P Leyland (eds), *Public Law in a Multi-layered Constitution* (Hart 2003), p. 79.

22 R Mulgan, *Holding Power to Account: Accountability in Modern Democracies* (Palgrave Macmillan 2003), p. 8.

23 A Benz, Y Papadopoulos and C Harlow, 'Special Issue: Accountability in EU multilevel governance' (2007) 13 *European Law Journal*, pp. 441–442.

24 C Lord, *Democracy in the European Union* (Sheffield Academic Press 1998).

25 M Moore and M Gates, *Inspectors-General: Junkyard Dogs or Man's Best Friend?* (Russel Sage Foundation 1986), p. 1.

26 M Power, *The Audit Society, Rituals of Verification* (Oxford University Press 1997).

27 D Osborne and T Gaebler, *Reinventing Government: How the Entrepreneurial Spirit is Transforming the Public Sector* (Plume 1992).

28 R Behn, *Rethinking Democratic Accountability* (Brooking Institution Press 2001).

A suitable definition of the term is provided by Bovens. Accountability is a 'relationship between an actor and a forum, in which the actor has an obligation to explain and to justify his or her conduct, the forum can pose questions and pass judgment, and the actor may face consequences'.[29] In other words, 'A is accountable to B when A is obliged to inform B about A's (past or future) actions and decisions, to justify them, and to suffer punishment in the case of eventual misconduct'.[30]

In its fundamental sense, therefore, accountability means being answerable for one's actions to some authority and, if necessary, having to suffer sanctions for actions not in accordance with the mandate granted by that authority. In concrete terms, this form of accountability can be broken down into four major elements: the setting of standards, the obtaining of an account, the judging of such an account and a decision about the consequences that arise from such a judgment.[31]

Requirements of accountability

The first feature of accountability is that there must be at least two different persons or bodies in an external relationship, in the sense that the account must be given to some other body or person outside the person or body being held accountable (the forum). Also, there needs to be a social interaction and exchange between the one who calls for the account and the one who is being held accountable. The former asks questions and scrutinises the other party, whereas the latter answers and may suffer the imposition of sanctions where necessary. This definition of accountability combines justification by the accountability holdee to the accountability holder, with availability to the latter of applying sanctions vis-à-vis the former.[32]

Another feature of accountability is reparation and/or effective redress.[33] Put simply, there is a strong need to put matters right in the event of errors. In fact, accountability, besides leaving the accountee liable for giving an explanation of actions and suffering the consequences for those actions where appropriate, entails that the accountee must, in addition, 'undertake to put matters right if it should appear that errors have been made. In other words it is explanatory and amendatory'.[34] This is in line with the argument that accountability operates prospectively and retrospectively and, as such, encompasses the 'fire watching'

29 M Bovens, 'Analysing and Assessing Accountability: A Conceptual Framework' (2007) 13 *European Law Journal* 4, p. 447.

30 A Schedler, 'Conceptualizing accountability', in A Schedler, *The Self-Restraining State: Power and Accountability in New Democracies* (Lynne Rienner Publishers 1997), p. 17.

31 *See* Davies, op. cit. n 7 *supra*.

32 *See* Schedler, op. cit. n 30 *supra*.

33 *See* Davies, op. cit. n 7 *supra*.

34 D Oliver, *Government in the United Kingdom: The Search for Accountability, Effectiveness, and Citizenship* (Oxford University Press 1991), p. 24.

function of legislation and regulation.[35] This statement brings into play the definition of control as 'periodic checking and examination of the activities of public officials by external actors possessed of formal or constitutional authority to investigate, to grand quietus or to censure, and in some cases even to punish'.[36]

However, accountability is often understood as a process that operates retrospectively in the sense that it involves giving an account of a prior conduct. Such views, however, have been challenged by approaches that see accountability as more of an on-going process.[37] Though accountability has mainly to do with wrongdoing that has taken place in the past, the objectives of the accountability process are increasingly achieved by more forward-looking methods, in order to prevent failures from happening again.

What can therefore be designated as the original or the core meaning of the term is the liability to give an account or explanation of actions and, where appropriate, to suffer the consequences, take the blame or undertake to put matters right if it should appear that errors have been made.[38]

Consequently, the emphasis on accountability can be either on 'giving an account' or on 'holding to account'.[39] The former concentrates on disclosing information and on justifying behaviour, leaving the possibility of sanction as an option only. The latter not only entails the obligation to disclose information and to justify actions but also, and more fundamentally, that the actors should be in a relationship with another forum which has the power to impose sanctions and to give rewards.[40]

Accountability and transparency

Accountability's *alter ego*, transparency, 'ensures that decisions are taken out of the "backroom"',[41] allowing firmer supervision as well as control of the exercise of delegated power. As such, transparency is considered essential to any democratic polity.[42] It is transparency that serves as a crucial tool for understanding the reasons behind governmental action and thereby facilitates construction of a reasoned argument by those opposed to the measure.[43]

35 *See* Brandsma, op. cit. n 2 *supra*.

36 C Lord, 'The hidden public sector: The "quangocratization" of the world', in G Kaufmann, G Majone and V Ostrom, *Guidance, Control and Evaluation in the Public Sector* (de Gruyter 1986), p. 766.

37 JM Moncrieffe, 'Accountability: Ideals, ideas, constraints' (2001) 8 *Democratization*, p. 26.

38 *See* Oliver, op. cit. n 3 *supra*.

39 RW Grant and RO Keohane, 'Accountability and abuses of power in world politics' (2005) 99 *American Political Science Review*, p 29; *See* Mulgan, op. cit. n 6 *supra*; *See* Harlow, op. cit. n 21 *supra*; *See* Oliver, op. cit. n 3 *supra*; *See* Scott, op. cit. n 4 *supra*.

40 *See* Mulgan, op. cit. n 6 *supra*.

41 *See* Fisher, op. cit. n 5 *supra*, p 503.

42 P Craig, *EU Administrative Law* (Oxford University Press 2006), p. 359.

43 *See* Fisher, op. cit. n 5 *supra*.

At the same time, transparency is essential for holding a government accountable for its actions. This can happen only when individual citizens are granted access to the relevant information enabling them to monitor the actions of the decision-makers.

Similarly, transparency can only be meaningful when enforcement mechanisms are attached to it.[44] Therefore an effective and independent judicial system is also 'a fundamental prerequisite for effective executive accountability'.[45]

> No society can be considered truly democratic if its citizens are denied the possibility of vindicating their legal rights in judicial proceedings, whether against the oppressive acts of a powerful legislature – even a democratically elected one – or against the unlawful practices of an overweening administration.[46]

In this regard, the Court of Justice of the EU plays a crucial role in public accountability. They contribute to transparency by bringing cases to public attention. It has been noted that:

> The fact that the citizens are aware of what the administration is doing is a guarantee that it will operate properly. Supervision by those who confer legitimacy on the public authorities encourages them to be effective in adhering to their [citizens'] initial will and can thereby inspire their confidence, which is a guarantee of public content as well as the proper functioning of the democratic system.[47]

Overall, accountability of the EU can only be properly understood through the lens of the access to documents rules. The public's right to hold decision-makers to account, by assessing the impact of the activities of the EU and by commenting upon those activities, can obviously be exercised if there are rules in place which allow people to access the relevant information. 'After all, without information on what decisions are being taken and by whom, it will not be possible for various accountability forums to hold actors to account.'[48] Transparency and openness enhance awareness and understanding of the ultimate objectives that the decision-making processes aim to achieve.[49] 'Without maximum access to

44 A Frost, 'Restoring Faith in Government: Transparency Reform in the United States and the EU' (2003) 9 *European Public Law*, p. 87.

45 *See* Mulgan, op. cit. n 6 *supra,* p. 76.

46 F Mancini and D Keeling, 'Democracy and the European Court of Justice' (1994) 57 *Modern Law Review*, pp. 175, 181.

47 Case C-353/99P, *Hautala* v. *Council* [2001] ECR I-9565, Opinion of Advocate-General Leger, para. 52.

48 G Brandsma, D Curtin and A Meijer, 'How transparent are EU "comitology" committees in practice?' (2008) 14 *European Law Journal*, p. 819.

49 I Harden, 'Citizenship and Information' (2001) 7 *European Public Law*, p. 165.

government information, citizens have no way effectively to evaluate and monitor the process by which laws and policies get made and enforced.'[50] In the words of the judiciary, 'the widest possible access to documents . . . is essential to enable citizens to carry out genuine and efficient monitoring of the exercise of the powers vested in the [Union] institutions.'[51] This concept is now set out in the second recital in the preamble of Regulation 1049/2001 on public access to documents held by the EP, the Council and the Commission,[52] which states that 'openness . . . guarantees that the administration enjoys greater legitimacy and is more effective and more accountable to the citizen in a democratic system'. Consequently, access to documents rules are used to assess the EU's legitimacy and to strengthen accountability.

50 S Kierkegaard, 'Open access to public documents: More secrecy, less transparency!' (2009) 25 *Computer Law & Society Report*, pp. 3, 4.

51 Case T-92/98, *Interporc* v. *Commission* [1999] ECR II–3521, para. 39.

52 Regulation 1049/2001 [2001] OJ L145/43.

2 Accountability within the Commission

Introduction

The analysis on accountability in the EU would have been incomplete without examining the most dramatic week, at least so far, in the history of the EU: the long running saga of allegations of maladministration that led to the fall of the Santer Commission. In particular, the media coverage given to the Commission back in 1999 was damaging to the reputation of the institution as well as to the EU as a whole. The events that led to the resignation of the Commission confirmed the pre-existing suspicions about bad administration and improper functioning within the Commission. This chapter, therefore, focuses on applying the notion of accountability explained in Chapter 1 with regard to the Commission. In particular, this chapter examines whether the general public and their elected representatives: the members of the European Parliament (EP) and the judiciary – as the accountability forums – can hold the Commission and its individual members, the actors, accountable for their actions or omissions. The chapter concludes that there are serious problems regarding the Commissioners' executive actions. Yet, as we shall see in Chapter 3, these deficits can be eliminated by enhancing the principle of transparency within the administration of the Commission.

The EP appointed the Committee of Independent Experts (CIE) to deal with the allegations of fraud, mismanagement and nepotism within the Commission. The CIE has considered, *inter alia*, the situation of all the Commissioners against whom allegations have been made in order to determine whether the allegations were cases of maladministration. The two reports published by the CIE in March and September 1999 revealed the existence of significant accountability deficits at the EU level of governance.[1] The CIE concluded that it was 'becoming difficult to find anyone [within the Commission] who has even the slightest sense of responsibility'.[2] Unsurprisingly, the findings of the CIE's investigation led to

1 C Harlow and R Rawlings, 'Promoting accountability in multilevel governance: A network approach' (2007) 13 *European Law Journal* 4, p. 542.

2 Committee of Independent Experts, 'First report on allegations regarding fraud, mismanagement and nepotism in the European Commission' (1999) para. 9.4.25.

the resignation of the Santer Commission on 15 March 1999. One of the most frequently quoted paragraphs of the first report of the CIE reads as follows:

> The studies carried out by the Committee have too often revealed a growing reluctance among the members of the hierarchy to acknowledge their responsibility. It is becoming difficult to find anyone who has even the slightest sense of responsibility . . . The temptation to deprive the concept of responsibility of all substance is a dangerous one. The concept is the ultimate manifestation of democracy.[3]

The Second Report focused on weaknesses in the Commission's services with particular reference to their management functions and found that at least part of the problem with the Commission was the result of a 'mentality' within the organisation. However, it was found that 'there are no specific ways of dealing with a problem of mentality, but the Committee believes it should encourage a process of reflection and internal discussion in this respect'.[4] It observed that the Commission was simply not designed to cope with the range and complexity of tasks it had been facing during the previous decade.

Bringing the Union closer to its citizens: the White Paper on European Governance (2000)[5]

As already explained above, the main problems that occurred during the process of ratification of the Maastricht Treaty[6] confirmed the extent to which the Union has become disconnected from its citizens as well as the widespread notion that the Union's decision-making process lacked legitimacy and that EU officials exercising public authority are not subject to accountability at all.[7] The downfall of the Santer Commission at least had the effect of placing accountability on the political agenda of the EU institutions. Consequently, in December 2000, the Inter-Governmental Conference (IGC) in Nice recognised 'the need to improve and to monitor the democratic legitimacy and transparency of the Union and

3 *Ibid.*, para. 9.4.25.

4 Committee of Independent Experts, 'Second report on reform of the Commission: Analysis of current practice and proposals for tackling mismanagement, irregularities and fraud' (1999) point 8.3.

5 European Commission, 'Reforming the Commission. A White Paper' COM (2000) 200 final/2, vols I and II.

6 Very near to the majority of the electorate voting in the referendum in 1992 chose to reject France's ratification of the Maastricht Treaty. Very long discussions occurred in the UK Parliament and there was a challenge to the German ratification in the German Constitutional Court.

7 S Peers, 'The New Regulation on Access to Documents: A Critical Analysis' (2001) 21 *Yearbook of European Law*, p. 385; *See* U Oberg, 'Public access to documents after the entry into force of the Amsterdam Treaty: Much ado about nothing?' (1998) 2 European Integration Online Papers; *See* I Osterdahl, 'Openness v. secrecy: Public access to documents in Sweden and the European Union' (1998) 23 *European Law Review* 4, p. 336.

its institutions, in order to bring them closer to the citizens of the Member States'.[8] Similarly, as regards the non-ratification of the Constitutional Treaty, the Constitutional Committee of the EP argued that the decline in support of the ratification was at least in part due to a sense of 'alienation, the serious difficulties encountered in understanding and participating, and a fear of helplessness in the face of imposed decisions which cannot be influenced or controlled'.[9]

The term accountability entered political vocabulary with a speech by the then incoming President of the Commission, Romano Prodi, to the EP in which he spoke of the need to increase transparency, efficiency and accountability of the Commission. Succeeding the discredited Santer Commission and faced with the very harsh findings of the CIE, the Prodi Commission was anxious to demonstrate its commitment to high standards of administration and accountability. The then new President of the Commission introduced a number of reforms in order to restore public faith. The main challenge faced by the then new Commission was obviously the reform of the Commission itself. At the same time, the appointment of Romano Prodi and the initiation of the Commission reform project aimed to provide a response to the criticisms noted by the CIE. The then Vice President, Neil Kinnock, was given specific responsibility to oversee the reform procedure, which resulted in the road map for renewal and eventually led to the Reform White Paper of 2000.

The White Paper included a New Code of Conduct for Commissioners with strict rules about the formation and the role of their private offices. Prodi's Commission tried to present itself as a force of change and therefore put a lot of effort into developing concepts of administrative renewal.[10]

The White Paper included accountability as one of the 'good governance values [amongst] openness, effectiveness and coherence'.[11] In the Commission's work programme for the White Paper entitled 'Enhancing Democracy in European Union', it was stated that 'the conclusions of the White Paper may address the Commission's position in the institutional set-up, its political character, its independence and its authority in view of improving European governance'.[12] Moreover, the proposal was to:

> Contribute to a renewed understanding of the tasks and 'core business' of the Commission that are enshrined in the Treaty (guardian of the Treaty; expression of general interest; monopoly to take initiatives) given the new context of interdependence and interaction between various levels of government.[13]

8 Treaty of Nice, Declaration on the Future of the Union, No. 23 para. 6.

9 A Cygan, 'Democracy and accountability in the European Union: The view from the House of Commons' (2003) 66 *Modern Law Review* 3, pp. 384, 385.

10 *See* European Commission, op. cit. n 5 *supra*.

11 *Ibid.*

12 *Ibid.*

13 *Ibid.*

The White Paper focused on the amendment to the previous Community method, criticising the Member States rather than the Commission itself for the existing deficits within the Union.[14] Yet, the White Paper recognised existing concerns regarding policy-making in the EU by highlighting the poor policy implementation, the democratic deficit within the Union and the lack of policy effectiveness, while calling for more consultation and transparency. In the White Paper, the Commission stressed a variety of measures to enhance the role of the Commission in policy-making, such as co-regulation with private actors. It also proposed to limit the role of the Council and the EP in relation to the executive regulatory activities and delegate these to new agencies controlled by the Commission alone. Clearly, the White Paper seeks to widen the decision-making role of the Commission and to reduce legislation by the Council and the Parliament while trying to reduce the role of comitology.[15]

The White Paper introduced a new decision-making mechanism (known as 'Activity-Based Management') to guarantee that responsibilities matched resources and that results can be evaluated. In setting out this strand of the reform agenda, the Commission made it clear that it would in future refuse to take on new responsibilities where it had not been given the resources to implement them. As we shall see in Chapter 4, at the heart of this new method of governance was the development of agencies that are now given significant areas of responsibilities. Furthermore, the White Paper involves the reform of the Commission's financial management system, with the aim of empowering departments to establish internal control systems, so that the responsibilities of all actors involved in financial management would become clear, allowing for systematic checks to be undertaken by the Commission's new Internal Audit Service. Finally, the third strand is the whole-scale reform of the Commission's human resources policy. The emphasis there is on 'performance, continuous training and quality of management, as well as improving recruitment and career development'.[16]

The legal framework on the Commissioners' accountability

But what does the Treaty provide with regards to the accountability of the Commission? Pursuant to Article 245(1) TFEU, '[t]he Members of the Commission shall refrain from any action incompatible with their duties'. Additionally, Article 245(2) TFEU covers the case of compulsory retirement of an individual Commissioner. It reads as follows:

14 D Wincott, 'Looking Forward or Harking Back? The Commission and the Reform of Governance in the European Union' (2001) 39 *Journal of Common Market Studies* 5, p 897; *See* C Harlow and R Rawlings, op. cit. n 1 *supra*.

15 For a detailed analysis of the accountability regime of comitology committees, see Chapter 5, this volume.

16 *See* European Commission, op. cit. n 5 *supra*.

> The Members of the Commission may not, during their term of office, engage in any other occupation, whether gainful or not. . . . [t]hey shall give a solemn undertaking that, both during and after their term of office, they will respect the[ir] obligations . . . in particular their duty to behave with integrity and discretion as regards the acceptance . . . of certain appointments or benefits. In the event of any breach of these obligations, the Court of Justice may . . . rule that the Member concerned be, according to the circumstances, either compulsory retired in accordance with Article 247 or deprived of his right to a pension or other benefits in its stead.

Similarly, Article 247 TFEU, which contains the only reference to the personal liability of Commissioners, provides that:

> If any Member of the Commission no longer fulfils the conditions required for the performance of his duties or if he has been guilty of serious misconduct, the Court of Justice may, on application by the Council acting by a simple majority or the Commission, compulsorily retire him.

At the same time, Article 234 TFEU provides for another kind of responsibility which the Commission owes to the EP, the 'censure' motion, as follows:

> If a motion of censure on the activities of the Commission is tabled before [the EP], [and] . . . is carried by a two-thirds majority of votes cast, representing a majority of the component Members of the EP, the Members of the Commission shall resign as a body.

Finally, pursuant to Article 17(6) TEU, 'a member of the Commission shall resign if the President so requests'.

It is clear from the Treaty provisions, quoted above, that the Commission owes legal accountability to the Court of Justice and political accountability to the Parliament. According to the CIE, those who have public power must be responsible for their actions as well as for the actions taken by their inferior officials, even if they had no personal knowledge of them. The CIE rightly distinguished administrative from political responsibility. In doing so, the CIE pointed out that the Commissioners bear the political and the Directors General the administrative responsibility. Hence, Commissioners are responsible for the overall policy and Directors General for the implementation of that policy. The CIE noted that 'Commissioners must continuously seek to be informed about the acts and omissions of the DG's for which they bear responsibility'.[17] In the wording of the CIE:

> Reprehensible conduct of the Commission as a body, or of Commissioners individually, and more particularly . . . mismanagement in detecting or

17 *Ibid.*, para. 9.3.4

> dealing with fraud, mismanagement or nepotism perpetrated by the administrative services of the Commission and by third parties working for the Commission, obviously involves the responsibility of the Commission as a whole, or of individual Commissioners.[18]

This aspect of political accountability is of course compatible with the accountability requirements explained in Chapter 1: those with positions of public power must always be accountable for their wrongdoings, policies and decisions as well as the decisions taken by their officials and DGs, even if they are not aware of such decisions. Overall, it is self-evident that Commissioners must be held accountable with regards to the organisation as well as the implementation of policies by the DGs.

The facts of the *Cresson* case

It is necessary at this stage to examine the role played by the Court of Justice in securing accountability of the Commissioners. The *Cresson* case[19] involved Mrs E. Cresson, an ex French Prime minister and EU Commissioner, who held office from 24 January 1995 to 8 September 1999. Her portfolio consisted of science, research and development, human resources, education, training and youth, together with the Joint Research Centre (JRC). The Commission took a legal action against Cresson based on ex Article 213 EC Treaty (now Article 245 TFEU). She was found to have breached her obligations under Article 245 TFEU as a European Commissioner by appointing a close friend, Mr Berthelot, in an act of favouritism and seeking to offer consultancy contracts to a lawyer friend, Mr Riedinger.

Mrs E. Cresson had requested the appointment of Mr Berthelot, a dentist, as a scientific advisor within her cabinet, but as the cabinet was already fully staffed, he was appointed as a 'visiting scientist' for the JCR. Mr Berthelot, however, worked as a close advisor to Mrs E. Cresson[20] rather than with the JCR, as well as working beyond his permitted contract dates. Strictly speaking, Mr Berthelot's work did not match his profile and was 'inadequate in quality, quantity and relevance'.[21] Furthermore, he had worked for Mrs E. Cresson for over two and a half years even though the regulations stated that visiting members could only work for a maximum of 24 months.[22] It was held that Mrs E. Cresson's appointment of Mr Berthelot was contrary to Article 213(2) EC, now 245(2) TFEU, and solely in the interest of helping her friends and not within the interests of the Commission.

18 *See* Committee of Independent Experts, op. cit. n 2 *supra*, para. 1.6.2.

19 Case C-432/04, *Commission* v. *Cresson* [2006] ECR I-6387.

20 Case C-432/04, *Commission* v. *Cresson* [2006] ECR I-6387, Opinion of Advocate-General Geelhoed, para. 7.

21 *See* Committee of Independent Experts, op. cit. n 2 *supra*, para. 8.1.35.

22 Case C-432/04, *Commission* v. *Cresson* [2006] ECR I-6387, Opinion of Advocate-General Geelhoed, para. 9.

At the very least, Mrs E. Cresson should have made inquiries as to the appropriateness of her actions and had thus acted negligently.[23]

The finding of the Court

The Court held that Mrs E. Cresson had acted improperly in the case of Mr Berthelot. He had been appointed as a 'visiting scientist' by a Commission department for which Cresson was responsible when in fact he was working exclusively for her as an 'advisor'. In her defence, Mrs E. Cresson claimed that she personally had not appointed Mr Berthelot but that the Commission itself had. The Court rejected that line of argument stating that the appointment was made at her personal and expressed request after she had been fully informed that Mr Berthelot could not be officially appointed as an advisor. With regards to Mr Riedinger, the Court dismissed the action because although contracts had been offered to him, they appeared to be relevant to the work of the Commission.

The Court made it clear that ex Article 213 EC (now Article 245 TFEU) requires Members of the Commission to respect their obligations, to be independent and to always act in the general interest of the EU. Individual Commissioners must ensure that the general interest of the EU preponderates at all time, not only over national interest but also over personal interest.[24] As already stated above, Article 245(2) TFEU empowers the Court to impose a penalty if there is a breach. The penalty can be either a compulsory retirement or the deprivation of any pension rights or other benefits instead. Yet, the Court of Justice did not clarify the system of accountability for the Commissioners' executive actions; it ruled that the recognition that Mrs E. Cresson had breached her obligations constitutes an adequate penalty itself. As a result, one could argue that when there is a breach of obligations arising from Article 245 TFEU, in the sense that a Commissioner does not act in the general interest of the Union but they are guided by personal or financial interest, they can still not be subject to any meaningful sanction. This is a classic case of an accountability deficit: the person under scrutiny does not face any sanctions as per the accountability requirements examined above.

Some mitigation to the problem is found to the fact that the Court of Justice required Mrs. Cresson to bear her own legal costs. At the same time, she faced negative consequences such as having to respond to journalists commenting on her actions. Yet, it is questionable whether these negative consequences are in proportion to the bad publicity caused to the Union.

Twenty years after Cresson*: the* Dalli *saga*

The *en bloc* resignation of the Santer Commission in 1999 against a background of allegations of fraud, maladministration and chronic mismanagement is still

23 *Ibid.*, para. 21.

24 *See* op. cit. n 19 *supra*, para. 71.

topical, almost two decades on. As we saw above, the European Commission has long been criticised for its administrative inadequacies and for the structural deficiencies in the Union's system of accountability. There have been a number of reports depicting the Commission as an institution suffering from structural and political irregularities.

On 11 May 2015, the General Court (GC) gave a significant judgment on a legal challenge brought by the former EU Health Commissioner, Mr John Dalli, against the Commission. Dalli argued that he was forced to resign, by the then President of the Commission, Jose Manuel Barroso, without being given enough time to consider his legal rights. Rather paradoxically, the GC ruled that Mr Dalli resigned voluntarily and dismissed the action as inadmissible.

This judgment raises long-lasting constitutional implications. With all due respect, the ruling comes as a surprise and fails to clarify issues in relation to the powers that can be lawfully exercised by the President of the Commission when he loses confidence in any of the members of his Commission. This section examines the appropriateness of the recent ruling and concludes that the GC lost a rather rare opportunity to rule on significant aspects of the Treaty powers granted to the President of the Commission to sack the individual Commissioners, and as a result also fails to remedy the accountability deficits of the Commission.

Facts of the case

Dalli, the former Maltese Commissioner, was accused of soliciting bribery for the amount of 60 million euros in exchange for seeking to influence future legislative proposals in favour of the tobacco maker, Swedish Match. Following a complaint to the Commission from the latter, the EU's Anti-Fraud Office (OLAF) initiated investigations into the serious bribery allegations. On 15 October 2012, OLAF sent its final report to the Commission highlighting that there was no conclusive evidence that the Commissioner was involved in requesting money from the tobacco manufacturer. Yet, there was some evidence confirming that Mr Dalli was at least aware of the fact that a Maltese entrepreneur was using his name for the purposes of getting financial benefits from the tobacco maker.

On 16 October 2012, Mr Dalli had a meeting with the President of the Commission where he was presented with two already drafted press releases by the Commission: one stating that Mr Dalli decided to resign 'voluntarily', while the other stated that Barroso requested him to resign by exercising his prerogative powers under Article 17(6) TEU. During their meeting, the President showed the covering letter of the OLAF's report to Mr Dalli. Nevertheless, access to the full report was refused on the grounds that it was confidential. Towards the end of their meeting, the President made it clear that he was going to force the applicant to resign if he was not going to do so voluntarily. The applicant asked for at least 24 hours to consult a lawyer and to find out what his legal rights were. Barroso said that he could give him no more than 30 minutes. Mr Dalli chose to resign.

Mr Dalli challenged the legality of the oral decision taken by Barroso to terminate his term of office as the EU Health Commissioner. The Court declared the action as inadmissible since there was no clarity in relation to the act whose annulment was sought. The Court could not distinguish whether Mr Dalli was seeking the annulment of the decision of the President to remove him from office pursuant to Articles 245 and 247 TFEU, or the allegedly oral decision taken by Barroso to request Mr Dalli's resignation under Article 17(6) TEU. In consequence, the action was dismissed as inadmissible.

Comment and analysis

The *Dalli* judgment is a lost opportunity by the Court to clarify the abovementioned provisions as regards accountability of the EU Commissioners. Surely, any failure by an individual Commissioner to meet the standards described in Article 245 TFEU, as set out above, can lead to significant damage to the public image of the Commission. This is not a hypothetical observation if one looks at the events leading up to the collective resignation of the Santer Commission and to the closely related *Cresson* judgment analysed above. Consequently, one can understand the concerns of President Barroso to avoid a repetition of the discredited Santer Commission in 1999. Barroso's commitment to high standards of administration is perfectly legitimate. What is not legitimate, however, is the process that led to the resignation of Mr Dalli. Notably, the Commission can only succeed if individual Commissioners operate impartially and independently, without influence from external sources, whether national governments or private individuals and without engaging privately with stakeholders to achieve financial benefits. This is the only way for the Commission to gain confidence from other institutions as well as Member States and citizens.

The Commissioners must meet the highest standards not just on external matters but on their conduct inside the Commission. They should perform their duties without division or external influence due to their high ranking and experience in the political arena. In particular, as already explained above, Article 245(1) TFEU requires Commissions to be free from any external influence. This point is vital if the Commission is to stay independent of Member States or individuals. But let's assume for a while that there was enough evidence that Mr Dalli obtained pecuniary advantages from the Swedish tobacco maker. Assume further that the OLAF report concluded that the Commissioner needed to be held accountable for infringing his duty to behave with integrity pursuant to Article 245 TFEU. Is the procedure that forced him to resign acceptable and does it respect the rule of law? Or does it confirm an exercise of abusive behaviour by the President? Forcing an individual Commissioner to resign without allowing him to consult a lawyer and without being given the opportunity to see the OLAF report constitutes a manifest violation of his basic right to respond to the evidence against him. Any employment lawyer will agree that this behaviour is a classic case of constructive dismissal. Surely this is not something that can be justified, particularly if this comes from the President of the Commission, an institution supposedly entrusted with the duty to guard and ensure that the rule of law is duly respected.

Unfortunately, the GC did not clarify the system of accountability for the Commissioner's actions. The Court rather simply decided to dismiss the action as inadmissible. The OLAF report and the factual background of the previously decided *Cresson* case reveal that a lot of irregularities can take place within the Commission and that there is a deficit in any meaningful notion of accountability of the Commission. The GC, with all due respect, made the wrong decision in refraining from clarifying what obligations are mandatory for EU Commissioners as set out within the Treaty framework. Additionally, and most importantly, the judgment fails to set the boundaries of the prerogative powers of the Commission's President to sack the members of his cabinet. Whether or not Commissioners can be held accountable for their decisions was completely ignored in *Dalli*.

Concluding remarks

Overall, the CIE reports as well as *Cresson* and *Dalli* clearly highlight that many irregularities exist(ed) within the Commission. Fully accountable Commissioners are absent. According to the Advocate General, the Court of Justice seemed to have made a wrong decision in not only refraining from sanctioning Mrs E. Cresson but also losing its chance to clarify what obligations are mandatory for EU Commissioners as set out within Article 213(2), now Article 245(2) TFEU.[25] This point is rather significant since the same mistake was made again by the Court almost a decade later. Finally, both cases, it seems, have not clarified the meaning of Commissioner's accountability. The lack of any meaningful notion of accountability is identified here as the key problem of the internal mechanisms in the Commission. The Treaty has not established a mechanism by which Commissioners can be held accountable, neither does it put the Commissioners in a position to effectively lead their departments. Fully accountable and fully influential Commissioners are the missing link in the search for democratic structures throughout the EU.

25 Case C-432/04, *Commission* v. *Cresson* [2006] ECR I-6387, Opinion of Advocate General Geelhoed.

3 The access to documents regime in the EU

In all my public and private acts as your president, I expect to follow my instincts of openness and candor with full confidence that honesty is always the best policy in the end.

(Gerald R. Ford)

Introduction

Having examined the meaning of accountability, this chapter focuses on the fundamental prerequisites of the accountability relationship: the legal rules with regard to access to documents. As already explained in Chapter 1, the access rules are considered to be an *essential* accountability requirement, since without information on what decisions are being taken and by whom, it is impossible for the various accountability forums to hold the actors to account. Hence, the principal focus here is upon transparency by means of access to 'government' information. The aim of the chapter is to investigate a significant question, albeit not being an uncomplicated task, regarding openness and transparency in the EU: How far and open can the Union's decision-making be and is it possible for citizens to find out what is happening within the EU's institutions, bodies, offices and agencies?

The chapter starts by examining the innovations of the Maastricht Treaty in 1992,[1] focusing on the major developments which attempted to establish a 'right' of public access to information, where transparency efforts have been most successful, and then goes on to the Code of conduct of access to EU documents introduced in 1993. An essential part of the analysis is to consider the *initial* contribution of the EU Courts to transparency by interpreting the decisions of the Commission and the Council to refuse access based on the Code of conduct. Also, the chapter examines the developments introduced by Regulation 1049/2001 (hereafter the Regulation) on access to documents of the EP, the Council and the Commission.[2] A significant part of this analysis is to investigate the way in which the jurisprudence of the judiciary has been developed over the last 20 years to ensure openness, accountability and legitimacy in the EU.

1 Treaty on European Union ('TEU' or Maastricht Treaty), OJ C 191 [1992], (entered into force 1 November 1993).

2 Regulation 1049/2001 [2001] OJ L 145/43.

The chapter questions whether the above-mentioned measures and the way they have been implemented by the EU organs and interpreted by the judiciary are adequate to ensure public awareness and participation in the decision-making process. A detailed investigation shows that the right of access has been increased to a considerable extent, especially when one compares the situation which existed before 1992 when secrecy and closed doors were the norm.[3] Had the Regulation been interpreted in a more liberal way by the EU Courts, the EU could have been more transparent. In what follows, the developments to date are described so that the question of what remains to be done for further improvements in the area can be properly assessed. The chapter concludes that the establishment through the case law of general presumptions against openness has long-lasting constitutional consequences for the right of access. The presumptions case law in particular for administrative documents has effectively changed the default position of the *widest possible* access set by the legislature to one of *non-disclosure.*

Historical overview of the legislative background

The main problems that occurred during the process of ratification of the Treaty of Maastricht,[4] and particularly the negative response from Danish public opinion, confirmed the widespread notion that the Union's decision-making process lacked accountability and legitimacy.[5] In consequence, accountability was placed high on the political agenda and forced the Heads of States and Government as well the other EU institutions to find alternatives that would bring the Union closer to its citizens. Access to documents was believed to be the solution to the problem.[6]

3 Case C-170/89, *BEVC* v. *Commission* [1991] ECR I-5709; *See* Oberg, Chapter 2, op. cit. n 7 *supra*; *See* D Curtin and H Meijers, 'The principle of open government in Schengen and the European Union: Democratic retrogression?' (1995) 32 *Common Market Law Review*, p. 391; *See also* T Bunyan, *Secrecy and Openness in the European Union* (Kogan Page 1999).

4 The negative response from the Danish electorate and also the very near majority of the electorate voting in the referendum in 1992 chose to reject France's ratification of the Maastricht Treaty. Long discussions occurred in the UK Parliament and there was a challenge to the German ratification in the German Constitutional Court.

5 *See* Peers, Oberg and Osterdahl, Chapter 2, op. cit. n 7 *supra*.

6 It must be noted here that the majority of the Member States, with the notable exception of Cyprus, have regulated the issue and introduced provisions on public access either at Constitutional or at legislative level. Constitutional provisions exist in Sweden, Spain, the Netherlands, Austria, Portugal, Belgium and Finland. Legislative provisions regulating access to documents exist in France, Denmark, Portugal, Ireland, Greece, Italy, Germany, the United Kingdom, Luxembourg, Czech Republic, Estonia, Hungary, Latvia, Lithuania, Malta, Poland, Portugal, Slovak Republic and Slovenia. A comparative analysis of the Union's public access to documents rules with public access legislation in the Member States reveals that the issue had already been regulated at the national level years before the EU legislation on the issue was introduced. *See*, for example, H Kranenborg and W Voermans, *Access to Information in the European Union: A Comparative Analysis of EC and Member State Legislation* (Europa Law Publishing 2005).

As already explained in Chapter 2, the public's right to hold decision-makers to account, by assessing the impact and by commenting upon their activities, can only be exercised when rules allow people access to the relevant information.[7] In this regard, transparency enhances awareness and understanding of the ultimate objectives that the decision-making processes aim to achieve.[8] 'Without maximum access to government information, citizens have no way effectively to evaluate and monitor the process by which laws and policies get made and forced'.[9] As the Court of First Instance, now the General Court, has already ruled, 'the widest possible access to documents . . . is essential to enable citizens to carry out genuine and efficient monitoring of the exercise of the powers vested in the [Union] institutions'.[10] This concept is now set out in Preamble 2 of the Regulation, which states that 'openness . . . guarantees that the administration enjoys greater legitimacy and is more effective and more accountable to the citizen in a democratic system'. In consequence, access to documents rules is used in this chapter as a lens to assess the Union's legitimacy and as a means of strengthening accountability.

The initial step, which proved to be the cornerstone of the public's fundamental right to information, was Declaration No 17 attached to the Final Act of the Maastricht Treaty, which stated that:

> The Conference considers that transparency of the decision-making process strengthens the democratic nature of the institutions and the public's confidence in the administration. The conference accordingly recommends that the Commission submit to the Council no later than 1993 a report on measures designed to improve public access to the information available to the institutions.[11]

Declaration No 17 illustrates the willingness for the establishment of a general 'right' of access to information and is commonly referred to in the legal literature as such.[12] This non-binding political statement constitutes a type of soft law and not a rule of law of higher order, which the previous rules would have rendered invalid if they had not been complied with.[13] Yet, the Advocate General Maduro

7 E Best, 'Transparency and European governance: Clearly not a simple matter', in V Deckmyn *Increasing Transparency in the European Union* (European Institute of Public Administration 2002) pp. 93–95.

8 *See* Harden, Chapter 1, op. cit. n 49 *supra*.

9 *See* Kierkegaard, Chapter 1, op. cit. n 50 *supra*, p. 4.

10 Case T-92/98, *Interporc* v. *Commission* [1999] ECR II–3521, para. 39.

11 *See* Chapter 3, op. cit. n 1 *supra*, Declaration 17.

12 S Peers, 'From Maastricht to Laeken: The political agenda of openness and transparency in the EU', in V Deckmyn, *Increasing Transparency in the European Union* (European Institute of Public Administration 2002); *See* A Tomkins, 'Transparency and the emergence of a European administrative law' (1999) 19 *Yearbook of European Law*, p. 217; *See also* D Curtin and H Meijers, op. cit. n 3 *supra*.

13 *See* Peers, op. cit. n 12 *supra*.

rightly opined that declarations attached to the Treaties can be used as a basis to clarify Treaty provisions, so long as they do not amend explicit stipulations provided in the Treaties.[14] This approach is in line with the case law which confirms that declarations can be used as a basis for interpretation of Treaty provisions.[15]

In response to Declaration No 17 and with the aim of bringing the Union closer to the citizens, the Commission first surveyed national law on access to documents and then released a communication on the issue.[16] In 1993, transparency was also emphasised by the inter-institutional Declaration on Democracy, Transparency, and Subsidiarity.[17] These endeavours constitute the early steps taken by the EU in an attempt to have more openness and transparency in the decision-making process. Amongst these, clearly the most important was the Code of conduct on access to documents which was later implemented by the Council[18] and the Commission.[19]

The accession of Austria, Finland and Sweden in 1995 and the appointment of the first European Ombudsman, Mr Jacob Soderman, increased the state of transparency in the EU.[20] In 1996, the Ombudsman began an own initiative inquiry regarding the adoption of access rules by other EU institutions, bodies, offices and agencies and argued that as long as the Union legislature had not adopted general rules on access to documents, the institutions and bodies were obliged to adopt access rules as part of their internal organisation.[21] This inquiry resulted in a draft recommendation that the other institutions and bodies should follow the example of the Council and the Commission and adopt their own internal rules on public access, considering that failure to do so could be maladministration. The outcome of this attempt was that all the Union institutions, bodies, offices and agencies, with the notable exceptions of the Court and the European Council, introduced rules regarding public access to their documents.[22] More recently, the Court adopted access rules for its administrative documents.

14 Case C-64/05 P, *Kingdom of Sweden* v. *Commission of the European Communities and Others* [2007] ECR I-11389, Opinion of Advocate-General Maduro, para. 7.

15 Case T-187/99, *Agrana Zucker und Stärke* v. *Commission* [2001] ECR II-1587, and order of the Court in Case C-321/01 P, *Agrana Zucker und Stärke* v. *Commission* [2002] ECR I-10027.

16 [1993] OJ L 156/5 and [1993] OJ L 166/4.

17 No 10 Bulletin of the European Communities (1993) pp. 118–120.

18 Decision 93/731 [1993] OJ L 340/43.

19 Decision 94/90 [1994] OJ L 340/41.

20 *See* Osterdahl, Chapter 2, op. cit. n 7 *supra*; *See* Harden, Chapter 1, op. cit. n 49 *supra*; *See* Kranenborg and Voermans, op. cit. n 6 *supra*.

21 *See* the Report (616/PUHAB/F/IHJ), available on the website of the European Ombudsman www.euro-ombudsman.eu.int, accessed 1 February 2016.

22 OJ 1998 C295/1 (Court of Auditors); OJ 1997 C243/13 (European Investment Bank); OJ 1999 L110/30 (European Central Bank); the European Agency for Health and Safety at work; Europol; OJ 1997 L339/18 (Economic and Social Committee); OJ 1997 351/70 (Committee of the Regions); OJ 1998 L90/43 (European Monetary Institute); European Centre for the Development of Vocational Training (cadefop); OJ 1997 C282/5 (European Environment Agency); OJ 1998 C46/5 (Translation Centre for Bodies of the European Union); European Monetary Centre for Drugs and Drug Addiction; European Agency for the Evaluation of Medicinal Products.

The pre-regulation regime: the Code of conduct

The basic principle enshrined in the joint Code of conduct governing access to the Commission and the Council was the 'widest possible access to documents' and also the narrowest interpretation of the exceptions, since the latter is a corollary of the former[23] and also a fundamental standard of legal interpretation.[24] However, this did not mean that the Code guaranteed an absolute right. On the contrary, it provided for documents to be refused where disclosure 'could' undermine the protection of certain public and private interests. Although the joint Code of conduct adopted by the Council and the Commission started with the assurance that 'the public will have the widest possible access to documents held by the Commission and the Council' the openness criterion was not the rule. Rather paradoxically, the Code's exceptions were defined broadly with the effect of changing the presumption of disclosure from positive rights with negative exceptions to a text which treated access as the exception.[25]

The Code contained a non-exhaustive list of mandatory exceptions,[26] which meant that the institutions must refuse access to documents that came within one of the exceptions, if the relevant circumstances were shown to exist. The rules provided for a radical change to the present situation of secrecy, thus the grounds for refusing access were drafted generously. The Code exceptions were covering:

- the protection of the public interest (exemplified by public security, international relations, monetary stability, court proceedings, inspections, and investigations);
- the protection of the individual and of privacy;
- the protection of industrial and commercial secrecy;
- the protection of the Union's financial interests; and
- the protection of confidentiality as requested by the natural or legal persons that supplied the information or as required by the legislation of the Member State that supplied the information.

Additionally, the institutions had discretion to refuse access in order to protect confidentiality in their proceedings. In consequence, the Code included two different types of exceptions, divided into mandatory and discretionary, depending on the nature of the interest which they sought to protect.

23 *See* Peers, Chapter 2, op. cit. n 7 *supra*.

24 P Cabral, 'Access to Member State documents in EC law' (2006) 31 *European Law Review*, pp. 378–381.

25 M De Leeuw, 'The regulation on public access to EP, Council and Commission documents in the European Union: Are citizens better off?' (2003) 28 *European Law Review*, p. 324.

26 Case T-610/97, *R Carlsen* v. *Council* [1998] ECR II-485, para. 48 whereas the President of the Court ruled that the mandatory exceptions regarding the protection of the public interest were not exhaustive and that an exception relating to the stability of the Community legal order existed, which also covers the legal advice given by the legal service of the institutions.

The mandatory exceptions, as quoted above, obliged the institutions to refuse disclosure of any documents that could undermine the protection of certain public or private interests. Pursuant to the discretionary exceptions, the institution concerned exercised discretion as to whether or not to disclose the documents requested in order to protect the confidentiality of its proceedings. The Court of First Instance ruled in *WWF*[27] that the mandatory exceptions were aiming to protect the interests of third parties and/or the interests of the public in general in the sense that if they possessed the documents concerned, they could deny access.[28] Under the discretionary exceptions, the only interest that was protected was the institution's own interest in the confidentiality of its deliberations.[29] This could justify the fact that regarding the mandatory exceptions there was no possibility of balancing the interests of the applicant against the interests of the institution.[30] As explained already, the balancing exercise was only required in the case of discretionary exceptions, whereas the institution was obliged to balance its own interest against that of the applicant. If the institution's interest outweighed the latter, access was denied.[31]

That the Code's exceptions were dangerously restrictive was understood quite early by the Netherlands,[32] and the legal basis of the Code was challenged in a Court case. It was argued that transparency constitutes an essential aspect of democracy and cannot be regulated by measures of internal organisation. The Netherlands were supported by the EP, the intervening party, who argued that the Council incorrectly relied on ex Article 207 of the EC Treaty and on Article 22 of its Rules of Procedure to regulate the fundamental right of the general public to have access to official documents. The same approach was taken by the Advocate General Tesauro who argued, in his opinion delivered on 28 November 1995, that the public's right to access the official documents is based on the principle of democracy, which constitutes one of the cornerstones of the Union recognised in Declaration No 17 of the Maastricht Treaty. The Court of Justice, however, dismissed the challenge on the grounds that the institutions could adopt those measures as part of their internal organisation.[33] At that time, the Treaty of

27 Case T-105/95, *World Wildlife Fund (WWF)* v. *Commission* [1997] ECR II-313; *See also* the case-note of M De Leeuw, 'WWF (UK) v. Commission of the European Communities' (1997) 3 *European Public Law*, p. 339.

28 D Curtin, 'Betwixt and between: Democracy and transparency in the governance of the European Union', in B De Witte et al., *Reforming the Treaty on European Union: The Legal Debate* (Brill 1996).

29 *See* Bunyan, op. cit. n 3 *supra*.

30 P Dyrberg, 'Current issues in the public debate on access to documents' (1999) 24 *European Law Review*, p. 157.

31 Case T-194/94, *Carvel* v. *Council* [1995] ECR II-2765, para. 65; *See* Case T-105/95, *WWF* v. *Commission* [1997] ECR II-313, para. 59.

32 The Netherlands, Denmark, Sweden and Finland have consistently pressed for greater openness within the Union, gaining strong inspiration from their national laws where the notion of citizens' rights is underscored.

33 Case C-58/94, *Netherlands* v. *Council* [1996] ECR I-2169; *See also* U Oberg, 'The EU citizens' right to know: The improbable adoption of a European Freedom of Information Act' (1999) 2 *Cambridge Yearbook of European Legal Studies*, p. 303.

Amsterdam was not in force and thus the institutions were entitled to have access rules governing citizens' rights based solely on internal procedural rules.[34]

The Code defined the term 'document' as any written text, whatever its medium, containing data and having been established by the institution in question. The rules also laid down the procedure to be followed in order to obtain a document. The institution had 30 days to decide on an application for access. Where the application was refused, the applicant could appeal. After the appeal, the institution in question had 30 days to decide on it. If the decision was to refuse access, the institution had to inform the applicant about the possibility of lodging a complaint with the European Ombudsman according to ex Article 195 of the EC Treaty, now Article 228 TFEU, or bringing an action before the Court of First Instance, based on ex Article 230 of the EC Treaty, currently Article 263 TFEU.

Even after the enactment of the Code, there was much dissatisfaction about the state of transparency in the EU.[35] The institutions were reluctant to interpret the Code in favour of transparency.[36] This attitude led to repeated refusals for access. As a result, the Court of Justice and the Court of First Instance handed down several judgments interpreting the Council and the Commission decisions denying access. In this regard, the contribution of the EU Courts has been, to a more or lesser extent, significant in supporting a culture of openness and accountability in the EU.[37] The Courts held, for example, that the institutions, after having adopted their internal rules on access, were abiding by them and any exceptions to the principle of the widest access must be justified on objective grounds and be strictly applied.[38] In addition to this, the Court ruled that the institutions were obliged to carry out a concrete and individual assessment of each of the requested documents

34 It must be noted here that it was only in 1997 that the EP adopted rules regarding access to its documents.

35 D Curtin, 'The fundamental principle of open decision-making and EU (political) citizenship', in O' Keeffe, *Legal Issues of the Amsterdam Treaty* (Oxford University Press 1999).

36 C Harlow, *Accountability in the European Union* (Oxford University Press 2002); *See* H Brunmayr, 'The Council's policy on transparency', in V Deckmyn and I Thomson, *Openness and Transparency in the European Union* (European Institute of Public Administration 1998).

37 H Ragnemalm, 'The Community courts and openness within the European Union' (1999) 2 *Cambridge Yearbook of European Legal Studies*, p. 29.

38 Case T-105/95, *WWF* v. *Commission* [1997] ECR II-313, para. 55. This was the first judgment on access to documents rules concerning the Commission. It established that the internal institutional rules on access to documents are capable of conferring rights on citizens and imposing obligations on the Commission. The CFI also ruled for the first time on the public interest exception concerning inspections and investigations and ruled that the documents relating to investigations which may lead to an infringement procedure according to Article 226 of the EC Treaty, now Art 258 TFEU, satisfy the conditions that must be met by the Commission in order to rely on the public interest exception according to Article 4(1) of the Code of conduct. *See* Case C-68/94, *Netherlands* v. *Council* [1996] ECR I-2169; Joined cases, C-174/98 P & 189/98 P, *Netherlands and Van der Wal* v. *Commission* [2000] ECR I-1, para. 27; and Case C-353/99 P, *Hautala* v. *Council* [2001] ECR I-9565, para. 25; *See* RW Davis, 'The Court of Justice and the right of public access to Community-held documents' (2000) 25 *European Law Review*, p. 303.

before deciding whether or not to release them.[39] Also, as already explained above, if the institutions were relying on a discretionary exception, they were required to balance the interest of the applicant against their interest in protecting confidentiality. Access should be granted if the applicant's interest outweighed the institution's interest.[40] Finally, the institutions had to disclose the part of the documents not covered by the exceptions. This is known as the principle of partial access, which was first developed by the Courts after this possibility was not provided for in the Code.[41] In this regard, 'the principle of transparency is intended to secure a more significant role for citizens in the decision-making process and ensure that the administration acts with greater propriety, efficiency and responsibility'.[42] As already explained in Chapter 1, the principle of transparency strengthens democracy and enhances the respect for fundamental rights.[43]

Concrete and individual examination of the requested documents

Under the Code of conduct, there is consistent jurisprudence that 'the legal rule is that the public is to have access to the documents of the institutions and the power to refuse access is the exception'.[44] At the same time, the exceptions needed to be interpreted and applied restrictively so as not to defeat the general principle of the widest possible access found in the Code and in the Council and the Commission decisions implementing it.[45] To implement the above-mentioned rule, the institutions were required to examine the documents concretely and individually and to state reasons based on the Code's exceptions if access was to be refused in respect of each of the requested documents.[46] The risk of the public or private interest being undermined must be reasonably foreseeable and not purely hypothetical.[47] This exercise was aimed at helping the applicant assess the reasons on which access was denied and to enable the Court to exercise its power of review. Thus, refusal could only be based on an analysis of factors relating to each of the requested documents individually.[48]

39 Case T-174/95, *Svenska Journalistforbundet* v. *Council* [1998] ECR II-2289, para. 112.

40 Case T-194/94, *Carvel* v. *Council* [1995] ECR II-2765, para. 65 and Case T-105/95, *WWF* v. *Commission* [1997] ECR II-313, para. 59.

41 Case C-353/99 P, *Hautala* v. *Council* [2001] ECR I-9565.

42 Case T-211/00, *Kuijer (II)* v. *Council* [2002] ECR II-485, para. 52.

43 Case T-309/97, *Bavarian Lager (I)* v. *Commission* [1999] ECR II-3217, para. 36.

44 Case T-211/00, *Kuijer (II)* v. *Council* [2002] ECR II-485, para. 55; *See* B Vesterdorf, 'Transparency – Not Just A Vague Word' (1999) 22 *Fordham International Law Journal*, p. 902.

45 Case T-174/95, *Swenska Journalistforbundet* v. *Council* [1998] ECR II-2289, para. 110; Case T-105/95, *WWF* v. *Commission* [1997] ECR II-313, para. 56; Case T-124/96 *Interporc (I)* v. *Commission* [1998] ECR II-231, para. 49.

46 Case T-83/96 *Van der Wal* v. *Commission* [1998] ECR II-545, para. 43; Case T-124/96, *Interporc (I)* v. *Commission* [1998] ECR II-231, para. 52.

47 Case T-211/00, *Kuijer (II)* v. *Council* [2002] ECR II-485, para. 56.

48 Case T-211/00, *Kuijer (II)* v. *Council* [2002] ECR II-485.

The Court[49] ruled that, in exceptional cases, the requirement of concrete and individual examination could be limited under the 'administrative burden rule', according to which the document-by-document examination may be abandoned and that the institutions were allowed to balance the work that would be required against the public interest in gaining access. In other words, excessive administrative work may allow an institution to derogate from the access requirement.[50]

The case law of the EU Courts also established that, although based on the power of internal organisation, the Council and the Commission decisions contained enforceable rights for individuals, and exceptions to the general rule of public access should be construed and applied strictly in a manner that did not defeat the application of the general rule.[51] In this regard, the Court of First Instance ruled in *Kuijer II*[52] that the Council had wrongly applied the exception mentioned in Article 4(1) of the Council Decision 93/731 relating to the protection of international relations. According to the CFI, the Council failed to consider the consequences of releasing the requested documents upon the EU's relationship with specific third countries. Instead of making this specific examination, the Council refused to release the documents based on very general statements and assumptions rather than on analysis of factors which specifically and effectively may undermine the exception relating to international relations. Thus, the Court found that the Council did not examine specifically whether there was a risk that would prejudice the Union's relations with third countries.

The principle of partial access

As already explained, the exceptions of the Code were required to be interpreted in a way which facilitated the right to access and respected the principle of proportionality. These requirements could only be fulfilled by granting partial access to the documents not covered by the exceptions. Yet, in exceptional circumstances where the administrative burden of redacting the parts that may not be disclosed proved to be particularly heavy thereby exceeding the limits of what may reasonably

49 Case C-353/99 P, *Hautala* v. *Council* [2001] ECR I-9565, para. 30; Case T-14/98, *Hautala* v. *Council* [1999] ECR II-2489, para. 86; Case T-188/98, *Kuijer* v. *Council* [2000] ECR II-1959, paras 55–56; Case T-211/00, *Kuijer* v. *Council (II)* [2002] ECR II-485, para. 57.

50 J Heliskoski and P Leino, 'Darkness at the break of noon: The case law on Regulation No. 1049/2001 on access to documents' (2006) 43 *Common Market Law Review*, p 735; *See also* A Flanagan, 'EU freedom of information: Determining where the interest lies' (2007) 13 *European Public Law*, p. 595.

51 Case T-105/95, *WWF* v. *Commission* [1997] ECR II-313; Case T-174/95, *Svenska Journalistforbundet* v. *Council* [1998] ECR II-2289.

52 Case T-211/00, *Kuijer (II)* v. *Council* [2002] ECR II-485.

be required,[53] the institutions could rely on the administrative burden rule and refuse access.[54]

The first legal challenge: Article 4.2 of the Council Decision[55]

The way according to which the Code of conduct was interpreted by the institutions proved to be fairly contentious. The early cases reveal that the Council and the Commission had a very restrictive view on what documents could be disclosed to the applicants. During the early case law, Article 4.2 of the Council Decision proved to be particularly problematic, granting to the Council the power to abuse its position by finding that the deliberations of its meetings could not be disclosed. It was Article 4.2 that formed the basis for the first legal challenge. It provided that 'access to a Council document may be refused in order to protect the confidentiality of the Council's proceedings'.

On 2 February 1994, John Carvel asked the Council for documents from three meetings of the Justice Council. On 28 February, the General Secretariat of the Council replied with very little information. Following a confirmatory application from John Carvel, the Council rejected the application on the grounds that the documents concerned 'refer directly to the deliberations of the Council and its preparatory instances. If it did allow access, the Council would fail to protect the confidentiality of its proceedings'.[56]

The Court of First Instance annulled the decision of the Council refusing the applicant's access to preparatory reports, minutes, attendance and voting records of the Justice Council of 29 and 30 November 1993. The Court held that when an applicant requests documents that fall under the confidentiality exception, then the latter has an obligation to balance its interest regarding the confidentiality exception against the applicant's interest to have access to those documents. If the protection of confidentiality outweighs the applicant's interest, then access is refused. Hence, a blanket refusal to grant access to a class of documents infringes Article 4(2) of the Council Decision 93/73.[57] The first judgment ensuring openness over secrecy in the Council meetings had been won and does constitute the first step forward towards more accountability and transparency.[58]

53 Case T-211/00, *Kuijer (II)* v. *Council* [2002] ECR II-485, para. 57.

54 Case C-353/99 P, *Hautala* v. *Council* [2001] ECR I-9565, para. 30; Case T-14/98, *Hautala* v. *Council* [1999] ECR II-2489, para. 86; Case T-188/98, *Kuijer* v. *Council* [2000] ECR II-1959, paras 55–56; Case T-211/00, *Kuijer* v. *Council (II)* [2002] ECR II-485, para. 57. On this point, *see also* Flanagan, op. cit. n 50 *supra*.

55 93/731/EC: Council Decision of 20 December on Public Access to Council Documents (1993), available at eur-lex.europa.eu/legal-content/EN/TXT/?uri=CELEX%3A31993D0731, accessed 26 June 2016.

56 Case T-194/94, *Carvel* v. *Council* [1995] ECR II-2765, para. 22.

57 Case T-194/94, *Carvel* v. *Council* [1995] ECR II-2765, para. 65.

58 T Bunyan, 'Secrecy and openness in the European Union: The ongoing struggle for freedom of information', available at www.statewatch.org/secret/freeinfo/index.html, accessed 28 January 2016.

The authorship rule: Article 2.2 of the Council Decision

The authorship rule constituted a rather significant restriction on the right of access to documents. Pursuant to this rule, access to documents which each of the two institutions did not draw up shall be denied and must be directed to the author. The result of this restriction was that any requests to the Commission or the Council relating to documents in their possession, but 'authored' by another institution or body, or by any international organisation or Member State, or natural or legal person, were refused on the basis of the 'authorship rule'. Any such requests were directed to the author.

The authorship rule was confirmed by the early case law. In *Rothmans*,[59] the Court of First Instance ruled for the first time on the 'authorship rule' by holding that requests regarding documents prepared (authored) by third persons must be directed to those persons and that the institutions merely possessed the documents and had no authority to disclose them. The Court highlighted that this exception constituted a restriction to the right of access to documents and must be treated as such and be interpreted and applied strictly. Thus, for the purposes of the access rules and by applying the general principle of the widest possible access to documents, the Court ruled that comitology committees assisting the Commission in implementing the legislation are part of the Commission and not separate entities.[60] The validity of the authorship rule was upheld by the Court of First Instance in *Interporc II*.[61]

The Ombudsman's decisions on access to documents

The Ombudsman's decisions on complaints against refusal of access to documents show a similar pattern.[62] For instance, the Council contested the Ombudsman's competence to deal with a series of complaints from the British journalist, Tony Bunyan, on behalf of Statewatch, concerning documents relating to cooperation in justice and home affairs. The Ombudsman considered that the correct interpretation and application of Decision 93/731 was a matter of the then Community law and not a third pillar matter, even if the documents in question concerned

59 Case T-188/97, *Rothmans* v. *Commission* [1999] ECR II-2463.

60 Case T-188/97, *Rothmans* v. *Commission* [1999] ECR II-2463, paras 56–62; *See* C Bergström, *Delegation of Powers in the European Union and the Committee System* (Oxford University Press 2005); Bovens, Chapter 1, op. cit. n 29 *supra*; A Türk, 'Transparency and comitology', in C Demmke and C Engel, *Continuity and Change in the European Integration Process* (European Institute of Public Administration 2003).

61 Case T-92/98, *Interporc Im- und Export GmbH* v. *Commission ('Interporc II')* [1999] ECR II-3421.

62 J Soderman, 'The role and impact of the European Ombudsman in access to documentation and transparency of decision-making', in V Deckmyn and I Thomson, *Openness and Transparency in the European Union* (European Institute of Public Administration 1998), p. 75; *See* Tomkins, op. cit. n 12 *supra*.

actions under the third pillar.[63] This approach was confirmed by the Court in a case which its own jurisdiction contested on the same basis.[64]

The Ombudsman also ruled that the authorship rule did not apply to documents of which the Council was a joint author and that the term 'repeat applications' in the Code did not include applications for different documents. Similarly, the Ombudsman found that the decision to seek a fair solution in the case of an application for very large documents did not apply to applications for a large number of documents.[65] Furthermore, the Ombudsman did not consider a mere reference to the fight against organised crime to be an adequate justification for applying a mandatory exception. Neither was it sufficient merely to state that a document contains 'detailed national positions' when applying the exception for maintaining the confidentiality of the institution's deliberations.[66] Finally, the Council established the public register for its own documents following a recommendation from the Ombudsman.[67]

The Treaty of Amsterdam (Article 1 TEU)

The next step towards more transparency came with the Treaty of Amsterdam, which provided that decisions need to be taken as openly and closely *as possible* to the citizen (Article 1 TEU). More importantly, under old Article 255 EC, any EU citizen and any natural or legal person residing or having its registered office in a Member State could have access to EP, Council and Commission documents. Access was to be denied for the protection of certain public and private interests to be determined by the Council under the then co-decision procedure. Currently, Article 15 TFEU requires all the EU organs to conduct their work openly. There is, therefore, a generic Treaty obligation upon the institutions to function openly. These Treaty amendments show clearly the political consensus to incorporate the principle of transparency in the EU. What is less clear, however, is the exact status of transparency in the EU legal order, due to national divergences on the issue.[68]

More recently, the appointment of Timmermans, a strong advocate for greater transparency, as the new vice-president of the Commission, sent the signal for higher ethical standards and increased transparency as regards EU lobbying with

63 Case 1087/96 [1998] EOAR 41.

64 Case T-174/95, *Svenska Journalistforbundet* v. *Council* [1998] ECR II-2289, paras 85–86.

65 Case 1053/96, [1998] EOAR 167; *See also* Case 1056/96, [1998] EOAR 172.

66 Case 1057/96, [1998] EOAR 178.

67 2000/23/EC Council Decision on the improvement of information on the Council's legislative activities and the public register of Council documents, OJ 2000 L9/22.

68 A Guggenbuhl, 'A miracle formula or an old powder in new packaging? Transparency and openness after Amsterdam', in V Deckmyn and I Thomson (eds), *Openness and Transparency in the European Union,* (EIPA 1998); *See* RW Davis, 'Public access to Community documents: A fundamental human right?' (1999) 3 *European Integration Online Papers*, p. 8.

stakeholders.[69] In consequence, Commission's officials can now only meet with registered industry representatives, consumers and non-governmental organisations that seek to influence decision-making in their favour.[70] Yet, the situation in relation to the online register for expert groups[71] is significantly different.[72] The register appears to be incomplete and outdated, as some of the experts do not exist and others that do exist are not listed on the register. Accountability deficits in this field exist because of the lack of transparency regarding their exact number, composition and meetings.[73] This lack of transparency is unacceptable given that expert groups are now crucial as conduits of expertise for the Commission and (indirectly) as sources of information for the EP and the Council, when holding the Commission accountable.

Regulation 1049/2001 and the relevant case law

Regulation 1049/2001 governs, at the time of writing, the 'fundamental'[74] right of citizens and residents in the EU to access, in principle, all the documents drawn or held by the EP, Council and the Commission.[75] The adoption of this legislative

69 *See* ec.europa.eu/transparencyregister/public/, accessed 29 January 2016.

70 R Mack, 'Lobbying effectively in Brussels and Washington: Getting the right result' (2005) 9 (4) *Journal of Communication Management*, p. 339.

71 Expert groups have been defined as 'a committee or group set up by and terminated by the Commission of its own accord or a committee/group that is regarded to be the Commission's expert group although not financed, chaired or set up by the Commission'. *See* T Larsson, *Precooking in the European Union – The World of Expert Groups* (Fritzes Offentliga Publikationer 2003), p. 14.

72 *See* ec.europa.eu/transparency/regexpert/, accessed 1 February 2016.

73 S Peers and M Costa 'Accountability for delegated and implementing acts after the Treaty of Lisbon' (2012) 18 (3) *European Law Journal*, p. 427.

74 There is much debate on the fundamental aspect of the access to documents right in the EU. Applicants have repeatedly argued before the Courts on the fundamental nature of such a right. Legal scholars have advocated also for the fundamental nature of the right of access to documents in the EU. *See*, for example, D Curtin, 'Citizens' fundamental right of access to EU information: An evolving digital passepartout?' (2000) 37 *Common Market Law Review*, p. 7; *See* Davis, op. cit. n 68 *supra*; M Bromberg, 'Access to documents: A general principle of Community law' (2002) 27 *European Law Review*. The Court of Justice, however, acknowledges the importance of this right, but it has never accepted its fundamental aspect. The whole discourse on the fundamental aspect of the access to documents right now resides in the past, because the Treaty of Lisbon has become law. Article 6 of the TEU recognises the Charter of Fundamental Rights as legally binding, granting it the same legal value as the Treaties. The Charter includes in Article 42 a right of access to documents. In addition, Article 15 of the Treaty on the functioning of the EU, which is the equivalent of the ex Article 255 of the EC Treaty, is significantly widened. For example, it covers the Union institutions, bodies, offices and agencies; and the Court of Justice, the European Central Bank and the European Investment Bank are also covered by this provision for their administrative tasks.

75 Although in principle the beneficiaries of the right of access to documents are EU citizens and residents, Article 2(2) of the Regulation grants discretion to the EU institutions bound by it to grant access to any natural or legal person not residing or not having its registered office in a Member State. The institutions responded positively to this option. *See* Decision 2001/840 of the Council OJ 2001, L 313/40, Decision 2001/937 of the Commission OJ 2001, L 345/94 and the Decision of the EP OJ 2001, L 374/I.

measure was a real triumph for the advocates of transparency in the EU.[76] The pre-Regulation case law has, to a large extent, been incorporated into this Regulation, and the interpretation of the old rules is still applicable unless clearly stated otherwise.[77] This is justified by Recital 3 of the Regulation's Preamble, which states that the Regulation 'consolidates the initiatives which the institutions have already taken'. Essentially, the jurisprudence towards the right of access has developed two approaches. The first one was described as 'marginal review', whereas the second was called as the 'foreseeability standard'.[78] The former approach relates to the fact that the institutions exercise wide discretion when they apply the exception[79] and, in consequence, judicial review is significantly restrained. The latter confirms the requirement for the widest possible access, so long as the risk of harm to the protected interest is not merely hypothetical.

As already explained, pursuant to settled case law and in view of the objectives of the Regulation, the exceptions set out in Article 4 of the Regulation must be interpreted and applied strictly. Thus, when the institution decides to rely on any of the exceptions mentioned in Article 4, 'it must explain how access to that document could specifically and effectively undermine the interest protected by an exception'.[80] The purpose of the Regulation, as set out in its Article 1, is:

> [t]o define the principles, conditions, and limits on grounds of public or private interest governing the right of access to EP, Council, and Commission documents . . . in such a way as to ensure the widest possible access to documents . . . to establish rules ensuring the easiest possible exercise of this right . . . and to promote good administrative practice on access to documents.[81]

For this purpose, any European citizen and any natural or legal person residing or having its registered office in any of the Member States can apply to access any documents.[82]

76 *See* Harden, Chapter 1, op. cit. n 49 *supra.*

77 *See* Peers, Chapter 2, op. cit. n 7 *supra*; H Kranenborg, 'Is it time to revise the European regulation on public access to documents?' (2006) 12 (2) *European Public Law*, p 251; *See* joined cases T-391/03 and T-70/04, *Franchet and Byk* v. *Commission* [2006] ECR II-2023, paras 82, 88 where the court applied and further developed the prior jurisprudence concerning the exceptions of the access rules.

78 D Adamski, 'How wide is "the widest possible"? Judicial interpretation of the exceptions to the right of access to official documents revisited' (2009) 46 (2) *Common Market Law Review*, p. 521.

79 Case T-211/00, *Kuijer (II)* v. *Council* [2002] ECR II-485, para. 53: 'When the Council decides whether the public interest may be undermined by releasing a document, it exercises a discretion which is among the political responsibilities conferred on it by provisions of the Treaties'; *See* C-266/05 P, *Sison* v. *Council* [2007] ECR I-1233, para. 15: 'in areas covered by the mandatory exceptions to public access to documents, provided for in Art. 4(1) (a) of Regulation 1049/2001, the institutions enjoy a wide discretion'; Case T-14/98, *Hautala* v. *Council* [1999] ECR II-2489, para. 44.

80 Case T-121/05, *Borax* v. *Commission* [2009] ECR II-27.

81 *See* Flanagan, op. cit. n 50 *supra.*

82 Article 2(2) of Regulation 1049/2001 [2001] OJ L 145/43.

The Regulation reflects the overall intention specified in the second subparagraph of ex Article 1 TEU quoted above, currently Article 1 of the TEU, to mark a new stage in the process of creating an even closer union amongst the peoples of Europe, in which decisions are taken as openly as possible and as closely as possible to the citizen. Similarly, as it is noted in Recital 2 of the Regulation's Preamble, there is a direct link of the fundamental right of European citizens and residents to have access to documents held by the EU institutions with the democratic nature of those institutions.

Article 2 of the Regulation sets out the basic provisions, and its wording is analogous to the wording of ex Article 255 (1) of the EC Treaty, whereas Article 2(3) defines the scope of the Regulation and reads as follows:

> This Regulation shall apply to all documents held by an institution, that is to say, documents drawn up or received by it and in its possession, in all areas of activities of the EU.

This provision marks a significant change to the pre-Regulation regime. Article 2(3) provides that documents *drawn* or *received* by the institutions fall within the scope of the Regulation. This broader access constitutes an important obvious step forward in respect of the former situation, which covered only access to documents *drawn* up by the institutions.[83] As explained already, according to the authorship rule, requests for the release of documents not authored by the institution that possessed them were directed to the authors. Yet, this welcome abolition does not mean that the right of access to documents is an absolute right. The institutions may still rely on Article 4 to justify denial to grant access.

There are four types of exceptions: mandatory, 'discretionary', the protection of the decision-making process and, finally, documents originating from third parties and Member States. Article 4(1) is written in mandatory terms and provides that:

> [t]he institutions shall refuse access to a document where disclosure would undermine the protection of:
>
> (a) the public interest as regards:
>
> - public security;
> - defence and military matters;
> - international relations;
> - the financial, monetary or economic policy of the Community or a Member State;
>
> (b) privacy and the integrity of the individual, in particular in accordance with the Community legislation regarding the protection of personal data.

83 *See* Peers, Chapter 2, op. cit. n 7 *supra*; *See also* De Leeuw, op. cit. n 25 *supra*.

The first category of exceptions (Article 4(1) of the Regulation) precludes access to any of the documents falling within it and calls for no balancing of interests at stake. If the institutions can prove that the documents fall into this category, refusal is automatically justified.[84] As regards the privacy exception, the personal data legislation provides for limits.[85] The CFI, now the General Court, was called on to interpret the relationship between Regulation 1049/2001 and Regulation 45/2001[86] and ruled that disclosure can only be denied if the privacy or the integrity of the person would be undermined. In consequence, the CFI carried out a balancing exercise between the two fundamental rights at stake: public access and data protection. It highlighted the importance of the access right and reiterated that any limitations must be construed and applied restrictively so as not to defeat the general principle enshrined in Regulation 1049/2001.[87] At the same time, the right to data protection must be protected. As a result, the Court ruled that names, titles and functions of public office holders, civil servants and interest representatives in relation to their professional activities shall be disclosed, because disclosure does not lead to an interference with the private life of the persons, neither would those persons have any grounds to believe that they enjoyed confidential treatment.[88]

Unfortunately, from an openness point of view, the Court of Justice set aside the judgment of the General Court on the grounds that the assessment of whether the protection of privacy, and the integrity of the individual protected by Article 4(1) (b) of the Regulation, should not be confined to Article 8 of the European Convention on Human Rights (ECHR), but must take into account the EU legislation on data protection. Under Regulation 45/2001, Bavarian Lager did not provide any justification in favour of obtaining the requested data and therefore the Commission and the Court were not in a position to assess whether the applicant's interest outweighed the 'data subject's legitimate interest and to examine whether the latter's interest might be prejudiced, as required by Article 8(b) of 45/2001'.[89]

84 *See* Peers, Chapter 2, op. cit. n 7 *supra*; De Leeuw, op. cit. n 25 *supra*; H Kranenborg, 'Access to documents and data protection in the European Union: On the public nature of personal data' (2008) 45 *Common Market Law Review*, p. 1079; Joined Cases, T-110/03, T-150/03 and T-405/03, *Sison* v. *Council* [2005] ECR II-1429; *See also* Case T-211/00, *Kuijer (II)* v. *Council* [2002] ECR II-485; Case T-14/98, *Hautala* v. *Council* [1999] ECR II-2489; Joined Cases C-514/07 P, C-528/07 P and C-532/07 P, *Sweden and Others* v. *API and Commission* [2010] ECR I0000; Case C-139/07 P, *Commission* v. *Technische Glaswerke Ilmenau* [2010] ECR I-0000.

85 *See* Kranenborg, op. cit. n 84 *supra*.

86 L 145/29, available at eur-lex.europa.eu/legal-content/EN/ALL/?uri=CELEX%3A62013CC0615, accessed 30 June 2016.

87 Case T-194/04, *Bavarian Lager* v. *Commission* [2007] ECR II-4523, para. 94; *See also* Kranenborg, op. cit. n 161 *supra*.

88 Case T-194/04, *Bavarian Lager* v. *Commission* [2007] ECR II-4523, paras 131, 132, 136.

89 Case C-28/08 P, *Commission* v. *Bavarian Lager* [2010] ECR *Commission* v. *Bavarian Lager* [2010] ECR I-6055, para. 80.

The Article 4.1 case law on the mandatory exceptions consistently applies the marginal review standard, since judicial review is:

> [l]imited to verifying whether the procedural rules have been complied with, the contested decision is properly reasoned, and the facts have been accurately stated, and whether there has been a manifest error of assessment of the facts or misuse of powers.[90]

Yet, the exceptions set out in Article 4 must be interpreted and applied strictly to secure the *effet utile* of the access right. It follows from this that when the institution decides to rely on any of the exceptions, 'it must explain how access to that document could specifically and effectively undermine the interest protected by an exception'.[91] This delicate balancing task has been deemed essential, and access cannot be denied without first appraising the requested documents on a case-by-case basis. Despite this careful and consistent emphasis in support of transparency, there is a parallel development of a set of general presumptions (against openness), which reveals the existence of a paradox. Arguably, general presumptions defeat the very purpose of the widest access, which has been emphasised categorically during the past 20 years in the case law.[92] More fundamentally, this approach reveals that the EU Courts have taken a rather limited line on openness, which necessarily contributes to the debate about the lack of accountability in the EU. To substantiate this, the application of the exceptions regarding sensitive, legislative, administrative and judicial documents, as per settled case law, is discussed below.

Sensitive documents: The Sison *case*

The *Sison*[93] case was the first case where the Court had to examine the mandatory exceptions relating to public security and international relations under the Regulation. As explained already, in principle, the Regulation covers all the documents drawn or held by the EP, Council and the Commission. Pragmatically, however, certain documents are subject to special procedural rules before they can be released. In this regard, Article 2(5) provides that 'sensitive documents as defined in Article 9(1) shall be subject to special treatment'. The pre-Regulation understanding of the nature of the discretion related to the mandatory

90 Case T-14/98, *Hautala* v. *Council* [1999] ECR II-2489, para. 72. This has been confirmed as regards the Regulation. *See* Joined Cases T-110/03, T-150/03 and T-405/03, *Sison* v. *Council* [2005] ECR II-1429, para. 46; *See* Case C-226/05 P, *Sison* v. *Council* [2007] ECR I-1233, paras 34 and 64.

91 Case T-121/05, *Borax* v. *Commission* [2009] ECR II-27.

92 *See* Joined Cases C-514/11 P and C-605/11 P, *LPN and Finland* v. *Commission* [2013] ECLI:EU:C:2013:738.

93 Joined Cases T-110/03, T-150/03 and T-405/03 *Sison* v. *Council* [2005] ECR II-1429.

exceptions[94] has played a key role in *Sison* and led the Court to adopt a conservative interpretation of the public security and international relations exceptions. Pursuant to the reasoning of the Court, the power to review the legality of the institutions' decisions regarding Article 4(1) (a) is:

> [l]imited to verifying whether the procedural rules and the duty to state reasons have been complied with, the facts have been accurately stated, and whether there has been a manifest error of assessment of the facts or a misuse of powers.[95]

In *Sison*[96], the applicant had been refused access relating to three successive Council decisions implementing a Regulation on specific restrictive measures directed against persons with a view to combating terrorism.[97] The applicant's name had been included in all three Council decisions and his funds and financial assets were frozen.

Mr Sison challenged the legality of the Council's decision not to grant him access to the documents that had led the Council to adopt Decision 2002/848, as well as the Council's refusal to disclose the identity of the states which had provided the Council with certain documents in that connection. The applicant, based on the short and formulaic response, argued that the Council, contrary to settled case law, had never conducted a concrete and individual examination of the documents requested.[98] As a result, the applicant was unable to ascertain the reasons put forward by the Council, and the Court was unable to exercise its power of review. The Council, however, argued that the existence of a specific procedure dealing with the request for sensitive documents shows that concrete examination had taken place. The Court agreed with the Council and adopted a very conservative interpretation of the public security and international relations exception.

Regarding the disclosure of the identity of the states that had provided the Council with documents in relation to the adoption of the Decision 2002/848, the Court was satisfied by the fact that the documents were sensitive and also that the originators of the documents had expressed their opposition to the disclosure.

94 According to settled case law, the institutions enjoy wide discretion in the context of a decision denying access based on the protection of public interest regarding international relations. *See* Case T-14/98, *Hautala* v. *Council* [1999] ECR II-2489, para. 44 and Case T-211/00, *Kuijer* v. *Council* [2002] ECR II-485, para. 55.

95 Joined Cases T-110/03, T-150/03 and T-405/03, *Sison* v. *Council* [2005] ECR II-1429, para. 47; Case T-14/98, *Hautala* v. *Council* [1999] ECR II-2489, para. 44 and Case T-211/00, *Kuijer* v. *Council* [2002] ECR II-485, para. 55; *See* De Leeuw, op. cit. n 25 *supra*.

96 Joined Cases T-110/03, T-150/03 and T-405/03, *Sison* v. *Council* [2005] ECR II-1429.

97 Council Regulation (EC) No 2580/2001 of 27 December 2001 on specific restrictive measures directed against certain persons and entities with a view to combating terrorism L 344/70.

98 Joined Cases T-110/03, T-150/03 and T-405/03, *Sison* v. *Council* [2005] ECR II-1429, para. 57.

In his appeal, Mr Sison tried to set aside the CFI's judgment, though the Court of Justice reiterated that the Union institutions enjoy wide discretion in the areas covered by Article 4(1)[99] and thus dismissed the appeal.

The second category, set out in Article 4(2), is not really discretionary, since it is written in the same mandatory way ('shall refuse') as the exceptions in Article 4(1), but is subject to a public interest override in favour of disclosure. The decision-making exception provided by Article 4(3) is the equivalent of the confidentiality exception under the Code of conduct. The former imposes a higher threshold for non-disclosure. Specifically, it requires that the disclosure 'significantly undermines' the decision-making. Accordingly, the balance is tipped towards disclosure.

Article 4(2) reads as follows:

> [t]he institutions shall refuse access to documents where disclosure would undermine the protection of:
>
> - commercial interests of natural or legal person, including intellectual property
> - court proceeding and legal advice
> - the purpose of inspections, investigations and audits
>
> unless there is an overriding public interest in disclosure.

The latter clause constitutes an 'exception to the exception'[100] and, if applicable, the requested documents need to be released. However, the CFI interpreted this provision strictly and held in *Turco*[101] and in other cases[102] that the overriding public interest provided by Article 4(2) must be in addition to the public's right to be informed. This case law, however, cannot be considered as good law any longer after the ruling of the Court of Justice in the *Turco's* appeal.[103]

Legislative documents relating to legal advice: Turco *case*[104]

The applicant, Mr Turco, requested access to an opinion of the Council's legal service relating to a proposal for a Council Directive laying down minimum standards for the reception of applicants for asylum in Member States. He was refused access on the basis that the release of the opinion would undermine the protection of legal advice regulated by the second indent of Article 4(2)

99 Case C-266/05 P, *Sison* v. *Council* [2007] ECR I-1233, paras 32–34.

100 *See* Kranenborg and Voermans, op. cit. n 6 *supra*.

101 Case T-84/03, *Turco* v. *Council* [2004] ECR II-4061, para. 83; *See* Heliskoski and Leino, op. cit. n 50 *supra*.

102 Case T-36/04, *Association de la presse internationale asbl (API)* v. *Commission* [2007] ECR II-3201, paras 95, 97.

103 Joined cases C-39/05 P and C-52/05 P, *Sweden and Turco* v. *Council* [2008] ECR I-4723.

104 Case T-84/03, *Turco* v. *Council* [2004] ECR II-4061.

of the Regulation. The Council argued that its interest in protecting internal legal advice outweighed the public interest in disclosure.[105] In addition to this, the Council argued that such a public interest cannot constitute the mere fact that the release of the document concerned would be in the general interest of increasing openness and transparency of the institutions' decision-making process. This criterion, according to the Council, would apply to all written opinions of the Council's legal service. Finally, the Council argued that the release of the opinion concerned would give rise to uncertainty of the validity of the legislative act adopted following such advice.[106]

The applicant and one of the intervening governments,[107] Finland, argued that denial of access should be based on a concrete and individual examination of the documents requested and not relate to all legal advice on legislative acts in general.[108] The Court ruled that, in principle, denial of access must be based on concrete and individual examination, but, however, the Council's generality was justified by the fact that giving additional information would deprive the exception relied upon of its effect.[109] The CFI ruled also that the rationale behind the legal advice exception is to avoid uncertainty, by raising doubts, over the legality of EU legislation[110] along with securing independence of the opinions of the institutions' legal service.[111] As far as the public interest override is concerned, the Court found that the legal advice can derogate from the established duty, incumbent on the institutions, to carry out a concrete assessment of the requested documents. By doing so, the CFI placed the burden of proof regarding the override upon the applicants.[112] What is more surprising, however, was the outcome of the Court that the override could not be invoked in the general interest of transparency, openness, democracy and citizens' participation in the decision-making process.[113] These principles, according to the Court, have already been implemented and underlie the transparency Regulation.[114]

The above-mentioned reasoning is hardly convincing. The CFI here says that the purpose of the exception is to prevent disclosure of the underlying legal advice in order to avoid uncertainty as to the legality of the acts adopted following such advice, and that any reference in the statement of reasons to the content of the opinion would deprive the exception of its effect. To paraphrase,

105 *Ibid.*, para. 5.
106 *Ibid.*, para. 8.
107 The other two intervening governments were Denmark and Sweden.
108 Case T-84/03, *Turco* v. *Council* [2004] ECR II-4061, para. 36.
109 *Ibid.*, para. 57.
110 *Ibid.*, para. 74.
111 *Ibid.*, para. 79.
112 *See* Curtin, op. cit. n 74 *supra*.
113 *See* Adamski, op. cit. n 78 *supra*.
114 Case T-84/03, *Turco* v. *Council* [2004] ECR II-4061, para. 83. *See also* Osterdahl, Chapter 2, op. cit. n 7 *supra*.

the CFI is of the view that a way to protect legal certainty is to prevent the public from finding out that acts of uncertain legality have been issued and are maintained.

The approach followed by the CFI in this case is in direct contradiction with the settled case law which sets out the principles governing the access to documents' regime. As already explained, the widest possible access enhances citizens' participation in the decision-making process. In fact, the same Court has ruled that 'the widest possible access to documents . . . is essential to enable citizens to carry out genuine and efficient monitoring of the exercise of the powers vested in the Community institutions'.[115] How can citizens exercise these rights when access to legal advice is refused as a matter of principle? Can any legal system be based on principles which prevent citizens from scrutinising the legality of any acts? On the contrary, there is a strong public interest override as regards the right to seek the annulment of measures of uncertain legality. To that end, protecting legal certainty cannot be considered as a panacea for an act which might very well be invalid.

The applicant also argued that the correct exception for the protection of the Council's legal advice is Article 4(3), which aims to protect the institution's decision-making process.[116] The CFI had rejected the application of Article 4(3) to the case of legal advice relating to legislative acts on the basis that to do so would empty Article 4(2) of relevancy. The CFI ruled that Article 4(2) does not relate to legal advice taken for the purpose of Court proceedings, but was designed to cover both situations.[117] This reasoning is not wholly convincing and it may make more sense to see legal opinion given as part of the legislative process as another form of *travaux preparatoires*, restricting Article 4(2) to legal advice relating to Court proceedings.[118] However, such an argument contradicts the fact that in Article 4(2) legal advice and Court proceedings are mentioned separately. It is worth mentioning that the Code of conduct was only referring to the Court proceedings exception; legal advice was inserted by the Regulation. Had the legislature wanted to protect Court proceedings alone, it would have had every opportunity to do so by choosing not to include an exception relating to legal advice. In any event, there can be legal advice not related to legislative proceedings, even legal advice given by in-house lawyers to companies and obtained by the Commission under competition proceedings, as long as such advice is not protected as privileged under EU law.

115 Case T-92/98, *Interporc* v. *Commission* [1999] ECR II-3521, para. 39.

116 Case T-84/03, *Turco* v. *Council* [2004] ECR II-4061, para. 33.

117 *Ibid.*, para. 67; the same approach was also taken by the Advocate-General, Poiares Maduro, in his opinion in the *Turco* case delivered on 29 November 2007, Case C-64/05 P, *Kingdom of Sweden* v. *Commission of the European Communities and Others* [2007] ECR I-11389, Opinion of Advocate-General Maduro.

118 *See* Heliskoski and Leino, op. cit. n 50 *supra*; L Penny, 'News: How accessible is it? An examination of the public's right to access information in the European Union' (2007) 18 *Entertainment Law Review*, p. 1.

The second ground put forward by the CFI appears no less problematic. The CFI found that the disclosure of the introductory paragraph of the Council's legal service opinion confirms that concrete and individual examination has taken place.[119] If the reasoning adopted here by the CFI becomes the accepted norm, then the access right will be drastically diminished of any substance in the sense that any partial access would always constitute evidence that an individual and concrete assessment had taken place. Finally, the CFI placed the burden of proof regarding the public interest override on the applicants, by ruling that the override could not be invoked in the general interest of transparency, openness, democracy and citizens' participation in the decision-making process. These principles, according to the Court, have already been implemented and underlie the transparency Regulation. Thus, the overriding interest capable of justifying disclosure must be distinct from those principles.[120]

For the above-mentioned reasons, it seems unfortunate that the reasoning of the Court was framed in such general language, especially because the Court in *Turco* ruled for the first time on the legal advice exception as well as on the public interest override provided by the Regulation in a number of exceptions. One would have wished the Court to confirm in a more explicit manner that not all the legal advice should escape the duty incumbent on the institutions to carry out a concrete assessment of documents of this kind.

Fortunately and in the interests of transparency, the Court of Justice, in the joined cases of *Sweden and Turco* v. *Council*,[121] set aside the CFI's judgment and upheld the appeal. The Court highlighted the importance of the principle of transparency in the decision-making process. What the Court did not do, however, was to rule that this principle constitutes a general principle of EU law. Also, the whole judgment has no reference to Article 42 of the Charter of fundamental rights which recognises the right of access to documents and, under the Treaty of Lisbon, has the same legal value as the Treaties themselves. Despite these deficiencies, the Court of Justice has delivered a significant judgment in support of openness and transparency, which further clarifies that the exceptions from the general rule of access must be interpreted and applied strictly.

The Court of Justice addressed how the EU institutions should deal with disclosure requests relating to legal advice laid down in the second indent of 4(2) of the transparency Regulation. It was held that when the institutions are asked to disclose such a document, they must carry out a specific three-staged procedure that corresponds to the three criteria outlined in that provision.[122]

119 Case T-84/03, *Turco* v. *Council* [2004] ECR II-4061, para. 75.

120 *Ibid.*, para. 83.

121 Joined cases C-39/05P and C-52/05P, *Sweden and Turco* v. *Council* [2008] ECR I-4723; *See* R Van Ooik, 'The growing importance of agencies in the EU: Shifting governance and the institutional balance', in D Curtin and R Wessel, *Good Governance and the European Union: Reflections on Concepts, Institutions and Substance* (Intersentia 2005); *See also* Adamski, op. cit. n 78 *supra*.

122 Joined cases C-39/05 P and C-52/05 P, *Sweden and Turco* v. *Council* [2008] ECR I-4723, para. 37.

First, the institution must consider and satisfy itself that the requested document does indeed relate to legal advice and whether any parts of the requested documents are covered by the exception.[123] The second stage is the requirement to consider whether disclosure of any parts of the document would undermine the protection of such an advice.[124] Regarding the latter requirement, the Court, using a teleological interpretation, ruled that the term legal advice must be understood in the light of the purpose of the Regulation. Under this purpose, the exception 'must be construed as aiming to protect an institution's interest in seeking legal advice and receiving frank, objective and comprehensive advice'.[125] The assessment of the risk of that interest being undermined should consider what is reasonably foreseeable and not purely hypothetical. Finally, if the outcome of the above assessment is that disclosure of the document would undermine the ability of the institution to receive frank and objective legal advice, it is incumbent on the institution to balance the interest in non-disclosure against any possible overriding interest, bearing in mind the purpose of the transparency legislation to secure the widest possible access to documents, giving a reasoned judgment for its decision.[126]

The Court of Justice in the *Turco* appeal held that the CFI was erred in law by finding that the *raison d'être* of the legal advice exception is not to fuel doubts over the legality of legislation. In fact, the Court of Justice has ruled that preventing disclosure can lead to the contrary and raise doubts in the citizens' minds over the legality of the decision-making process. Pursuant to the wording of the judiciary:

> [i]t is in fact rather a lack of information and debate which is capable of giving rise to doubts in the minds of citizens, not only as regards the lawfulness of an isolated act, but also as regards the legitimacy of the decision-making process as a whole.[127]

By upholding this appeal, the Court of Justice highlighted the importance of the access to documents rules and reintroduced the cornerstone of this regime, which is based on the ability of the public to assess the impact, comment upon and influence the development of policies, an activity which cannot take place without maximum access to information.

Nevertheless, regarding the protection of the institutions' interest in seeking and receiving frank, objective and comprehensive legal advice, the Court of Justice's justification appears to be particularly problematic. It is difficult to understand how the public's access to legal advice can affect the objectiveness

123 *Ibid.*, para. 38.
124 *Ibid.*, para. 40.
125 *Ibid.*, para. 42.
126 *Ibid.*, para. 44.
127 *Ibid.*, para. 59.

of it. Anyone studying accountability will argue that disclosure of this kind of document can only lead to professional behaviour, because of the fact that the drafters of the legal advice will always have in mind that the advice will be accessible. Arguably, it may even make more sense to interpret the legal advice exception more strictly, on a case-by-case basis, and limit it for the very sensitive cases.

More interestingly, the Court of Justice ruled that the overriding public interest pressing for disclosure of the legal advice needs to be no different from the principle of openness, transparency, democracy and civil participation in the decision-making process which already underlie the Regulation.[128]

The approach taken in *Turco* was indeed promising in terms of transparency and was described as 'spectacularly' progressive.[129] It clearly provided the foundations to disclose legal advice given in the remit of the executive action of the EU institutions as well. This was upheld by the General Court and recently confirmed by the Court of Justice in *In't Veld*.[130] Yet, it is deemed necessary to revisit the wider contribution of *Turco*. A further and detailed examination indicates significant shortcomings in the judgment. In particular, the 'general presumptions' line of reasoning as introduced by *Turco* raises significant questions as to the fundamental nature of the access right. In this regard, the Court established that:

> [i]t is in principle, open to the Council to base its decisions . . . on general presumptions which apply to certain categories of documents, as considerations of a generally similar kind are likely to apply to requests for disclosure relating to documents of the same nature.[131]

The Court effectively ruled that the Council, and arguably by analogy all the other institutions, can deny access based on general considerations as opposed to the well-established duty for a specific and detailed examination. In consequence, post *Turco*, there was every possibility that the institutions, the Commission in particular, would rely on general considerations in order to avoid carrying out a concrete appraisal of the requested documents. The Court, with great respect, set the foundations to depart from the principle of transparency and disregard almost two decades of jurisprudence. Indeed, later developments, examined further below, provide sufficient evidence to question the validity of the earlier finding that the judgment was spectacularly progressive.

128 Joined Cases C-39/05 P and C-52/05 P, *Sweden and Turco* v. *Council* [2008] ECR I-4723, para. 74.

129 *See* Adamski, op. cit. n 78 *supra*.

130 Case T-301/10, *Sophie In't Veld* v. *Commission* [2013] ECLI:EU:T:2013:135; Case C-350/12 P *Council* v. *Sophie In't Veld* [2014] ECLI:EU:C:2014:2039.

131 Joined Cases C-39/05 P and C-52/05 P, *Sweden and Turco* v. *Council* [2008] ECR I-4723, para. 50.

Administrative documents: the end of the one-by-one examination?

Despite the adoption of the Regulation, the state of transparency in the EU is still unsatisfactory. The institutions rely continuously on a culture of secrecy and take every opportunity to deny access. This is particularly the case as regards administrative documents. In *Verein für Konsumenteninformation*,[132] a consumers' organisation, had sought access to the Commission's administrative file containing 47,000 pages. The Commission refused access to the entire file on the grounds that partial access 'would have represented an excessive and disproportionate amount of work for it'.[133] In essence, the Commission denied access without even looking at the file, not even attempting to browse through the documents. But assume for a while that the Commission was right and the request was particularly burdensome. Assume further that the request could even paralyse the proper functioning of the institution. Should it result in the public being deprived of the fundamental right of access in such generic terms? Can it be considered as acceptable for the institutions to reduce the standards of transparency without invoking the exceptions provided by the Regulation?

The Regulation does not provide in any provision for the requirements of concrete and individual assessment to be abandoned under any circumstances. While Article 6(3) provides for an informal consultation aiming to find a fair solution, Article 7(3) provides that the time limit for handling an application can, under certain circumstances, be extended. Similarly, the Court noted that in the absence of a fair solution mentioned in Article 6(3), the Regulation provides no ruling similar to the one developed through the jurisprudence of the Courts relating to the administrative burden.[134] The Court moved on to note that the principle of proportionality may justify refusal of a concrete and individual examination to avoid cases where a manifestly unreasonable number of documents is requested which could result in paralysis of the proper functioning of the institution.[135]

Pursuant to the reasoning of the Court, Article 6(3) reflects the possibility that where a very large number of documents are requested, the institution can 'reconcile the interests of the applicant with those of good administration'.[136] As a result, there can be cases that require no individual examination. The Court observed that the possibility of non-concrete assessment must satisfy four requirements:

1 The administrative burden entailed by concrete and individual examination must be heavy and exceed the limits of what may be reasonably required.
2 The burden of proof rests within the institution relying on its unreasonableness.

132 Case T-2/03, *Verein für Konsumenteninformation* v. *Commission* [2005] ECR I-1121.
133 *Ibid.*, para. 20.
134 *Ibid.*, para. 96.
135 *Ibid.*, para. 101.
136 *Ibid.*

3 The institution must consult with the applicant in order to ascertain his interest and consider how it might adopt a measure less onerous than a concrete and individual examination.
4 The institution must prioritise the most favourable option for the applicant's right of access.[137]

With great respect to the judgment, the validity of the criteria, quoted above, can be questioned. Legally, the requirements lack proper foundation on the legislation. Had the legislature wanted to incorporate the pre-Regulation case law on administrative burden, it would have had every opportunity to do so. Yet, the legislature did not do so because they could hardly see how this restriction could fit with the principle of the widest possible access and with the corollary fundamental legal standard to interpret the exceptions narrowly.

Similarly, in 2010, *TGI*[138] concerned a request for access to certain large state aid files held by the Commission. The Court of Justice, by citing *Turco* this time, confirmed the 'settled case law' as regards the existence of a general presumption against disclosure.[139] *TGI* upheld the validity of the presumption and established that administrative documents are now essentially exempted from the document-by-document appraisal and that the public interest override will never apply unless particularly pertinent.[140]

More recently, the validity of the general presumption was upheld in *LPN*.[141] Citing this time *TGI* and *Turco*, *LPN* confirmed the existence of the presumption in the administrative file, in what appears to be a new development, to cover infringement proceedings.[142] On appeal, the applicants, LPN and Finland, argued that the Commission denied access without carrying out, in violation of settled case law, a concrete and individual assessment of the requested documents.[143] The Court ruled:

> [t]hat it can be *presumed* (emphasis added) that the disclosure of the documents concerning the infringement proceedings during the pre-litigation stage risks altering the nature of that procedure and changing the way it proceeds and, accordingly, that disclosure would in principle undermine the protection of the purpose of investigations, within the meaning of the third indent of Article 4(2) of Regulation No 1049/2001.[144]

137 *Ibid.*, paras 112–115.
138 Case C-139/07 P, *Commission* v. *Technische Glaswerke Ilmenau* [2010] ECR I-5885; Case C-477/10 P, *Commission* v. *Agrofert Holding a.s.* [2012] ECLI:EU:C:2012:394; Case C-404/10 P, *Commission* v. *Editions Odile Jacob SAS* [2013] ECLI:EU:C:2012:393; Case T-392/07, *Guido Strack* v. *Commission* [2013] ECLI:EU:T:2013:8.
139 Case C-139/07 P, *Commission* v. *Technische Glaswerke Ilmenau* [2010] ECR I-5885, para. 61.
140 Case C-139/07 P, *Commission* v. *Technische Glaswerke Ilmenau* [2010] ECR I-5885, para. 62.
141 Case C-514/11, *LPN and Finland* v. *Commission* [2013] ECLI:EU:C:2013:738.
142 Case T-29/08, *LPN* v. *Commission* [2011] ECR II-6021, para. 126.
143 Case C-514/11, *LPN and Finland* v. *Commission* [2013] ECLI:EU:C:2013:738, para. 35.
144 *Ibid.*, para. 65.

The presumptions case law, upheld in *LPN*, is fairly vague and in direct contrast with the Treaty framework, in particular with the requirements to take decisions as openly as possible pursuant to Article 1 TEU as well as with the overall wording of the Regulation. The Regulation provides no basis for the establishment of general presumptions. The Court of Justice's position regarding the administrative functions imposes significant constitutional ramifications on the fundamental aspect of the access right and incorporates limitations without the required level of explanation and clarity. The Court also did not take into account the overriding public interest as regards the infringement proceedings. As a result, the judgment makes one wonder if such an override cannot be established in an area where possible violations of EU law by Member States might take place, then it remains difficult to conceive of a scenario where the override would ever be accepted by the Court.

Interestingly, *LPN* treats in a rather paradoxical way a respectable non-governmental organisation as a mere 'busybody' unable to invoke the override successfully. This latest jurisprudence reveals the existence of a paradox. We saw the Court confirming categorically over the last 20 years that openness secures public oversight of the EU's decision-making, describing it as one of the fundamental credentials of the Union's democratic society. Yet, we have evidence that the Court provides little or no contribution in relation to the opening up of the functioning of the institutions. The judgment significantly decreases public access and leaves intact the possibility of the Commission, and by analogy the other institutions, refusing access to the entire administrative file without even looking at the individual documents.

Article 4(5) of the Regulation: documents originating from Member States

This section explores the nature of the Member State documents exception regulated by Article 4(5) of the Regulation.[145] An argument is made that the Court of Justice in the *IFAW*[146] appeal was right to rule that the exception does not provide Member States with an unconditional right of veto power to object to the disclosure of documents originating from them. Such a request for non-disclosure can only be justified by reference to Articles 4(1) to (3) of the Regulation and, in any case, contrary to what has been previously decided, cannot be interpreted as an absolute and unqualified power to prevent access regarding documents drafted by Member States.

Recital 15 of the Regulation provides that national legislation on access to official documents shall remain unaffected since 'it is neither the object nor the

145 Prior to the delivery of the *IFAW* appeal, it was argued by legal scholars that the Court was correct in interpreting that Article 4(5) confers upon Member States the power to request an institution not to disclose the documents originating from it without its agreement. In this regard, *See* B Driessen, 'Access to Member State documents in EC law: A Comment' (2006) 31 *European Law Review*, p 906; For a criticism of this approach *See* Cabral, op. cit. n 24 *supra*.

146 Case C-64/05 P, *Sweden* v. *Commission* [2007] ECR I-11389, para. 47.

effect of that Regulation to amend national legislation on access to documents'.[147] Similarly, Article 4(5), which specifically refers to the case of documents drafted by Member States and communicated to the institutions, provides that 'a Member State may request the institution not to disclose a document originating from that Member State without its prior agreement'. The latter provision mirrors what was agreed in Declaration No 35 annexed to the final Act of the Treaty of Amsterdam. Unsurprisingly, this ambiguous provision has been the object of judicial interpretation.[148] Initially, the Court, based on the principle *in claris non fit interpretatio* and in order to avoid departing from the language employed in the text, ruled that documents originating from Member States qualify for a *special* protection under the Regulation.[149] Yet, literally the word 'request' does not provide much support for a special protection: granting a special treatment to documents drafted by the Member States and giving them a power of veto is in a direct contradiction with the widest possible access as well as with the wording of the Regulation.

Interpreting 'request' to the effect that Member States have a veto power is also *not* in line with the clear distinction between Article 4(5) and Article 9(3). The latter requires release of sensitive documents subject to the originator's consent.[150] Had the Union legislator wanted to grant a veto power to the Member States, it would have had every opportunity to do so by adopting a similar wording as the originator's consent found in Article 9(3). The different wording adopted for these two situations, it seems, cannot justify similar treatment. This reasoning has been rejected by the Court of Justice on the grounds that contrary to what Article 9(3) requires:

> Article 4(5) does not make the prior agreement of the Member State an absolute condition of the disclosure of a document, but makes the possible need for such agreement subject to a prior expression of will by the Member State concerned.[151]

Yet, this view does not provide much support for the different wording employed by Article 4(5) and Article 9(3), and it may make more sense for the judiciary to interpret these two provisions differently, taking into account their wording.

147 Recital 15 of Regulation 1049/2001; Case T-187/03, *Isabella Scippacercola* v. *Commission* [2005] ECR II-1029, para. 34.

148 Case T-76/02, *Mara Messina* v. *Commission* [2003] ECR II-3203; Case T-168/02, *IFAW Internationaler Tierschutz-Fonts Gmbh* v. *Commission* [2004] ECR II-4135; Case T-187/03, *Isabella Scippacercola* v. *Commission* [2005] ECR II-1029.

149 *Ibid.*

150 *See* Peers, Chapter 2, op. cit. n 7 *supra*.

151 Case C-64/05 P, *Sweden* v. *Commission* [2007] ECR I-11389, para. 47; *See also* Flanagan, op. cit. n 50 *supra*.

The Court in *Messina*[152] clarified what constitutes a Member State. In this case, an Italian law lecturer sought to access certain documents exchanged between the Italian authorities and the Commission regarding a state aid scheme. The Commission refused to grant access on the basis that the requested documents were drafted by the Italian authorities, which objected to the disclosure and invited the applicant to direct the application to the Italian authorities.[153] The applicant argued that Italy's refusal was signed by one of the various directors of one of many national ministries and as such could not be sufficient to bind a Member State 'in the light of the exceptional nature of the power given to the State by Article 4(5) of the Regulation No 1049/2001'.[154] The CFI, however, did not accept this line of reasoning and emphasised that it was not within the Commission's power to rule on the division of competences by the institutional rules of the Member States.[155]

The same judicial approach was followed in *Scippacercola*.[156] In this case, the applicant requested from the Commission documents relating to the project for the new Athens International Airport, a project that had been co-financed by the Cohesion Fund. The Commission refused access again on the basis that the Greek authorities rejected the disclosure of the document. The applicant claimed that the concerned documents did not constitute Member States' documents, because they were drafted by private consultants on behalf of a bank, which assisted the competent Greek authorities during the preparation of the project, and, as such, they cannot be treated as documents originating from a Member State. The CFI, however, did not accept that argument. It held that, in order for an application to be financed from the Cohesion Fund, it must be submitted by a Member State[157] and the document would not have been received by the Commission had the Greek authorities not submitted their application.[158]

Overall, it is evident from the jurisprudence of the Courts that the notion of the Member State has been broadly defined. It is questionable, however, whether such a broad scope runs counter to the well-established principle of the widest possible access laid down in Article 1(a) of the Regulation and to its corollary, the narrowest interpretation of the exceptions. More fundamentally, the Member State veto does not fit well with the general purpose of Article 1 of the EU Treaty to take decisions as openly and as closely as possible to the citizen. Contrary to these provisions, the CFI in *Messina*[159] and *Scippacercola*[160] accepted that 'any person working for the state's central administration but also for regional or local

152 Case T-76/02, *Mara Messina* v. *Commission* [2003] ECR II-3203.
153 *Ibid.*, para. 8.
154 *Ibid.*, para. 30.
155 *Ibid.*, para. 46.
156 Case T-187/03, *Isabella Scippacercola* v. *Commission* [2005] ECR II-1029.
157 Case T-187/03, *Isabella Scippacercola* v. *Commission* [2005] ECR II-1029, para. 37.
158 *Ibid.*, para. 40.
159 Case T-76/02, *Mara Messina* v. *Commission* [2003] ECR II-3203.
160 Case T-187/03, *Isabella Scippacercola* v. *Commission* [2005] ECR II-1029.

governments may make such a request, no matter what functions that person exercises'.[161] With great respect to the above-mentioned judgments, one can reasonably argue that the notion of Member State 'should be as narrow as possible so as to guarantee that, within the Member States' national administrations, only persons holding positions of authority in departments of the central administration are able to exercise the power granted by Article 4(5)'.[162]

The CFI in the *Messina*[163] case did not rule explicitly that Article 4(5) grants the Member States a power to veto the disclosure of the documents originating from them. However, it did so with its later ruling in the *IFAW*[164] and in the *Scippacercola*.[165] In *IFAW*, the CFI ruled that documents drafted by third parties can only be disclosed with the consent of the author, unless it is obvious that they can or cannot be disclosed. In the wording of the judiciary: 'consultation of the third party is, as a general rule, a precondition for determining whether the exceptions to the right of access provided for in Article 4(1) and (2) of the Regulation are applicable in the case of third-party documents'.[166] Similarly, the CFI made it clear that 'a request made by a Member State under Article 4(5) . . . [is] an instruction to the institution not to disclose the document in question'.[167] Such request constitutes a binding instruction and leaves no discretion to the institution to decide otherwise. The Court held that if the institutions were entitled to proceed to the disclosure despite the Member State's objection, it would risk Article 4(5) becoming a dead letter.[168]

Similarly, the CFI ruled that:

> [t]he Member State is under no obligation to state the reasons for any request made by it under Article 4(5) of the Regulation and, once it has made such a request, it is no longer a matter for the institution to examine whether non-disclosure of the document in question is justified.[169]

This approach contradicts the fundamental principle to state reasons enshrined in the Regulation as well as the principle developed by the jurisprudence of the Courts that the exceptions must be applied and interpreted narrowly and be based on a concrete and individual examination.

161 *See* Cabral, op. cit. n 24 *supra*.
162 *Ibid.*
163 Case T-76/02, *Mara Messina* v. *Commission* [2003] ECR II-3203.
164 Case T-168/02, *IFAW Internationaler Tierschutz-Fonts Gmbh* v. *Commission* [2004] ECR II-4135.
165 Case T-187/03, *Isabella Scippacercola* v. *Commission* [2005] ECR II-1029.
166 Case T-168/02, *IFAW Internationaler Tierschutz-Fonts Gmbh* v. *Commission* [2004] ECR II-4135, para. 55.
167 *Ibid.*, para. 58.
168 Case T-168/02, *IFAW Internationaler Tierschutz-Fonts Gmbh* v. *Commission* [2004] ECR II-4135.
169 *Ibid.*, paras 58–59.

Regulation prior to the *IFAW*[170] appeal, was fully consistent with its wording and mirrors the EU's legislator explicit choice.[171] The Advocate General, however, has stated that, in his opinion, the wording of the legislation is unclear and that 'request' cannot be considered as a veto power.[172] Others have suggested that 'this provision confers upon Member States a power of veto'.[173] Yet, many scholars have suggested the opposite: that the wording of Article 4(5) leaves no doubts that it confers nothing more than the requirement of consultation and that the institution is free to proceed with the disclosure of the requested documents communicated by the Member State.[174] Indeed, one could argue that if Article 4(5) is construed to mean that Members States enjoy unlimited discretion on the disclosure of documents communicated to the institutions, it results in the reintroduction of the authorship rule provided for in the Code of conduct.[175]

Based on the earlier case law, which after the adoption of the *IFAW*[176] appeal cannot be considered as good law, the CFI ruled that if 'request' was interpreted to mean that the institutions were required to take into account the opinion of the Member State without necessarily following such an opinion, this would have resulted in equalising Article 4(4)[177] with Article 4(5) and as such rendering the provision of the latter a dead letter.[178] This argument, again, seems to be problematic. Under Article 4(5), Member States always have the possibility to express their views on the disclosure of documents originating from them, even in cases where the institutions consider it obvious that access must be granted or denied. On the contrary, such an obligation does not exist for documents originated from any other third parties under Article 4(4).

The above arguments, although extremely interesting from a historic viewpoint, now constitute a discussion for the past. The Court of Justice has ruled in the *IFAW*[179] appeal that the Member States are obliged, under the duty of loyal cooperation, not to jeopardise the EU rules on access to documents and thus clarified that Article 4(5) does require a joint implementation and cooperation amongst the administration of the Member States and the EU institutions. If an institution receives an application for access relating to a document drafted by any of the Member States, then a dialogue must take place in order to decide whether access must be granted. If the Member State is objecting to the disclosure, it is

170 Case C-64/05 P, *Sweden* v. *Commission* [2007] ECR I-11389.

171 *See* Cabral, op. cit. n 24 *supra*.

172 Case C-64/05 P, *Kingdom of Sweden* v. *Commission of the European Communities and Others* [2007] ECR I-11389, Opinion of Advocate-General Maduro.

173 *See* Cabral, op. cit. n 24 *supra*.

174 See Harden, Chapter 1, op. cit. n 49 *supra*; *See also* Peers, Chapter 2, op. cit. n 7 *supra*.

175 See the previous analysis on the authorship rule.

176 Case C-64/05 P, *Sweden* v. *Commission* [2007] ECR I-11389.

177 Article 4(4) of the Regulation provides that the documents drafted by third parties shall be disclosed after consulting the originators unless it is clear that they shall or shall not be disclosed.

178 Case T-168/02, *IFAW Internationaler Tierschutz-Fonts Gmbh* v. *Commission* [2004] ECR II-4135, para. 58.

179 Case C-64/05 P, *Sweden* v. *Commission* [2007] ECR I-11389.

required to do so within the time limits of Article 7(1) of Regulation and justify such objection on the exception found in Articles 4(1–3).[180] By not doing so, the institution is obliged to grant access to the documents unless it considers that refusal must be denied, following an assessment of this Article. If the Member State provides a reasoned refusal, then the institution is obliged to incorporate this into its decision on access in order for the judicial review or the complaint procedure to the EU Ombudsman to take place.[181] At the same time, the Member State must respect the time limits of the Regulation, and it must state reasons if it wishes to object to the disclosure. More interestingly, however, the Court of Justice held that the Member State may rely on its national rules on access to documents in order to justify the denial. According to the Court of Justice, 'there is nothing in the Regulation to exclude the possibility that compliance with certain rules of national law . . . could be regarded as an interest deserving protection on the basis of the exception laid down by that Regulation'.[182]

Judicial documents

The approach of the Court in relation to its own documents is fairly restrictive. Currently, it is presumed that disclosure of judicial documents is capable of causing harm, in a foreseeable way, to the outcome of Court proceedings. In *API*,[183] a non-profit-making organisation of foreign journalists made a request to have access to the Commission's submissions regarding, *inter alia*, a number of ongoing cases and one which, although closed, was related to a pending case.[184] The Commission, based on Article 4(2) of the Regulation, denied access. In particular, the Commission argued that disclosure would adversely affect its position and would expose it to undue pressure from members of the public. It concluded that disclosure 'would undermine the protection of . . . court proceedings and legal advice'.[185]

As regards the documents in relation to infringement proceedings, the Commission argued that disclosure would 'undermine the protection of

180 Case C-64/05 P, *Sweden* v. *Commission* [2007] ECR I-11389, para. 88.

181 *Ibid.*, paras 89–90.

182 *Ibid.*, para. 84.

183 Case T-36/04, *Association de la presse internationale asbl (API)* v. *Commission* [2007] ECR II-3201.

184 Case T-209/01, *Honeywell International* v. *Commission* [2005] ECR II-5527 and Case T-210/01, *General Electric* v. *Commission* [2005] ECR II-5575; Case T-342/99, *Airtours* v. *Commission* [2002] ECR II-1785; Case C-203/03, *Commission* v. *Austria* [2005] ECR I-935; Case C-466/98, *Commission* v. *United Kingdom* [2002] ECR I-9427; Case C-467/98, *Commission* v. *Denmark* [2002] ECR I-9519; Case C-469/98, *Commission* v. *Finland* [2002] ECR I-9627; Case C-471/98, *Commission* v. *Belgium* [2002] ECR I-9681; Case C-472/98, *Commission* v. *Luxembourg* [2002] ECR I-9741; Case C-475/98, *Commission* v. *Austria* [2002] ECR I-9797 and Case C-476/98, *Commission* v. *Germany* ('the *Open Skies* cases') [2002] ECR I-9855.

185 Case T-36/04, *Association de la presse internationale asbl (API)* v. *Commission* [2007] ECR II-3201, para. 15.

investigations',[186] the purpose of which is to reach an amicable resolution of the dispute. The same position was adopted by the Commission to cases relating to open infringement proceedings as well as the closed cases where the Member State had not yet complied with the judgment.

The CFI, now the General Court, annulled in part the Commission's decision, refusing access to the pleadings in proceedings before the CFI and the Court of Justice. It was first highlighted that the purpose of the Regulation was to allow the widest possible access and that the exceptions must be interpreted and applied strictly in respect to each individual document.[187] With regards to the exception of Court proceedings, however, the Court ruled that the Commission could provide a blanket refusal in relation to all written documents so long as the oral argument had not yet been presented. The rationale behind this is to safeguard the interest of the litigant to be free from all external pressure until the case reaches the stage of hearing.[188] Similarly, the CFI ruled that where denial of access is based on a connection between a completed and a pending case, the Commission could not refuse access without assessing concretely and individually why disclosure would undermine the Court proceedings. Regarding the infringement proceedings, the Court ruled that the interest of amicable resolution of the dispute could justify a blanket refusal as long as the judgment had not yet been delivered.[189] Overall, the CFI took the view that the objective of reaching an amicable settlement continued to justify a refusal even after the hearing and covers the period before the delivery of the judgment.

With great respect, the Court's ruling was wrong to find that the Commission was in a position to refuse access to the whole category of judicial documents without following a concrete and individual examination and without stating detailed reasons. The blanket refusal, accepted by the Court, justified by the fact that the litigant needs to protect its litigious interest and stay free from external pressure, seems to misinterpret the rationale of the access to documents regime.[190] More importantly, it leaves the access to documents rules at a vulnerable stage. As already explained, the mere fact that a document referred to in the application for access concerns an interest protected by an exception does not justify application of that exception. The exceptions are applicable only if the institution had previously assessed whether access would specifically and actually undermine the protected interest and, if so, there was no overriding public interest under Article 4(2) and (3). The risk of the protected interest being undermined must not be purely hypothetical. Consequently, the examination which the institution must undertake needs to be carried out in a robust manner and be apparent from the

186 *Ibid.*

187 Case T-36/04, *Association de la presse internationale asbl (API)* v. *Commission* [2007] ECR II-3201, para. 54; *See* Adamski, op. cit. n 78 *supra.*

188 *Ibid.*, para. 115.

189 *Ibid.*, para. 133.

190 P Leino, 'Just a little sunshine in the rain: The 2010 case law of the European Court of Justice on access to documents' (2011) 48 (4) *Common Market Law Review*, p. 1215.

reasons given. Only a concrete and individual examination, as opposed to an abstract, overall examination, would enable the institution to assess the possibility of granting the applicant partial access pursuant to Article 4(6) of the Regulation. The institution's obligation to undertake this type of assessment is applicable to all the exceptions found in paragraphs 1 to 3 of Article 4.

Sweden, API and the Commission brought an appeal against the judgment of the General Court. The Court confirmed that judicial documents are covered by a presumption against openness and that disclosure of the pleadings would undermine their protection, covered by the exception of the second indent of Article 4(2), while those proceedings remain pending.[191] Therefore, documents relating to Court proceedings are excluded, in principle, from the access to documents rules and the Commission bears no obligation 'to carry out a concrete assessment of each document requested in order to determine whether, given the specific content of that document, its disclosure would undermine the court proceedings to which it relates'.[192]

With this judgment, the Court of Justice significantly curtailed the already limited access right to Court proceedings. Post *API*, the burden of proof to rebut the presumption of non-disclosure rests with the applicant, whereas previously the institutions had the burden to prove that concrete and individual examination was not necessary.[193] This is deeply unsatisfactory for the state of transparency and, in conjunction with the finding that the overriding public interest can only be taken into account so long as it is particularly pertinent, effectively leaves no access right to judicial documents.[194] Overall, the outcome of the Court is problematic for two principal reasons. First, it decreases dramatically public access to judicial documents and sets the default position to non-disclosure; and second, and more fundamentally, requires the applicant, rather illogically, to discharge the burden of the presumption, given that the plaintiff has no sight of the documents.

While there is a clear strand in case law about the general presumptions, there are still cases in which the EU Courts have rejected the idea of the presumption and pointed to the opposite direction on the grounds that disclosure could not distort the administrative process.[195] Notably, the General Court ruled more recently in *Breyer*[196] that the Commission should not automatically refuse access to documents submitted to the EU Courts and highlighted that the

191 Joined Cases C-514/07 P, C-528/07 P and C-532/07 P, *Sweden and Others* v. *API and Commission* [2010] ECR I-8533, para. 94.

192 *Ibid.*, para. 104.

193 Case T-2/03, *Verein für Konsumenteninformation* v. *Commission* [2005] ECR I-1121.

194 Joined Cases C-514/07 P, C-528/07 P and C-532/07 P, *Sweden and Others* v. *API and Commission* [2010] ECR I-8533, para. 157.

195 Case C-506/08 P, *Sweden* v. *Commission and MyTravel Group plc. (MyTravel)* [2011] ECR I-6237; Case T-250/08, *Batchelor* v. *Commission* [2011] ECR II-2551; Joined Cases T-109/05 and T-444/05, *NLG* v. *Commission* [2011] ECR II-2479.

196 Case T-188/12, *Patrick Breyer* v. *Commission* [2015] ECLI:EU:T:2015:124.

presumption of non-disclosure only applies while the Court proceedings remain pending. The aftermath of *Breyer*, although it is very early to say with certainty, seems to suggest that the Court is ready to reconsider its approach on the presumptions. Nevertheless, general considerations leading to the presumption of non-disclosure are well-established and very difficult to rebut.[197] In practice, the nature of the requested documents gives rise to different judicial treatment. As already explained above, while the case law significantly increased public access as regards legislative documents, it has set the default position for non-legislative documents to non-disclosure. These fundamental discrepancies over the nature of the documents question the contribution of the Courts in respecting the standards of transparency mandated by the legislature and highlight the overall problematic state of transparency in the EU.

In April 2008, the Commission published a legislative proposal to recast the Regulation.[198] Following the publication of the Commission's proposal, the EP adopted a number of amendments and, following the EP's request, the Commission adopted a later proposal.[199] On 15 December 2011, the EP approved the proposal.[200] The weak points of the current regime, as already explained above, stem predominantly from the broad exceptions enshrined in the Regulation. Thus, in the amendment process, emphasis must be based upon the task of clarifying the exceptions. Rather regrettably, the procedure to recast the current access regime provides evidence to the contrary, and the proposal itself is far from securing transparency.

In particular, Article 2(6) of the Commission's proposal reduces dramatically the current standards, since it would leave outside the scope of the Regulation documents relating to individual decisions and investigations until the decision has been taken and the investigation has been closed or the act has become definitive. In addition, 'documents containing information gathered or obtained from natural or legal persons by an institution in the framework of such investigations shall not be accessible to the public even after the closure of the investigation'. At present, Article 4(2) of the Regulation provides that the disclosure of documents which would undermine the protection of inspections, investigations and audits shall be refused, unless there is an overriding public interest following disclosure. If the proposed provision is adopted, this would constitute a step backwards in

197 Case C-514/11, *LPN and Finland* v. *Commission* [2013] ECLI:EU:C:2013:738; Case T-82/09, *Dennekamp* v. *Parliament* [2011] ECR II-418; Joined Cases C-514/07 P, C-528/07 P and C-532/07 P, *Sweden and Others* v. *API and Commission* [2010] ECR I-8533; Case C-139/07 P, *Commission* v. *Technische Glaswerke Ilmenau* [2010] ECR I-5885.

198 Proposal for a Regulation regarding public access to European Parliament, Council and Commission documents, COM (2008) 229 final (30 April 2008), 2008/0090(COD).

199 Proposal for a Regulation regarding public access to European Parliament, Council and Commission documents, COM (2011) 137 final (30 March 2011), 2011/0073(COD).

200 For a general criticism of the Commission's proposal, see N Diamandouros, 'Contribution of the European Ombudsman to the Public Hearing on the Revision of Regulation 1049/2001 on Public Access to Documents', speech delivered in the EP on 2 June 2008.

terms of the existing *status quo*, since this provision would not be protected by an overriding public interest in disclosure.

Article 4(3) of the Regulation: the decision-making exception

Article 4(3) first indent provides that: 'Access to a document, drawn up by an institution for internal use or received by an institution, which relates to a matter where the decision has not been taken by the institution, shall be refused'. Similarly, the second indent of Article 4(3) states that documents 'containing opinions for internal use as part of deliberations and preliminary consultations within the institution concerned shall be refused even after the decision has been taken'. This exception may be invoked when it additionally passes a 'stricter'[201] qualified harm test: 'disclosure of the document would seriously undermine the institution's decision-making process'.

In *MyTravel Group*,[202] the CFI ruled on the Commission's refusal to grant access to documents relating to professional opinions concerning the opportunity for the Commission to challenge a judgment rendered in the area of competition law. The Commission based its denial on Article 4(3), arguing that the freedom of the authors would be threatened having known that their opinions may be accessible to the general public.[203] The CFI upheld the Commission's refusal and highlighted that if the authors of the documents were aware of the fact that their professional opinions may be screened by the public, they may engage in informal consultations with the institution in order to avoid drawing up documents that might involve the addressee being exposed to a risk. The CFI ruled that:

> It appears logical and probable that the Member of the Commission responsible for competition would be induced to cease making requests for the written, and potentially critical, views of his advisers . . . [and] merely to hold oral and informal discussions, which would not require the drawing up of a 'document' . . . [This attitude, however,] would cause significant damage to the effectiveness of the Commission's internal decision-making process.[204]

The later judgments of the CFI in the *Williams*[205] and *Borax*[206] cases confirmed the approach followed in the *MyTravel Group* case. Arguably, the CFI's reasoning appears to be at least problematic and constitutes a significant reduction of

201 *See* Kranenborg and Voermans, op. cit. n 6 *supra*.

202 Case T-403/05, *MyTravel Group* v. *Commission* [2008] ECR II-2027.

203 Case T-403/05, *MyTravel Group* v. *Commission* [2008] ECR II-2027, para. 14; D Adamski, 'How Wide Is "the Widest Possible"? Judicial Interpretation of the Exceptions to the Right of Access to Official Documents Revisited' (2009) 46 *Common Market Law Review*, p. 521.

204 Case T-403/05, *MyTravel Group* v. *Commission* [2008] ECR II-2027, para. 54.

205 Case T-42/05, *Williams* v. *Commission* [2008] ECR II-156.

206 Case T-121/05, *Borax* v. *Commission* [2009] ECR II-27. However, the approach in *Borax* is much more pro-transparency.

standards in the field of citizens' participation in the institutions' decision-making process, which supposedly needs to reflect their democratic nature. If the CFI says that public scrutiny of the institutions' advice would affect the objectiveness of that advice, this reasoning does not appear to be rational. Any practising lawyer will provide evidence to the contrary and argue that the public scrutiny of any advice protects the institutions' interest in receiving frank advice.[207] Yet, practising lawyers may prefer to protect their own advice as in-house counsel to be available to the Commission in competition cases.[208] In any case, the fact that the authors of the documents are aware that there is a possibility for their opinions to be scrutinised secures that the professional advice given to the institutions was based on evidence and sound argumentation and minimises the risk for the institutions to receive unprofessional advice.

The *MyTravel Group* judgment has now been overturned on appeal by the Court of Justice.[209] It was held that the CFI, now the General Court, should have required the Commission to indicate the reasons why the closure of the administrative procedure 'did not exclude the possibility that refusal of access to the report might remain justified having regard to the risk of the said decision-making process being seriously undermined'.[210]

Concluding remarks

There is no doubt that the EU has taken important steps to ensure transparency of the decision-making process. If one compares the pre-Regulation rules, where the CFI held, for example, that transparency did not require the adoption of secondary legislation and that decisions on access to documents could properly be based purely on the institution's Rules of Procedure with the current situation, it can be safely argued that progress has been made. Currently, it is obvious that 'we have gone from a situation of a mere favour being granted to the individual by the institutions in the exercise of their discretionary power to one of a true subjective fundamental right granted to the individual'.[211]

The Regulation improved the position governing access in several aspects. The most important developments introduced by the Regulation are the abolishment of the authorship rule and the requirement of having public registers. The judiciary has contributed to the development of transparency to a greater or a lesser extent. In a more limited way, for example, by avoiding carefully not ruling on the fundamental aspect of the access to documents and by refraining to rule on whether EU law recognised a general principle of the right of access.

207 *See* Adamski, op. cit. n 78 *supra*.

208 Case C-550/07 P, *Akzo Nobel Chemicals and Akcros Chemicals* v. *Commission and Others* [2008] ECR I2649.

209 Case C-506/08 P, *Sweden/MyTravel* v. *Commission* [2011] ECR I-6237.

210 *Ibid.*, para. 89.

211 Case C-52/05 P, *Sweden and Turco* v. *Council* [2008] ECR I-4723, Opinion of Advocate-General Leger, para. 40.

But, nevertheless, one should not underestimate the contribution of the judiciary. A significant number of Council and Commission decisions denying access have been annulled by the Court of Justice and the CFI.

Yet, the extent to which the jurisprudence acknowledges the existence of general presumptions is fundamentally wrong. As a result of this, the institutions can now offer a wide justification, often relating to the entire administrative file, and provide no evidence that they considered less onerous ways of dealing with the request. This is especially true in the light of the significant number of cases involving general presumptions as regards the administrative functions of the institutions. In practice, the presumptions' case law establishes a clear distinction between legislative and non-legislative documents and confirms, contrary to the wording of the Regulation, the widest possible access with regards to the former category. More regrettably, the on-going procedure to recast the existing legislation indicates that, in the years to come, we may be in a completely new situation, not necessarily a better one. Therefore, for the time being, emphasis should be based during the amendment process on eliminating the existing exceptions found in the Regulation, as it is clear that the weak points of the access to documents regime stem predominantly from those exceptions.

4 Accountability of the EU decentralised agencies

Introduction

Having examined in the previous chapter the access to documents rules, a prerequisite of accountability, it is important to assess the accountability regime of the decentralised agencies because the Council and the EP are no longer the de facto legislative forums. In fact, the Council, the EP and the Commission delegate a whole range of powers to agencies which have been set up to regulate areas that vary all the way from disease prevention and economics to energy and telecommunications, to mention but a few areas. Therefore, the analysis on accountability would not be comprehensive without examining the case of agencies established and active at the EU level of governance. In doing so, this chapter first sets the scene relative to the agencies' regime and second, explores whether the key institutions and main delegators, being the Commission, the Council and the EP, supervise agencies' actions and monitor sufficiently the implementation of tasks entrusted to agencies. It will be shown that agencies suffer from fundamental accountability problems. Delegating tasks to agencies without securing accountability constitutes a prima facie threat to the principle of the institutional balance. Before going into depth with these issues, however, a general background is provided below.

Historical overview

The gradual enlargements of the EU, along with the expansion of its competences and workload, have resulted in an unprecedented creation of agencies in diverse fields. The number of agencies has multiplied at a scarily increasing pace and clearly '[t]he creation of European agencies is one of the most remarkable institutional developments at the EU level in recent years'.[1] The functions they provide from the collection of information and delivering of

1 M Busuioc, 'Accountability, control and independence: The case of European agencies' (2009) 15 *European Law Journal*, 599–615, p. 600. For a more recent analysis on this, see S Peers and M Costa, 'Accountability for EU decentralized agencies: Mind the independence gap' *European Public Law* (forthcoming).

opinions to decision-making powers, inspections and investigations. Agencies with decision-making powers are entitled to adopt binding measures which may very well have adverse effects upon third parties, such as individuals, regulators and Member States.[2] These agencies are referred to as decentralised agencies and are considered to be highly specialised, autonomous and independent.[3] It would be misleading to argue that the technique of delegating tasks to agencies is something entirely new.[4] What is new, however, is their massive expansion since 'the EU's appetite for creating new agencies seems limitless'.[5]

From their inception, the main EU institutions, in particular the Commission and the Council, have used the opportunity of delegating tasks to external committees extensively to carry out tasks that usually require highly specialised knowledge and/or scientific expertise.[6] The development of agencies aimed at reducing some of these institutions' administrative tasks, leaving them free to concentrate on their major strategic policies. As a result, agencies were delegated the powers to take decisions based on complex knowledge, so that technical issues could be removed from any political considerations.[7]

The rationale behind the agencification process

The range of issues over which the EU has responsibilities means that, in pragmatic terms, it is not realistic for the Treaties to provide for all the detailed measures that need to be undertaken.[8] Similarly, legislative harmonisation was also soon understood as an insufficient instrument for dismantling barriers to trade, necessary for the achievement and maintenance of the internal market.[9] Yet, it was clear that the Commission could not exercise any additional

2 The Office of Harmonisation in the Internal Market (OHIM) and the European Aviation Safety Agency (EASA) as well as the European Supervisory Authorities (ESAs), among other agencies, have the powers to adopt legally binding decisions.

3 *See* R Van Ooik in Curtin and Wessel, Chapter 3, op. cit. n 121 *supra*; *See also* G Majone, 'Functional interests: European agencies', in M Shackleton, *The Institutions of the European Union* (Oxford University Press 2002); M Everson, G Majone, L Metcalfe and A Schout, *The Role of Specialised Agencies in Decentralising EU Governance*, (1999) Report to the Commission.

4 See Craig, Chapter 1, op. cit. n 42 *supra*, p. 359.

5 D Gerardin and N Petit, 'The development of agencies at EU and national levels: Conceptual analysis and proposal for reform' (2004) 4 *Jean Monnet Working Paper*, available at centers.law.nyu.edu/jeanmonnet/papers/04/040101.pdf, accessed 15 June 2015.

6 X Yataganas, 'Delegation of regulatory authority in the EU: The relevance of the American model of independent agencies', *Jean Monnet Working Paper* 3/01, available at www.jeanmonnetprogram.org.paper/01/010301.htlm, accessed 20 July 2015.

7 A Kreher, 'Agencies in the European Community: A step towards administrative integration in Europe' (1997) 4 *Journal of European Public Policy*, p. 239.

8 G Majone, 'The new European agencies: Regulation by information' (1997) 4 *Journal of European Public Policy*, p. 263.

9 E Vos, 'Reforming the European Commission: What role to play for EU agencies?' (2000) 37 *Common Market Law Review*, p. 1116.

administrative tasks because of time constraints as well as the lack of technical expertise required for each specific sector.[10] Any possible solution to the severe mismatch between the EU's specialised functions and the administrative instruments at its disposal[11] had to respect Article 4 of the original Treaty of Rome (post-Lisbon Article 13 TEU), which named the institutions and provided them with their powers. The lack of a Treaty basis providing for the genesis of agencies was seen in the legal literature as an obstacle to their creation.[12] Yet, that lack did not prevent their numbers from mushrooming. Article 308 EC Treaty,[13] post-Lisbon Article 352 TFEU, was frequently used as the appropriate legal basis. Article 308 EC Treaty provided that:

> If action by the Community should prove necessary to attain, in the course of the operation of the common market, one of the objectives of the Community, and this Treaty has not provided the necessary powers, the Council shall, acting unanimously on a proposal from the Commission and after consulting the European Parliament, take the appropriate measures.

However, the recent tendency is to use a more detailed Treaty provision. The choice of the appropriate legal basis constitutes a crucial factor for accountability requirements and has two fundamental consequences.[14] First, if an agency is created based on a specific legal basis, it is more likely that the ordinary legislative procedure and qualified majority voting will apply since the scope of the pre-Lisbon co-decision procedure, now known as the ordinary legislative procedure, was considerably extended by the Treaty of Lisbon, for example to cover areas such as agriculture, fisheries (Article 43(2) TFEU) and the common commercial policy (Article 207 TFEU). Therefore, the agency's functions will be narrow, mirroring the particular basis used for its creation. Second, reliance on Article 352 TFEU requires unanimity in the Council and only the consent of, previously only consultation with, the EP.

The lack of a Treaty basis for the establishment of agencies created a considerable tension between the institutions as well as the Member States.[15] For instance, in the case of the European Network and the Information Security

10 E Chiti, 'The Emergence of a Community Administration: The Case of European Agencies' (2000) 37 *Common Market Law Review*, p. 309.

11 M Everson, 'Independent Agencies: Hierarchy Beaters?' (1995) 1 *European Law Journal*, p. 193.

12 K Lenaerts, 'Regulating the regulatory process: "Delegation of powers" in the European Community' (1993) 18 *European Law Review*, p. 23.

13 Agencies established under Article 308 EC Treaty: CEDEFOP, EUROFOUND, OHIM, CPVO, EMEA, EU-OSHA, EMCDDA, EFT, CDT, EAR, GSA, FRA.

14 *See* Curtin, Chapter 1, op. cit. n 11 *supra*; the institutional design of the agencies established under the previously named Community pillar was taken by the legislature (Council and the EP) under a publicly available proposal by the Commission.

15 Now the Treaty of Lisbon explicitly mentions EU agencies.

Agency (ENISA), the UK government argued that only Article 308 was the appropriate legal basis for the creation of the agency. The Court,[16] however, ruled that ex Article 95 was the correct legal foundation. Pursuant to the reasoning of the Court, the main objective of that agency was the completion of the internal market as an area without any internal frontiers in the field of information technology. Nevertheless, even where agencies were initially founded on the basis of Article 352 TFEU (as it now is), the more specific legal bases were often used for later amendments to the legislation constituting those bodies.

The EU responded to the concerns with regards to expansion of competences with the delegation of powers to independent agencies with distinct legal personalities, subject of course to scrutiny and control by the Council, the Commission and the EP. In reality, the agencies' autonomous regime is restrained by the Court of Justice's jurisprudence, which clearly does not allow for the delegation of discretionary powers to agencies that were not mentioned in the Treaties. In substantive terms, their autonomy depends and varies from one agency to another. The Court of Justice, with the well-known *Meroni* principle and more recently with *ESMA*,[17] clarified that the Commission, and by analogy all the other institutions, can delegate some of their executive tasks to bodies not mentioned in the Treaty, subject to severe limitations. In any case, it was clearly pointed out by the Court that discretionary powers cannot be delegated. The Commission or the Council must be in a position to exercise sufficient control over the delegated powers and they will remain accountable if they do not do so effectively.[18]

Different types of agencies

The Community (as it was then) established the first generation of agencies in the mid-1970s.[19] Most agencies, however, were created in the early 1990s,[20] and

16 Case C-217/04, *UK* v. *EP and Council* [2006] ECR I-3771.

17 Case 9/56, *Meroni & Co Industrie Metallurgiche SpA* v. *High Authority* [1958] ECR 133; Case C-270/12, *United Kingdom* v. *Council & Parliament* [2014] ECLI:EU:C:2014:18.

18 Case 9/56, *Meroni & Co Industrie Metallurgiche, SpA* v. *High Authority of the European Coal and Steel Community* [1958] ECR 133, para. 152.

19 The European Centre for the Development of Vocational Training (CEDEFOP) and the European Foundation for the Improvement of Living and Working Conditions (EUROFOUND) were the first two agencies established by the Community, as it was then.

20 In the early 1990s, the EC/EU created the following agencies: The Office for Harmonization in the Internal Market (OHIM), the Community Plant Variety Office (CPVO), the European Medicines Agency (EMA), the European Agency for Safety and Health at Work (EU-OSHA), the European Environment Agency (EEA), the European Monitoring Centre for Drugs and Drug Addiction (EMCDDA), the European Training Foundation (EFT), the Translation Centre for the Bodies of the European Union (CdT), the European Police Office (EUROPOL), the European Monitoring Centre for Racism and Xenophobia (EUMC) and the European Agency for Reconstruction (EAR).

their number had almost doubled by the early 2000s.[21] Overall, it appears safe to say that 'more autonomous organs had been created by the EU in the early 2000s than in the preceding 50 years'.[22] The case of EU agencies and their mushrooming led to 'the new paradigm of European governance'.[23]

EU decentralised agencies are defined as 'independent bodies, entrusted by the European [Union] institutions with one or several tasks which they undertake under their own responsibility'.[24] All agencies have a general Director, sometimes referred to as president or executive Director. The Commission proposes candidates for Directors or selects from those proposed by the administrative board. The Director is responsible for the day-to-day management of the agency and is the agency's legal representative, bearing the overall responsibility for the respective agency's proper functioning. The administrative boards are the decision-making bodies of the agencies. Their composition usually comes from a representative from each Member State, the Commission, sometimes the EP and various stakeholders.[25]

From the early days (1960), the Council, the only legislator at the time, lacked extensive, detailed knowledge and the technical and scientific expertise required for the implementation of highly complicated legislative measures. It was also not possible for the Council to agree quickly and efficiently on all the technical requirements needed for every single piece of legislation due to workload

21 The European Union Institute for Security Studies (ISS), the European Union Satellite Centre (EUSC), the European Food Safety Authority (EFSA), the European Union's Judicial Cooperation Unit (EUROJUST), the European Maritime Safety Agency (EMSA), the European Aviation Safety Agency (EASA), the European Network and Information Security (ENISA), the European Centre for Disease Prevention and Control (ECDC), the European Railway Agency (ERA), the European GNSS Supervisory Authority (GSA), the European Defence Agency (EDA), the European Agency for the Management of Operational Cooperation at the External Frontiers (FRONTEX), the Community Fisheries Control Agency (CFCA), the European Police College (CEPOL), the European Chemicals Agency (ECHA), the European Institute for Gender Equality (EIGE), the Agency for the Cooperation of Energy Regulators (ACER), the European Foundation for the Improvement of Living and Working Conditions (EUROFOUND), the European Union Agency for Fundamental Rights (FRA), the European Asylum Support Office (EASO), the Agency for the operational management of large-scale IT systems in the area of freedom, security and justice (EU-LISA), and the Body of European Regulators for Electronic Communications (BEREC). In 2010 we saw the establishment of the European Banking Authority (EBA), the European Securities and Markets Authority (ESMA) and the European Insurance and Occupational Pensions Authority (EIOPA).

22 R Dehousse, 'Delegation of powers in the European Union: The need for a multi-principals model' Centre d' etudes europèennes de sciences Po, available at chairemadp.sciences-po.fr/pdf/seminaires/2007/Contribution_Renaud_DEHOUSSE.pdf, accessed 13 May 2010.

23 D Curtin, *Delegation to EU Non-Majoritarian Agencies and Emerging Practices of Public Accountability* in Geradin et al., *Regulation through Agencies in the EU: A New Paradigm of European Governance* (Edward Elgar 2005).

24 Rambøll Management, Euréval and Matrix, 'Evaluation of the EU decentralised agencies in 2009' (2009) Final Report: Volume I, Volume II, Volume III, Volume IV, p. 1.

25 *See* below about the content of the Common Approach.

limitations.[26] Delegation of the non-essential elements of legislation to the Commission was seen as a solution to mitigate these problems. However, delegation by the principal (in this case, the Council) to the agent (in this case, the Commission) can only be said to be desirable as long as the principal retains control of powers to monitor how the agent is carrying out its delegated tasks. As already pointed out, the leading cases on this point are the old *Meroni* case and, since January 2014, the *ESMA* judgment.[27] Loss of power by the Council is a sufficient reason to consider delegation as undesirable.[28]

The Council, by definition an intergovernmental institution, feared that delegation would see the supranational Commission acting contrary to the interests of the Member States when exercising its implementing powers. The Council therefore wished to exercise effective control over the Commission to limit, as far as possible, the Commission's discretionary powers and to ensure that the implementing measures reflected the opinions of the Member States.[29] It was the consideration of the Member States' interests via the route of expert advice that led to the birth of the pre-Lisbon comitology committees. These committees consisted of Member States' representatives with a certain expertise tasked with assisting and controlling the Commission in the exercise of implementing the powers delegated to it by the Council.[30] Equally, agencies' development aimed at reducing some of the Council's and the Commission's administrative tasks, allowing them to concentrate on their major strategic policies.

The extent to which agencies are empowered to adopt binding decisions also raises significant questions regarding agencies' compliance with the fundamental principle of subsidiarity,[31] particularly whether the same level of optimal regulation through the adoption of national standards could be better achieved at the domestic level. If so, regulation at the supranational level is not justified. In the case of the EU's recently created financial agencies,[32] in light of the recent financial crisis, it is very hard to imagine a scenario with cross-border implications threatening the stability of the whole or part of the euro system which could be better resolved through the adoption of national standards. This means that, again, the necessity of having these agencies cannot be neglected: agencies may lead to better efficiency; they carry out highly complicated tasks requiring

26 C Bergström, *Delegation of Powers in the European Union and the Committee System* (Oxford University Press 2005).

27 Case 9/56, *Meroni & Co, Industrie Metallurgiche SpA* v. *High Authority* [1958] ECR 133; *See United Kingdom* v. *Council & Parliament*, op. cit. n 305 *supra*.

28 A Türk, 'Transparency and comitology', in C Demmke and C Engel, *Continuity and Change in the European Integration Process* (EIPA 2003) p. 175.

29 *See* Harlow, Chapter 1, op. cit. n 21 *supra*.

30 *See* Chapter 5.

31 *See* Craig, Chapter 1, op. cit. n 14 *supra*.

32 In 2010, we witnessed the establishment of three European Supervisory Authorities (ESAs): the European Banking Authority; the European Insurance and Occupational Pensions Authority; and the European Securities and Markets Authority (ESMA).

knowledge and scientific expertise, all of which results in better use of resources.[33] As already stated, the CJEU ruled in *Meroni*[34] and *ESMA*[35] that delegation to autonomous bodies of wide discretionary powers presupposes the exercise of public power and cannot be accepted. Agencies' decision-making processes should be limited to the drafting of technical standards and not be related to the balancing of broad discretionary tasks or the exercise of a wide margin of appreciation which can disturb the institutional balance provided by the Treaty framework. If that happens, then delegation 'replaces the choices of the delegator by the choices of the delegatee, [and] brings about an actual transfer of responsibility'.[36]

Information gathering agencies

It was seen in Chapter 1 that in the aftermath of the resignation of the Santer Commission, the then president of the Commission, Romano Prodi, focused on the development of a number of agencies, which were entrusted with the task of collecting and assessing information.[37] Information agencies are set up for a limited period, they are regulated by a homogeneous general framework[38] and their main task is to implement EU programmes. Doing so requires no discretionary powers. As a result, the overall responsibility remains within the Commission, which overlooks the agencies' decisions and remains accountable for their actions. The Commission monitors closely the collection of information by these types of agencies and therefore they are not of concern to the accountability debate as long as they are not delegated with decision-making powers.

New generation agencies: decentralised agencies

Decentralised agencies differ significantly from information agencies. Initially, decentralised agencies were not subjected to a homogeneous regulatory regime but were established on an ad hoc basis, something which made their functioning and comprehension quite perplexing. In 2005, the Commission proposed an inter-institutional agreement on the governance of decentralised agencies.[39] The negotiations between the Commission, the Council and the EP on this proposal did not come to fruition and the Commission withdrew it in 2008. However,

33 G Majone, 'The agency model: The growth of regulation and regulatory institutions in the European Union' (1997) 3 *EIPASCOPE*, pp. 1–6.

34 *See Meroni & Co, Industrie Metallurgiche SpA* v. *High Authority*, op. cit. n 17 *supra*.

35 *See United Kingdom* v. *Council & Parliament*, op. cit. n 17 *supra*.

36 *See Meroni & Co, Industrie Metallurgiche SpA* v. *High Authority*, op. cit. n 17 *supra*.

37 P Craig, 'The constitutionalization of community administration' (2003) New York University School of Law, *Jean Monnet Working Paper* 3/03, available at www.jeanmonnetprogram.org/papers/03/030301.pdf, accessed 10 May 2015.

38 Regulation 58/2003 [2003] OJ L 11/2–3.

39 Draft Interinstitutional Agreement, COM (2005) 59 final.

after three years of negotiations, these three institutions eventually agreed upon the adoption of a 'Common Approach' on EU agencies, attached to a Joint Statement of the Commission, the EP and the Council adopted in July 2012.[40] This Common Approach does not apply to Common Foreign and Security Policy (CFSP) agencies or to Commission agencies with no decision-making powers. The Joint Statement acknowledges that the Common Approach is not binding, but states that the institutions 'will take the Common Approach into account' as regards all future discussions on decentralised agencies, 'following a case-by-case analysis'.

More importantly, decentralised agencies have the powers to adopt binding decisions vis-à-vis third parties. For instance, the European Securities and Markets Authority (ESMA) can adopt legally binding measures upon financial institutions of the Member States in the event of a threat to the proper functioning of the financial market or to the stability of the financial system of the EU. Additionally, the Office for Harmonisation in the Internal Market (OHIM) can be considered as a new generation of agency with explicit powers to adopt binding decisions.[41] Similarly, the European Aviation Safety Agency (EASA) has the power to issue certificates required for flying within EU air space.

One homogeneous characteristic of the decentralised agencies' regime is their internal structure. All agencies have a general Director, sometimes called a president or executive Director. The Director is responsible for the day-to-day management of the agency. The administrative board of the agency is formed by members of the Council, as well as members from the Commission, sometimes members of the EP and relevant stakeholders.[42] The EP also proposes candidates for Directors or selects from those proposed by the administrative board.

Accountability issues

The accountability debate with regards to agencies originates from the fact that implementing tasks originally entrusted by the Treaties to the Council or the Commission have now been delegated to newly created bodies. Whether delegation to agencies not originally mentioned in the Treaty respects the fundamental question of competence as well as whether the parent body is able to monitor the implementation process, is crucial in terms of accountability. How can delegation to bodies that were not created or mentioned in the Treaties be considered as lawful? To put it simply, the question of whether the transfer of responsibility from the delegator to the delegatee has taken place is of ultimate importance.

40 See Appendix II; also available at europa.eu/agencies/documents/joint_statement_and_common_approach_2012_en.pdf, accessed 17 November 2015.

41 There is, however, a recent agreement on legislation to give some non-binding powers to OHIM in relation to counterfeiting issues and piracy. *See* Council Document number 18680/11.

42 As far as agencies proposed and established by the Council as the principal are concerned, the Commission is not represented in the Administrative Board or involved in the appointment of the executive Director.

Naturally, the mushrooming of agencies resulted from the development of a series of mechanisms to ensure that 'no one controls agencies yet agencies are under control'.[43] The Commission, the Council, the EP, the Member States and the Court of Justice are empowered to secure political, financial and judicial accountability for the agencies' actions.[44]

Nevertheless, agencies have been heavily criticised in the literature as 'uncontrollable centres of arbitrary power'.[45] The lack of a constitutional legal basis exaggerated the criticism about agencies' accountability. It was argued that 'in any event, it is clear that EU independent agencies are independent in the sense of being relatively free of control by any other organs of the Community'.[46] The Treaty of Lisbon, however, has remedied this by integrating agencies into the Treaties and replaced 'institutions (and/or bodies)' with 'institutions, bodies, offices or agencies'.[47] Article 45 of the TEU specifically acknowledges the European Defence Agency. Additionally, Article 15 TFEU of the right of access to documents and Article 228 TFEU of the right to file complaints to the European Ombudsman are explicitly applied to EU agencies. A number of specific amendments have been introduced making general principles, such as transparency and the protection of personal data (Article 16 TFEU), also applicable to agencies. The most important of these amendments relates to judicial accountability: Articles 263 and 267 TFEU, as amended, empower the Court of Justice to review the legality of acts of agencies. Yet, the scientific opinions prepared by the agencies cannot per se be challenged directly since they are non-binding and, as such, they only constitute preparatory measures.[48] Nevertheless, the Court ruled that the scientific opinions prepared by the EMA are 'extremely important so that any unlawfulness of that opinion must be regarded as a breach of essential procedural requirement rendering the Commission's decision unlawful'.[49]

Accountability of agencies is linked to overall concerns about the EU's democratic deficit in the sense that agencies adopt significant decisions that touch upon adjudication, and at the same time they may escape accountability. The Commission responded to these concerns by confirming that:

43 T Moe, 'Interests, institutions and positive theory: The politics of NLBM' (1987) 2 *Studies in American Development*, p. 36.

44 *See* Curtin, Chapter 3, op. cit. n 35 *supra*.

45 *See* Van Ooik in Curtin and Wessel, Chapter 3, op. cit. n 121 *supra*.

46 M Shapiro, 'The problems of independent agencies in the United States and the European Union' (1997) 4 *Journal of European Public Policy*, p. 289.

47 See Articles 24, 123, 124, 127, 130, 228, 263 and 267 of the TFEU.

48 Case T-326/99, *Olivieri* v. *Commission* [2003] ECR II-6053; Cases T-311/06 RI, T-311/06 RII, T-312/06R and T-313/06R: Order of the President of the Court of First Instance of 1 March 2007, *FMC Chemical and Others* v. *EFSA* [2007] ECR II-21; Case C 95/86, *Ferriere San Carlo* v. *Commission* [1987] ECR 1413.

49 Joined cases T-144/00, T-76/00, T-83/00, T-84/00, T-84/00, T-85/00, T-132/00 and T-141/00, *Artegodan* v. *Commission* [2002] ECR 4945, para. 197; Case T-123/00, *Dr Karl Thomae GmbH* v. *Commission* [2002] ECR II-5193, para. 83.

> The independence of these agencies goes hand in hand with an obligation to meet their responsibilities. In order to strengthen the legitimacy of Community action, it is important to establish and delimit the responsibilities of the institutions and agencies . . . Moreover; the principle of accountability requires that a clear system of controls be put in place.[50]

As already explained in Chapter 1, the traditional notion of accountability requires that the powers of rule-making organisations are connected with a democratically elected parliament, since ‘appointed bodies enjoying a degree of independence from elected politicians are viewed as democratically suspicious at best and, at worst, democratically illegitimate’.[51] Consequently, it has been repeatedly pointed out that the crucial problem is decentralised agencies are not accountable to the public. More fundamentally, agencies are sometimes not even accountable to the citizens’ elected representatives as not all the founding regulations provide for the EP’s involvement. Similarly, the EP’s power to question the Director of an agency prior to its appointment is not always guaranteed.[52]

The institutions were therefore required to monitor closely the implementation of tasks by the agencies in order to comply with accountability requirements.[53] At the same time, ‘it is particularly important that [agencies] have genuine autonomy in their internal organisation and functioning if their contribution is to be effective and credible’.[54] In order to comply with the notion of accountability, the Commission or the Council cannot give instructions to agencies or oblige them to withdraw certain decisions. On the contrary, they are given considerable legal, budgetary and operational autonomy. Precisely because of this autonomy, agencies must be held directly responsible for their actions, most notably in view of their active contribution to the regulatory area. The direct corollary of this autonomy is the need to develop mechanisms of accountability.[55] To that end, ‘most founding acts [of agencies] expressly stipulate that the agency concerned will be completely independent from the makers of law and politics. The agency’s output may and should not be influenced by political considerations’.[56] In that context, agencies are expected to perform their tasks independently of their

50 European Commission, ‘Explanatory memorandum. Draft interinstitutional agreement on the operating framework for the European regulatory agencies’ COM (2005) 59 final, p. 2.

51 M Flinders, ‘Distributed public governance in the European Union’ (2004) 11 *Journal of European Public Policy* 520, p. 534.

52 The EP can question the proposed Director in the cases of: EASA, ENISA, ERA, Frontex, ECHA, European Asylum Support Office, EU Institute for Gender and Equality, EU Agency for Fundamental Rights, EUROPOL and the Agency for the Control of Energy Regulators.

53 S Puntscher Riekmann, ‘In search of lost norms: Is accountability the solution to the legitimacy problems in the European Union?’ (2007) 5 *Comparative European Politics*, p. 121.

54 Commission of the European Communities, ‘The operating framework for European regulatory agencies, Communication from the Commission’ COM (2002) 718 final.

55 M Shapiro, ‘The problems of independent agencies in the United States and the European Union’ (1997) 4 *Journal of European Public Policy*, p. 279.

56 *See* Van Ooik in Curtin and Wessel, Chapter 3, op. cit. n 121 *supra*.

political masters. Agencies' independence safeguards their policies and grants them a degree of immunity against external pressures. In the wording of the Commission, '[t]he main advantage of using the agencies is that their decisions are based on purely technical evaluations of very high quality and are not influenced by political or contingent considerations'.[57]

Giandomenico Majone, a strong supporter of EU agencies, argues that 'the delegation of important policy-making powers to independent institutions is democratically justified only in the sphere of efficiency issues, where reliance on expertise and on problem-solving style of decision-making is by far more important than reliance on direct political accountability'.[58] Majone also argues that the Commission must only identify the relevant areas in which further regulation is needed and details how technical regulatory issues are implemented and should be dealt with by agencies using scientific and/or technical experts.[59] It was argued, however, that there is 'no special claim to expertise when it comes to balancing broad, competing public interests'[60] and, in any case, 'scientific legitimacy is not a sufficient basis for the exercise of public authority'.[61]

At the same time, European agencies' independence raises significant constitutional questions about their accountability. Appropriate mechanisms to ensure the control of agencies' actions, subjecting them to a number of procedural and substantive constraints, must be developed. In cases where control mechanisms are weak or non-existent, agencies will act driven by their own interests. Yet, in cases where they are fully dependent on the Member States or on the Commission, agencies' acts will represent and favour the Commission's and Member States' interests. Thus, the equilibrium is seen as the solution to this institutional problem; namely, legal independence with sufficient accountability mechanisms controlling *ex ante* and *ex post* the agencies' behaviour. An interesting argument was made that the problem with agencies is the lack of independence by the parent institutions. It was argued that the parent institution can exercise pressure by means of not approving the agency's proposal, as well as by rejecting their funding if the delegator does not agree. Interestingly, a lack of independence by the parent institution was described as being the actual problem and not the lack of accountability.[62]

The gathering of information and the assessment of highly technical issues requiring specialised scientific knowledge, such as over the quality and safety of food by the European Food Safety Authority (EFSA), cannot be considered as something that does not respect the institutional balance provided by the Treaty.

57 Commission of the European Communities, 'The operating framework for the European regulatory agencies, Communication from the Commission' COM (2002) 718 final, p. 5.

58 G Majone, 'The new European agencies: Regulation by information' (1997) 4 (2) *Journal of European Public Policy*, pp. 263, 268.

59 *Ibid.*

60 *See* Craig, Chapter 1, op. cit. n 42 *supra*, p 184.

61 Case T-13/99, *Pfizer Animal Health SA* v. *Council* [2002] ECR-II 3303, para. 201.

62 *See* Busuioc, op. cit. n 1 *supra*.

Yet, delegation of tasks which imply the exercise of wide discretionary powers by an agency would indeed breach that balance. The Court of Justice held that 'such a delegation of powers can only involve clearly defined executive powers, the rules of which must be entirely subject to the supervision of the high authority'[63] (the precursor of the Commission).

Is there adequate parliamentary, judicial and administrative accountability regarding agencies' performance? If so, these mechanisms and a certain degree of openness, should amount to 'a[n] effective system of supervision and control [which] may mitigate legal objections against far reaching delegation of powers to independent agencies'.[64] Given this, it is essential that accountability mechanisms must exist so that agencies can be held accountable by the EU institutions, Member States and the general public (the principals). There are four types of measures by which the principals can secure accountability: 'contract design, monitoring and reporting, and additional institutional checks'.[65] However:

> [i]t is clear that the aim of accountability is not to achieve a direct control on the independent governance bodies: the very reason for which independence has been given to these bodies excludes the possibility of direct control of the political power.[66]

The establishment of agencies is the result of the adoption of an act, either by the legislature through an act of secondary legislation usually in the form of a Regulation, or through an international agreement in which the tasks, responsibilities and overall powers of the agency are described. The legal mandate should be the starting point to examine the accountability regime. That measure should secure oversight for an agency and state explicitly the powers of the agency: 'only where the accepted parameters of agency discretion are made explicit does there exist a yardstick for the evaluation of agency performance'.[67] Depending on who is taking the decision for the creation of the agency, and on what legal basis and in which policy area, will affect whether the agency will be more or less accountable.[68] The intention to set up a new agency, with the Commission as the principal and with the direct involvement of the EP under the ordinary legislative procedure, results in a more accountable agency. The EP, when involved in

63 Case 9/56, *Meroni & Co, Industrie Metallurgiche, SpA* v. *High Authority of the European Coal and Steel Community* [1958] ECR 133, para. 152.

64 *See* Van Ooik in Curtin and Wessel, Chapter 3, op. cit. n 121 *supra*.

65 R Kiewiet and M McCubbins, *The Logic of Delegation, Congressional Parties and the Appropriation Process* (University of Chicago Press 1991).

66 C Zilioli, 'Accountability and independence: Irreconcilable values or complementary instruments for democracy? The specific case of the European Central Bank', in G Vandersanden, *Melanges en hommage a Jean-Victor Louis* (Editions de I'Universite de 2003) p. 399.

67 *See* Everson, op. cit. n 11 *supra*.

68 M Busuioc, D Curtin and M Groenleer, 'Agency growth between autonomy and accountability: The European police office as a "living institution"' (2011) 18 *Journal of European Public Policy*, p. 848.

the process, retains a fundamental influence and can exercise political scrutiny: it ensures that the new agency has clearly defined powers, functions and operating procedures which allow for enhanced transparency and make control easier.

However, the existing measures designed to ensure that agencies are accountable appear to be insufficient. An underlying deficit identified in the existing literature is that agencies' independence, along with their discretionary tasks touching upon issues of adjudication, regulation and decision-making, operate at a distance from the reach of long-established controls. The obvious solution to this deficit is to provide an enhanced system of accountability mechanisms.

Accountability to the institutions and to the Member States

Accountability to the EP

Since the mid-1990s, with the Maastricht and Amsterdam Treaties, the EP has gradually contributed to the development of more participatory and transparent agencies.[69] As a result, stricter accountability requirements have been imposed entailing attendance before parliamentary committees as well as reporting procedures before the final approval of the agency's budget. In this regard, the budgetary procedure applies to the financing of the majority of agencies, thus giving the EP considerable influence. This significant role exercised by the EP can be seen in the founding Regulation of EFSA, which was formed under what was then the co-decision procedure. The Management Board of EFSA is appointed by the Council in consultation with the EP. In addition, four seats are guaranteed for interest groups and consumer organisations. More importantly, the Director, on appointment, must attend a hearing before the EP where they are expected to answer questions. Finally, the Regulation provides for open meetings and publication procedures. More systematic parliamentary scrutiny would be welcome however, as it would oblige agencies to give reasoned explanations. The insufficient participation of external stakeholders in the decision-making process of agencies constitutes another element of accountability that needs to be addressed. Similarly, more participation in the decision-making process from civil society, consumer groups and professional bodies will increase the legitimacy of the agencies' actions.

The Common Approach provides for a standard composition for agencies' Management Boards (point 10), which are a significant means of ensuring the agencies' accountability. They should have one representative from each Member State, two representatives from the Commission, one representative from the EP and a 'fairly limited' number of representatives from stakeholders. But the provisions on representatives from the EP and Commission are 'without prejudice' to existing rules, and the provisions on the EP and stakeholders apply 'where appropriate'.

69 S Borras, C Koutalakis and F Wendler, 'European agencies and input legitimacy: EFSA, EMEA and EPO in the post-delegation phase' (2007) 29 *Journal of European Public Policy*, p. 583.

The appointment of agency Directors

Currently, the executive Directors are appointed by the administrative boards following a publicly available proposal from the Commission. In this regard, the Common Approach provides that Directors be appointed by the Management Board on the basis of a shortlist drawn up by the Commission (point 16). Similarly, Article 39 of the founding Regulation for the establishment of the Civil Aviation Safety Agency provides that:

> The Executive Director shall be appointed on grounds of merit and of documented competence and experience relevant for civil aviation. The Executive Director shall be appointed or dismissed by the Management Board on a proposal from the Commission. The Management Board shall take its decision by a three-quarters majority of its members. Before being appointed, the candidate selected by the Management Board may be asked to make a declaration before the competent committee or committees of the EP and answer questions from its, or their, members.[70]

In addition, Article 26 of the Regulation establishing the EFSA provides that:

> The Executive Director shall be appointed by the Management Board, on the basis of a list of candidates proposed by the Commission after an open competition, following publication in the *Official Journal of the European Communities* and elsewhere of a call for expressions of interest, for a period of five years which shall be renewable. Before appointment the candidate nominated by the Management Board shall be invited without delay to make a statement *before the EP* (emphasis added) and answer questions put by members of this institution. The Executive Director may be removed from office by a majority of the Management Board.[71]

With regards to the European Agency for the Management of Operational Cooperation at the External Borders (FRONTEX), the EP requested to issue an opinion before the appointment of the designated Director.[72] The involvement of the EP in the appointment process of an agencies' Executive Director is a very welcome development and reflects its powers as a co-legislator. However, it is only in a few cases that the EP is involved in the appointment of the Director.[73]

In addition to the appointment of Directors, the budget of the agency must be subjected to political scrutiny. In this way, both the legislature and the executive are afforded the opportunity of informing themselves as to the proposed programme of the agency and thus of exercising a restraining financial hand at

70 Regulation 216/2008 [2008] OJ L79/1.

71 Regulation 178/2002 [2002] OJ L31/1.

72 European Parliament Document A5-0093/2004 Final.

73 *See* Appendix II.

the commencement of the budgetary year. Currently, the Commission oversees each agency's annual programme, and the Council and the EP both have the opportunity of accepting or rejecting an agency's annual programme. The ability of agencies to secure their own funding, via for example product licensing, cannot escape such control. Equally, political examination at the end of the year serves as a substantial inhibiting mechanism: has the agency performed those tasks it intended to? More political accountability is required, however. Enhanced scrutiny exercised by the EP will oblige agencies to provide reasoned explanations of their initiatives.

Concluding remarks

EU agencies have contributed significantly to the regulatory area because of their highly technical knowledge and scientific expertise. Nevertheless, the current accountability regime of agencies needs to be revised in order to balance the guarantee of agencies' political neutrality in regulating a specific sector with the requirements of accountability. Such a mechanism needs to clarify, for example:

> [w]ho will be responsible if a new medical product with European-wide approval causes problems. Blaming the European Agency for the Evaluation of Medicinal Products (EMEA) in London would be far too easy! It is, in fact, the Commission which takes the decision to approve a medical product, based on the *expertise* provided by the EMEA, the exact legal status of which is a complex matter.[74]

The current structure of governance depends on a variety of actors and, in reality, it would be simply wrong for just one of those actors involved in the decision-making process to be held accountable. Thus, more mechanisms need to be developed to ensure that everyone is being held accountable for their wrongdoings.

74 *See* Kreher, op. cit. n 7 *supra*, p. 535.

5 The invisible hand of the EU committee-based system

The case of delegated and implementing acts

Introduction

The previous chapter examined the accountability regime of EU agencies. The chapter concluded that EU agencies contribute significantly to the regulatory area due to their knowledge and scientific expertise. Clearly, without that knowledge, the internal market as we know it today would not have been possible. Yet, as already explained, the current accountability framework with regards to agencies needs to be amended to balance political neutrality with the requirements of accountability. Taking this finding further, the current chapter examines the problematic aspects of the procedures for adopting delegated and implementing acts, pre-Lisbon known as the comitology regime, often alleged and highlighted in the literature as non-transparent as well as non-accountable. The pre-Lisbon comitology system has been amended by the Implementing Acts Regulation.[1] Therefore, this chapter investigates whether the new procedures are sufficient to remedy the accountability deficits inherent in the field of implementing acts.

In addition, the new delegated acts procedure now grants the European Parliament (EP) more control powers, which effectively increases democratic control over non-legislative measures. From the EP's perspective, the new delegated acts procedure enhances accountability of the EU decision-making process as a whole. It is questionable, however, whether this political gain of the Parliament equally enhances, as one would have expected, accountability to the public and the Member States. The chapter concludes that accountability deficits in the field of delegated acts have been filled to a certain extent by giving more control powers to the Parliament, but this has actually resulted in less accountability for the Member States. More importantly, it is regrettable that the new delegated acts procedure does not enhance accountability to the public at all.[2]

1 Regulation (EU) No 182/2011 [2011] OJ L 55, 28.2.2011, pp. 13–18 of the European Parliament and of the Council of 16 February 2011 laying down the rules and general principles concerning mechanisms for control by Member States of the Commission's exercise of implementing powers.

2 On the topic of how accountable are the delegated and implementing acts in practice, *see* S Peers and M Costa 'Accountability for delegated and implementing acts after the Treaty of Lisbon' (2012)

Setting out the problem

The Lisbon Treaty has attempted to mitigate the accountability deficit inherent in the area of comitology. This chapter analyses the degree to which it has achieved this. First, the chapter looks at how the accountability issue was addressed pre-Lisbon. It then assesses the amendments incorporated by the Lisbon Treaty. Finally, it considers to what degree these new changes actually address the accountability deficit and whether they are likely to silence the critics.

As already explained in the previous chapters, the EU is continually accused of not being sufficiently accountable.[3] This has been particularly witnessed in the field of comitology committees.[4]

> The[se] committees [were] forums for discussion, consist[ing] of representatives from Member States chair[ed] by the Commission. They enabl[ed] the Commission to establish dialogue with national administrations before adopting implementing measures [and] . . . [to] ensur[e] that measures reflected as far as possible the situation in each of the countries concerned.[5]

The Treaty of Lisbon has brought a complete change to the previous system. Implementation of Article 291 TFEU required adaptation of the comitology system due to its incompatibility with the requirements of the new Treaty. The Commission, soon after the entry into force of the new Treaty, made a legislative proposal[6] for the implementation of Article 291 TFEU. The EP confirmed its agreement to consider the adoption of the new Implementing Acts

18 *European Law Journal*, pp. 427–460; A Alemanno and A Meuwese A, 'Impact assessment of EU non-legislative rulemaking: The missing link in "new comitology"' (2013) 19 *European Law Journal*, p. 76; J Bast, 'New categories of acts after the Lisbon reform: Dynamics of parliamentarization in EU law' (2012) 49 *Common Market Law Review*; G Brandsma, *Controlling Comitology. Accountability in a Multi-Level System* (Palgrave Macmillan 2013).

3 *See* Fisher, Chapter 1, op. cit. n 1 *supra*; A Arnull, 'Introduction: The EU's accountability and legitimacy deficit', in A Arnull and D Wincott, *Accountability and Legitimacy in the EU* (Oxford University Press 2003); *See* Harlow, op. cit. n 113 *supra*; W Van Gerven, 'Which form of accountable government for the EU?' (2005) 36 *Netherlands Yearbook of International Law*, p. 228; A Benz, Y Papadopoulos and C Harlow, 'Special issue: Accountability in EU multilevel governance' (2007) 13 *European Law Journal*, p. 442; C Lord, *Democracy in the EU* (Sheffield Academic Press 1998), p. 80; M Bovens, 'Analysing and assessing accountability: A conceptual framework' (2007) 13 *European Law Journal*, p. 447.

4 *See* Brandsma, op. cit. n 2 *supra;* C Neuhold, 'Taming the "Trojan horse" of comitology? Accountability issues of comitology and the role of the European Parliament' (2008) 12 *European Integration Online Papers*; G Brandsma, D Curtin and A Meijer, 'How transparent are EU "comitology" committees in practice?' (2008) 14 *European Law Journal*, p. 819.

5 *See* europa.eu/legislation_summaries/glossary/comitology_en.htm, accessed 10 August 2015.

6 European Commission, 'Proposal for a regulation of the European Parliament and of the Council laying down the rules and general principles concerning mechanisms for control by Member States of the Commission's exercise of implementing powers' COM (2010) 83 final.

Regulation with the Council in December 2010, and these came into force on 1 March 2011.[7]

The key point of the following analysis is to examine whether, following the Lisbon Treaty, EU citizens, along with their elected representatives, can exercise sufficient *ex ante* and *ex post* control over the delegated acts entrusted by the EU legislature to the Commission as per the accountability requirements discussed in Chapter 1. In addition, the accountability regime of the comitology committees, now regulated by the implementing acts of Article 291 TFEU, is examined. The Implementing Acts Regulation lays down the rules and general principles concerning the mechanism for controlling the Commission's implementing powers.[8] The powers possessed by the EP pre-Lisbon are compared and contrasted with the Implementing Acts Regulation in order to assess whether post-Lisbon accountability of the Commission, and the committees voting on the implementing measures, has been enhanced and whether the deficits identified by the literature on the previous comitology system have now been mitigated. It is argued that the EP lost a unique opportunity to secure a better text, in terms of accountability, rather than the one that has been adopted. After all, this was the first time the EP had equal powers at its disposal as the Council under the ordinary legislative procedure, something which gave it the opportunity during the negotiation process to secure a better text. However, the final version of the Implementing Acts Regulation does not correspond to 'its historical maturity being placed on the same footing as Council'.[9] In particular, the EP has lost a rather significant opportunity to improve the transparency standards in relation to the implementing acts.

The pre-Lisbon regime of comitology committees: the rationale for their development

The Commission is entrusted by the Treaties with the task of implementing the majority of legislation. Yet, in this process, the Commission has been assisted and simultaneously controlled by the comitology committees. These committees constitute a cardinal tool of EU governance. During 2014, for instance, 287 comitology committees met 773 times and voted 1,889 times.[10] The extent, therefore, to which these committees function as a mechanism of oversight upon the Commission's work illustrates the pressing need to ensure that they are subjected to adequate accountability mechanisms with regards to their activities.

For nearly as long as this committee-based system has been established as a mechanism of oversight, there has been a debate about its lack of accountability and transparency. There is a need to step into these concerns and examine

7 Regulation 182/2011 [2001] OJ L55/13.

8 *Ibid.*

9 *See* European Parliament Press Release, available at: www.europarl.europa.eu/sides/getDoc.do?language=EN&type=IMPRESS&reference=20100406STO72095, accessed 30 January 2016.

10 European Commission, 'Report from the Commission on the working of committees during 2014' COM (2015) 418 final.

the future of comitology committees by touching on a seminal constitutional question, namely whether comitology committees are post Lisbon subject to a sufficient accountability framework. The role of the EP as an accountability forum within such a mechanism needs to be secured and is examined herewith.

We saw in Chapter 4 that during the early days of the Community, as it was then, the Council, the only legislator at that time, lacked extensive, detailed knowledge and the technical and scientific expertise required for the implementation of legislative measures. It was also not possible for the Council to agree quickly and efficiently on all the technical requirements needed for every single piece of legislation due to workload limitation.[11] Delegation to the Commission of the non-essential elements was seen as a solution to mitigate these problems. The Council, by definition an intergovernmental institution, feared that delegation would see the supranational Commission acting contrary to the interests of the Member States while exercising its delegated implementing powers. The Council, therefore, wished to exercise effective control over the Commission to limit, as far as possible, the Commission's discretionary powers in the field and ensure that the implementing measures reflect the opinions of the Member States' experts.[12] It was therefore consideration of the Member States' interests via the route of expert advice that led to the birth of the comitology committees. The committees consisted of Member States' representatives with a certain expertise tasked with assisting and controlling the Commission in the exercise of implementing the powers delegated to it by the Council.[13]

Developed by necessity[14] and 'spreading like wildfire',[15] the first type of comitology committees came into existence in the areas of the Common Agricultural Policy and Common Commercial Policy, areas where highly detailed and up to date scientific and technical knowledge was needed most.[16]

The comitology system was eventually provided for in Article 145 EEC/EC, as inserted by the Single European Act, and subsequently renumbered Article 202 EC by the Treaty of Amsterdam. Article 202 EC provided that:

> The Council shall confer on the Commission, in the acts which the Council adopts, powers for the implementation of the rules which the Council lays down. The Council may *impose certain requirements* (emphasis added) in respect of the exercise of these powers. The Council may also reserve the right, in specific cases, to exercise directly implementing powers itself.

11 *See* Bergström, Chapter 3, op. cit. n 60 *supra*, p. 44.
12 *See* Harlow, Chapter 3, op. cit. n 36 *supra*.
13 However, assistance and control are, by definition, contradictory and the whole idea of helping and controlling may thus be counterintuitive.
14 It has to be noted here that the Treaties do not provide for the creation of comitology committees, which are established by secondary legislation on an ad hoc basis.
15 B Driessen, 'Delegated legislation after the Treaty of Lisbon: An analysis of Article 290 TFEU' (2010) 35 *European Law Review*, pp. 837–838.
16 *See* Bergstrom, Chapter 3, op. cit. n 60 *supra*.

> The procedures referred to above must be consonant with principles and rules to be laid down in advance by the Council, acting unanimously on a proposal from the Commission and after obtaining the opinion of the European Parliament.

The general 'principles and rules' referred to in Article 202 EC, quoted above, were set out initially in a Council decision of 1987,[17] which was replaced in 1999.[18] The 1999 decision was amended in 2006.[19]

Accountability deficits of the comitology regime

The above-mentioned schematic presentation is only a small part of the whole story. The development of comitology committees faced severe criticism[20] and led to a number of long-standing inter-institutional tensions. It would go beyond the scope of this chapter to examine in detail the shortcomings of each of the comitology decisions. Suffice to say here that the first comitology decision in 1987[21] provided complex procedures (seven in number) that the Commission had to follow before the adoption of the delegated implementing measures. The first comitology decision provided no further guidance as to which procedure should apply in each case. More importantly, it granted the Member States through the Council a dominant role and completely ignored the EP, leaving it outside of the established 'control system'. The EP, occupying the opposition side, feared[22] that already adopted legislative measures might be manipulated significantly in the implementation process without its involvement.

The exclusion of the EP from the control mechanisms of the comitology committees when general rules on such mechanisms were first adopted, led the EP to bring annulment proceedings before the Court of Justice against the first comitology decision on the grounds of alleged accountability deficits.[23] The pressing need for the EP to be on an equal footing with the Council became more obvious

17 Council Decision 87/373/EEC [1987] OJ L197/33.

18 Council Decision 1999/468/EC [1999] OJ L184/23.

19 Council Decision 2006/512/EC [2006] OJ L200/11. On the development of the comitology rules, *see* W Wessels, 'Comitology: Fusion in action. Politico-administrative trends in the EU system' (1998) 5 *Journal of European Public Policy*, p. 209; C Joerges and E Vos, *EU Committees: Social Regulation, Law and Politics* (Hart 1999); C Joerges and J Neyer, 'Transforming strategic interaction into deliberative problem-solving: European comitology in the food stuff sector' (1997) 4 *Journal of European Public Policy*, p. 609; E Vos, 'The rise of committees' (1997) 3 *European Law Journal*, p. 230; *See* Bergstrom, Chapter 3, op. cit. n 60 *supra*; *See* Brandsma, op. cit. n 2 *supra*; Neuhold, op. cit. n 4 *supra*.

20 *See* Türk, Chapter 3, op. cit. n 60 *supra*.

21 *See* Council Decision, op. cit. n 18 *supra*.

22 M Alfe, 'Institutional tensions in the evolution of the comitology system', in T Christiansen, TJ Oettel and B Vaccari, *21st Century Comitology: The Role of Implementing Committees in the Wider European Union* (European Institute of Public Administration 2009).

23 Case 302/87, *EP* v. *Council* [1988] ECR 5615, para. 29; the EP's action was inadmissible.

post Maastricht with the development of the co-decision procedure, which placed the EP on a similar footing to the Council and left its control powers relating to implementing measures unchanged. The EP considered that the Commission should not possess the power to amend or supplement a legislative act without the assent (tacit or explicit) of the legislator. However, the Court of Justice subsequently implicitly confirmed that the general comitology rules also applied to acts adopted by co-decision, although the EP had argued the opposite.[24]

The EP has consistently fought for increased control powers over the comitology committees, which it saw as a strategy of the Council to devalue the increased legislative powers of the EP. The latter considered comitology as a way to manipulate the implementation of measures already adopted under the (then) co-decision procedure, something which was affecting the accountability of the EP: MEPs could no longer be held accountable if the measures decided by them were significantly changed in the implementation process. In addition, such manipulation was affecting the ability of the EP to hold the executive to account because the implementing measures were de facto being taken by the committees, creating a massive accountability gap.[25]

The EP's demands for increased powers in the field were reflected in the first reform of the comitology decision in 1999,[26] which enhanced the position of the EP and also simplified and reduced the comitology procedures from seven to four.[27] This decision in particular granted the EP the right to be informed of agendas, voting results and draft measures (where the basic act was adopted pursuant to the then co-decision procedure), and to view summary records and attendance lists of the comitology committees.[28] The EP was also given the power to adopt *ultra vires* resolutions indicating that the Commission had exceeded its implementing powers foreseen in the basic act (if that act was adopted by means of the co-decision procedure).[29] This type of soft control is closely related to the principle of the institutional balance provided by the Treaties and is upheld by a consistent line of case law.[30]

According to the management procedure (Article 4), the Commission could adopt the implementing measures which would apply immediately, but if the opinion of the committee was negative (a qualified majority vote (QMV) of the Member States' representatives against the proposal was required to block it) then the Council was entitled to take a different decision within a period of up to three months, which was set by each basic act. The regulatory procedure (Article 5) was based on the idea that the committee needed to approve the draft

24 Case C-259/95, *EP* v. *Council* [1997] ECR I-5303.
25 *See* Neuhold, op. cit. n 4 *supra*.
26 *See* Council Decision, op. cit. n 18 *supra*.
27 The decision also included new rules on public accountability.
28 Art 7(3), Council Decision, op. cit. n 18 *supra*. The EP also had to be informed when the Commission proposed measures or proposals to the Council.
29 *See* Articles 5(5) and 8, Council Decision, op. cit. n 18 *supra*.
30 P Craig, 'Democracy and rulemaking within the EC: An empirical and normative assessment' (1997) 3 *European Law Journal*, p. 105.

measure before the Commission could adopt it, thus a QMV of the representatives in favour of the measure was necessary. If the committee blocked a draft measure, it had to be forwarded to the Council, which had the chance to adopt or oppose it by a QMV. If the Council failed to do either within the specified period, then the Commission had to adopt the measure. But the EP had no role in such cases. There was also a safeguard procedure (Article 6), which required the Commission to inform the Member States and the Council of the draft measures. A Member State could then refer the draft decision to the Council, which could control the decision-making of the Commission by blocking or approving it, or taking a different decision by QMV.

The Commission argued for abolishing comitology committees because the management and regulatory committees could prevent it from adopting implementing measures without the committee's approval.[31] It proposed as a replacement 'a simple legal mechanism [which] allows Council and European Parliament as the legislature to monitor and control the actions of the Commission against the principles and political guidelines adopted in the legislation'.[32]

The EP pressed for further reforms, as it still considered that an act adopted under the co-decision procedure (as it was then) which provided for the comitology procedure should not be considered lawful as long as control could not be exercised by both arms of the legislator equally. Addressing these objections, the 2006 amendments to the comitology decision[33] granted more control powers to the EP by introducing the Regulatory Procedure with Scrutiny (RPS), which reflected its powers as a co-legislator by giving it the power to revoke implementing measures. More specifically, the 2006 decision provides that where the basic act in question was adopted under the co-decision procedure and called for the adoption of a measure of 'general application designed to amend non-essential elements of that instrument, *inter alia* by deleting some of those elements or by supplementing the instrument by the addition of new non-essential elements', the new RPS would apply.[34]

Under this procedure, the Commission must submit a draft measure to a committee.[35] If the committee supports the proposal by QMV, then it is forwarded to the Council and the EP, and they both have three months to decide on adoption of the measure. After the expiry of the three-month period, the Commission can proceed with adoption.[36] Under the RPS, the EP and/or the Council has the power to block the draft measure when certain conditions are met: when the draft measure exceeds the implementing powers provided in

31 European Commission, 'White Paper on European governance' COM (2001) 428, p. 31.

32 *Ibid.*

33 *See* Council Decision, op. cit. n 19 *supra*.

34 *See* Article 2(2) as inserted by the 2006 amendment, Council Decision, op. cit. n 19 *supra*.

35 *See* Article 5a(2) as inserted by the 2006 amendment, Council Decision, op. cit. n 19 *supra*.

36 *See* Article 5a(3) as inserted by the 2006 amendment, Council Decision, op. cit. n 19 *supra*. The Council can block the measure by a QMV against, and the EP can block it if a majority of its members vote against.

the basic act; when the draft measure is not compatible with the general aim or the content of the basic act; and finally, when the principles of subsidiarity and proportionality are being violated. If the measure is blocked by either the EP or the Council (or both), the Commission may resubmit an amended draft of the implementing measure to the committee, or present a legislative proposal.

In cases where a committee gave a negative or no opinion, the draft measure is forwarded to the Council.[37] The Council then has three options: to adopt, to oppose or to take no action in relation to the measures concerned; it is *not* limited to opposing the measure only on certain substantive grounds. If the Council votes against the measure by QMV, then it cannot be adopted; if the Council decides to adopt the draft measure by QMV, then the measure is forwarded to the EP; if the Council does not act (i.e. because there is no QMV for or against the measure), then the Commission must forward the draft measure to the EP. In the latter two cases, the EP can then reject the measure by a majority of its members, on the same grounds set out above. Thus, if the Commission does not have the support of the comitology committee, the issue is referred first to the Council, but the EP still has the power to block it.

There is also the possibility of an urgent version of the RPS, which provided for the Commission to adopt a measure immediately, with a short period for the Council or EP to veto the measure concerned on the grounds that it was ultra vires, etc. In that case, the Commission would have to repeal the measure concerned, although it could 'provisionally maintain the measures in force if warranted on health protection, safety or environmental grounds'.[38]

Since the introduction of the RPS in 2006, the Commission has examined all the basic acts adopted under the co-decision procedure in order to apply the RPS to the existing *acquis communautaire*. The adaptation process was completed by 2008.[39] In practice, interestingly enough, the first veto under the RPS was exercised by the Council when it objected to six draft measures that had been agreed by the comitology committees.[40] For its part, the EP has blocked draft measures under the RPS in the areas of financial services[41] and energy labelling.[42]

37 *See* Article 5a(4), Council Decision, op. cit. n 19 *supra*.

38 *See* Article 5a(6), Council Decision, op. cit. n 19 *supra*.

39 There was an initial list of 25 measures to be amended urgently (2006 OJ C255/1). The remaining acts were amended by 'omnibus' legislation: Regulations 1137/2008 (2008 OJ L311/1), 1103/2008 (2008 OJ L304/80), 219/2009 (2009 OJ L87/109) and 596/2009 (2009 OJ L188/14). A proposal for a fifth omnibus Regulation (COM (2009)142, 30 March 2009) became obsolete due to the entry into force of the Treaty of Lisbon.

40 One related to the Water Framework Directive (2000 OJ L327/1) and five to the inclusion of active substances under the Biocides Directive (Directive 98/8/EC (1998 OJ L123/1). *See* the Commission's report on comitology for the year 2008 (COM (2009) 335, 3 July 2009), pp. 7–8.

41 The opposing resolution was adopted in the European Parliament plenary session on 16 December 2008 (P6_TA-PROV(2008)0607). In 2008, the EP and Council between them blocked 7 RPS measures out of 71 (COM (2009) 335, *ibid.*).

42 'Report from the Commission on the Working of Committees during 2009', (COM (2010) 354, 2 July 2010), pp. 8–9. In 2009, the EP blocked 1 RPS measure out of 131, whereas the Council blocked none.

Also, the EP has brought a case against the Council, arguing that one adopted measure is *ultra vires* the basic act. The Court of Justice annulled the measure on the grounds that the measure should have been adopted jointly by the EP and Council acting together under the ordinary legislative procedure.[43]

Lifting the veil of secrecy

Apart from the accountability deficits resulting from the exclusion of the EP from the control mechanisms of the implementing measures, other than the RPS procedure, comitology committees' meetings were (and still are) taking place behind closed doors. Furthermore, access to documents rules prior to 1999 was simply non-existent. Comitology committees and their working procedures were carried out away from any type of public scrutiny. A select committee of the House of Lords reported that these committees were unknown, since no list of such committees was 'publicly available nor is there an authoritative account of what each does'.[44] However, in 1999, the Court of First Instance,[45] now the General Court, ruled that the 1993 rules on access to documents applied to those committees. Therefore, the public can have access to all the comitology documents unless any of the exceptions provided for in the access to documents regulation applies.

The above-mentioned inter-institutional controversy resulted in the insertion of Article 7 of the 1999 comitology decision.[46] This provision grants the EP the right to be informed of agendas, vote results and draft measures and to view summary records and attendance lists of the comitology committees. Moreover, since 2000, the Commission has published an annual report containing information on the number of such committees, their meetings and voting procedures. In addition, since 2001, an online comitology register is also available. The EP has also the power to adopt *ultra vires* resolutions indicating that the Commission has exceeded its implementing powers foreseen in the basic act. As already stated above, this type of monitoring is ensuring compliance with the institutional balance requirement provided by the Treaties and upheld by a consistent line of case law.[47]

As for judicial review as regards comitology documents, the Court of First Instance (as it was then) ruled in *British American Tobacco*[48] that the applicant's interest in obtaining comitology documents outweighed the Commission's own interest in safeguarding the confidentiality of its proceedings. As we saw

43 Case C-355/10, *EP* v. *Council* [2012] ECLI:EU:C:2012:516, The EP mustered a majority of the *vote* against the draft measure, but not the majority of its *members*, as required by the RPS rules.

44 House of Lords, Select Committee on European Communities, Delegation of Powers to the Commission: Reforming Comitology, 3rd Report.

45 Case T-188/97, *Rothmans* v. *Commission* [1999] ECR II-2463.

46 *See* Council Decision, op. cit. n 18 *supra*.

47 *See* Craig, op. cit. n 30 *supra*.

48 Case T-111/00, *British American Tobacco* v. *Commission* [2001] ECR II-2997, para. 38.

in Chapter 3, the latter rule was later replaced by an exception where giving access to documents would 'seriously undermine' a 'decision-making' process, but the Court ruled that if the Commission seeks to rely on this exception as regards comitology documents, it must show that there is a real risk, which is reasonably foreseeable and not hypothetical, that outside pressure would seriously undermine the effectiveness of its discussions; the preparatory or informal nature of its work was not grounds to refuse access as such.[49] Equally, documents concerning the views expressed in the comitology process must be disclosed even despite experts' desire to hide their identities, and even if they concern scientific advice.[50]

The post-Lisbon regime

The Treaty of Lisbon provided for a complete change of the previous comitology system, entailing the creation of a new type of measure (delegated acts) as well as revising the Treaty framework regarding implementing measures. The relevant Treaty provisions are Article 290 TFEU for the delegated acts and Article 291 TFEU for the implementing acts. They provide as follows:

> *Article 290*
>
> 1 A legislative act may delegate to the Commission the power to adopt non-legislative acts of general application to supplement or amend certain non-essential elements of the legislative act.
>
> The objectives, content, scope and duration of the delegation of power shall be explicitly defined in the legislative acts. The essential elements of an area shall be reserved for the legislative act and accordingly shall not be the subject of a delegation of power.
>
> 2 Legislative acts shall explicitly lay down the conditions to which the delegation is subject; these conditions may be as follows:
>
> (a) the European Parliament or the Council may decide to revoke the delegation;
>
> (b) the delegated act may enter into force only if no objection has been expressed by the European Parliament or the Council within a period set by the legislative act.
>
> For the purposes of (a) and (b), the European Parliament shall act by a majority of its component members, and the Council by a qualified majority.
>
> 3 The adjective 'delegated' shall be inserted in the title of delegated acts.

49 Case T-144/05, *Muniz* v. *Commission* [2008] ECR II-335.

50 Cases T-121/05, *Borax* v. *Commission* [2009] ECR II-27 and Case T-166/05, *Borax* v. *Commission* [2009] ECR II-28; *see* S Peers and M Costa, op. cit. n 2 *supra*.

Article 291

1 Member States shall adopt all measures of national law necessary to implement legally binding Union acts.
2 Where uniform conditions for implementing legally binding Union acts are needed, those acts shall confer implementing powers on the Commission, or, in duly justified specific cases and in the cases provided for in Articles 24 and 26 of the Treaty on European Union, on the Council.
3 For the purposes of paragraph 2, the European Parliament and the Council, acting by means of regulations in accordance with the ordinary legislative procedure, shall lay down in advance the rules and general principles concerning mechanisms for control by Member States of the Commission's exercise of implementing powers.
4 The word 'implementing' shall be inserted in the title of implementing acts.

The Treaty of Lisbon, contrary to the prior situation under the EC Treaty, introduced a hierarchy of legal norms. By doing so, the Treaty made a distinction between legislative and non-legislative acts. Delegated and implementing acts fall into the latter category. The power to adopt, under Article 290 TFEU, delegated acts of general application can *only* be delegated to the Commission. The delegated acts are based on a basic legislative act delegating the power to adopt a non-legislative act in order to supplement or amend some of the non-essential elements of the basic act. Pursuant to Article 290 TFEU, the basic act must define clearly the objectives, content, scope and duration of the delegation. These criteria need to be defined in the basic act on a case-by-case basis and cannot be delegated to the Commission. It should be noted that only the Commission can adopt delegated acts and not the Council.

The issue of whether regulations, directives and decisions originated from the EU legislative or executive power was, pre-Lisbon, a very difficult and time consuming herculean task, especially for the general public; an exercise which reflected the overall non-transparent manner of the EU decision-making process. The EU's legal order has now been clarified with the introduction of a hierarchy of legal norms, and citizens can now easily differentiate, at least in theory, between legislative and non-legislative acts.

The limited EP influence over the control of comitology committees has now been rectified by granting more control powers in relation to the delegated acts. Thus, as far as Article 290 TFEU is concerned, control powers are granted jointly to both arms of the EU legislator, something that places the Council and the EP on an equal footing. Both arms of the legislature are entrusted with the ability to block any draft measures. The procedure for the adoption of delegated acts has replaced the RPS of the comitology proceedings. The delegated acts process is now applicable in all areas of legislative activity, whereas under the comitology system the RPS was limited in the ex co-decision procedure. This interpretation follows from the wording of Article 289(3), which defines a legislative act as one adopted under the legislative procedure as either ordinary or special. Similarly, the delegated acts procedure can apply as regards the implementation of acts adopted under the special legislative procedure. Therefore, the delegated acts process is being inserted in acts which were not previously subject to co-decision.

Finally, delegated acts are not covered by any binding horizontal framework, something which leaves the co-legislator free to decide about the objectives, duration and scope of the delegation on an ad hoc basis, taking into account the specific characteristics of each case. Consequently, post Lisbon, in cases where the Commission amends the basic legislative act, comitology committees have ceased to exist, except on a transitional basis, if those committees were set up by a pre-Lisbon act.

There are several other issues in relation to the application of Articles 290 and 291 TFEU which have brought significant changes to the previous comitology system and alter the accountability framework. First, the Commission has argued, rightly, that these two provisions are mutually exclusive. This interpretation derives from the wording and the different purpose of each of these Articles. Under Article 290, for example, the legislator delegates powers to the Commission that would ordinarily have been exercised by the legislator, i.e. supplementing or amending a legislative act. This explains the fact that under this Article control powers can only be exercised by the Council and the EP. On the other hand, under Article 291, only the Member States can control measures which interfere with their tasks of implementing EU law. Therefore, it is clear that the Commission cannot be controlled by the Member States in relation to the delegated acts or by the Council in relation to implementing acts.

Second, while there was hitherto no procedure for adopting delegated acts as such, the EU's previous comitology rules recognize, as from 2006, a separate category of implementing acts, which are 'measures of general scope designed to amend non-essential elements of the [legislative act], inter alia by deleting some of those elements or by supplementing the instrument by the addition of new non-essential elements'.[51] These measures needed to be adopted under RPS from 2006, which gives extra powers to the EP, although it gives a more dominant role to Member States through the Council. The circumstances in which the delegated acts procedure applies are very similar to the circumstances in which RPS applied pre-Lisbon. However, the delegated acts procedure can apply for the implementation of any types of legislative acts, including those adopted under the special legislative procedure. This interpretation follows from the wording of Article 289(3), which defines a legislative act as one adopted under the legislative procedure which can be either ordinary or special. This has also been the practice to date.[52]

51 *See* Council Decision, op. cit. n 19 *supra*. For the points mentioned in this section, *see also* S Peers and M Costa, op. cit. n 2 *supra*, pp. 427–460.

52 Regulation 973/2010 [2010] OJ L285/4.

Third, the Treaty of Lisbon provides the essential elements of the delegation, which shall be explicitly defined in the legislative act and constitute the explicit and clear will of the Treaty's drafters. A contrary interpretation of this proviso will be reviewable by the Court of Justice. It is noteworthy to comment on the Commission's communication on the implementation of Article 290 of the TFEU where it considers that Article 290 'does not require the Commission to be subject to strict cut-off dates'. The EP, the Council and the Commission in Spring 2011 agreed upon a common understanding which sets out the framework for the use of the delegated acts procedure, including model clauses which the institutions 'undertake to refer [to] as far as possible' when making use of this process.[53] The common understanding provides that the delegation of power can be for limited or unlimited periods. Where the period is limited, the basic act 'should in principle' provide for the delegation to be extended tacitly for periods of identical duration unless there is an objection by either legislator within three months before the end of that period, following a report on the delegation by the Commission nine months before the end of that period. The institutions also agreed that the standard period for the EP and/or the Council to object to a draft delegated act 'should in principle' be two months, and 'not less than that', with a two-month extension possible at the behest of the EP or the Council. If both legislators inform the Commission of their intention not to object before the end of this period, the delegated act may be published and enter into force earlier. The common understanding also includes provisions for an urgency procedure.[54] Acts adopted under this procedure enter into force without delay and apply unless there is an objection by either legislator within a specified time period.

Fourth, as noted already, the delegated acts procedure applies regardless of the legislative procedure used to adopt a basic legislative act, as compared to the RPS system, which only applied where the basic act was adopted by means of the co-decision procedure. So it follows that the delegated acts procedure now applies in many places where the regulatory procedure *without* scrutiny previously applied. In particular, the delegated acts procedure now applies in place of the 'ordinary' procedures in the previous comitology rules where (a) the former co-decision procedure did not apply and (b) the measures to be adopted are of 'general application' and 'supplement or amend certain non-essential elements of [a] legislative act'.

However, as regards the EP, the scope of this change is less dramatic than it first appears, since the scope of the co-decision procedure, now known as the ordinary legislative procedure, was considerably extended by the Treaty of Lisbon, for example, to cover areas such as agriculture and fisheries (Article 43(2) TFEU) and the common commercial policy (Article 207 TFEU). So the RPS process

53 Council document 8640/11, 4 April 2011. *See* Appendix III.

54 This 'should be' limited to 'exceptional cases, such as security and safety matters, the protection of health and safety, or external relations, including humanitarian crises'.

would in any event have been extended to such areas, even if the delegated acts procedure had not been invented. On the other hand, the delegated acts procedure is wider in scope than the RPS to the extent that the new procedure applies to areas that *still* fall within the scope of special legislative procedures. But, as discussed below, in practice, the EP will not be granted control powers over the delegation in such cases.

The new procedure also applies where the Council had previously delegated *to itself* the power to adopt measures which are of 'general application' and 'supplement or amend certain non-essential elements of [a] legislative act'. Again, this change is not as significant as it first appears, since delegation to the Council was the exception under the comitology rules and, in particular, the EP rarely (if ever) accepted the Council's delegation of implementing powers to itself as regards legislation adopted by means of the co-decision procedure.

Having said that, the move to the delegated acts procedure fundamentally alters the control powers of Member States, both *de jure* and de facto. As noted already, Member States have lost all *de jure* power as compared to the previous rules, since they cannot as such control delegated acts. They have also lost considerable de facto power, since the usual requirement under the previous rules that such measures had to be *supported* by a QMV of Member States' representatives in a comitology committee has gone, leaving only the power of the Council, made up of Member States' representatives, to *block* a proposed delegated act by QMV.

Fifth, it is necessary, in order to ensure that legislative acts are not amended without control of the legislature, to amend all relevant pre-Lisbon measures so that the new rules can apply. To this end, the Commission has stated that all pre-Lisbon legislation providing for the RPS will be converted to the delegated acts procedure.[55] Furthermore, the Commission also provided an indicative timetable listing its planned proposals to convert other pre-Lisbon legislative measures which provide for the adoption of implementing measures to the delegated acts procedure.[56] A number of these proposals have already been submitted,[57] including a proposal regarding the common commercial policy that brought most legislation in this area within the scope of the general rules on implementing acts for the first time, removing the Council's powers to adopt trade defence measures or to overrule the Commission, and leaving such powers with the Commission only.[58]

Initially, the pre-Lisbon comitology provisions were converted to the regime of the new Implementing Acts Regulation, except for those cases where the RPS

55 *See* the Commission's statement [2011] OJ L55/19.

56 *See* Council document 18097/10, 22 Dec 2010, which lists 153 such measures.

57 For instance, *see* COM (2010) 738 final, 10 Dec 2010; COM (2010) 733 final, 10 Dec 2010; and COM (2010) 728 final, 9 Dec 2010.

58 COM (2011) 82, 7 Mar 2011.

applied,[59] until replaced by the delegated acts procedure.[60] To the extent that the procedures concerned now fall within the scope of the delegated acts rules, this is surely illegal, because, for the reasons discussed above, legislation adopted after the entry into force of the Treaty of Lisbon *must* provide for the adoption of delegated acts, not implementing acts, where the acts concerned fall within the scope of Article 290.

Next, an important question as regards Article 290 TFEU is whether the possibilities for control of the Commission listed in that Article are exhaustive or not.[61] On this point, when the Treaty states that the power to adopt delegated acts *may* be conferred on the Commission, it presumably means, in light of the general context of Article 290 (as discussed above), that the legislators have an option to confer this power upon the Commission; they could instead have fully retained the power to adopt such measures themselves pursuant to the legislative procedure. Next, the Treaty *requires* ('shall') the objectives, etc. of the delegation to be specified, and equally rules out the delegation of essential elements of the legislation. The legislation 'shall' lay down the conditions to which the delegation is subject, but these conditions 'may' be revocation or prior control before adoption of a delegated act.

The obvious meaning of the word 'may', as contrasted with the word 'shall' in the same Article, is that the two types of control referred to expressly in Article 290(2) are *not* the only types of control which the legislators can impose. This also follows from the context of Article 290: since the legislators decide whether or not to delegate their legislative power, it must follow that they have the power to decide on the conditions which apply when they delegate it, provided that the conditions are explicit and that the limits in Article 290(1) (and the basic distinction between Articles 290 and 291, i.e. control can only be exercised by the EP and/or the Council) are complied with. It might even be argued that the final sentence of Article 290(2), which provides that the EP and Council 'shall' apply particular voting rules, need not always apply either, since that sentence refers back to provisions which are themselves only options.

This discussion is relevant because the EP and Council might well wish to develop other forms of control besides those listed in Article 290(2). In particular, the Council has already adopted a regulation by means of a special legislative procedure, which provides powers of control over delegated acts only for itself, and not for the EP.[62] This could only legally be justified if the list of control mechanisms in Article 290(2) is non-exhaustive, and in that case

59 *See* Article 13, op. cit. n 1 *supra*.

60 *See* Article 12, *ibid*.

61 *See* Commission document COM (2009) 673, 9 Dec 2009 and EP resolution (INI/2010/2021) of 5 May 2010; *See* P Craig, *The Lisbon Treaty: Law, Politics, and Treaty Reform* (Oxford University Press 2010); *See* Driessen, op. cit. n 15 *supra*.

62 Regulation 973/2010 [2010] OJ L 285/4, Articles 6–10. There are further proposals to this end: *see*, for instance, the proposal for a Common Consolidated Tax Base (COM (2011) 121, 16 Mar 2011), Articles 127–130.

it must follow that other types of alternative control mechanisms are possible too. From the point of view of accountability, limiting control powers to the Council is acceptable where the Council alone is conferring the power on the Commission, but arguably, since Article 290(2) is non-exhaustive, it remains an option: the Council might equally chose to share that power jointly with the EP if it wishes. The latter argument is stronger where the EP has the power of consent as regards Council legislation adopted by means of a special legislative procedure.

Control mechanisms of delegated acts

A basic fact to be born in mind is that the Lisbon Treaty introduced important innovations and has improved the control powers granted to the EP in the area of delegated legislation. It is Article 290 TFEU which greatly improves democratic accountability by enhancing the EP's position. First, the EP and the Council acting together under the ordinary legislative procedure set the '*ex ante* specification of standards in the primary law'.[63] Second, the legislator is directly involved in the monitoring of compliance with the conditions set in the legislative act, and it is empowered to exercise ex post control 'should the measure not be to the liking of the EP or the Council'.[64] Article 290 TFEU provides for two control mechanisms for the case of delegated acts. The first is that the delegation can be revoked by the EP or the Council, whereas the second refers to the ability of either the EP or the Council to oppose the delegated act for coming into force within a time limit specified in the basic legislative act. Several points need to be addressed here.

First of all, for the first time in the history of the comitology committees, direct control powers can now be exercised independently by both arms of the legislature. Starting from the fact that delegation can be revoked by either the EP or the Council, 'the EP has achieved its historical maturity being placed on the same footing as Council' where concerns about the EU's democratic deficit, which were obviously connected with the limited Parliamentary influence given the Council's dominant role, seem now to be alleviated. This is impressive, at least in theory. Therefore, Article 290 of the TFEU grants to the legislature a significant and direct power of control subject to the ability of the co-legislature to use it. However, the issue here is whether the co-legislator is in a position to substitute the opinions given by Member States' experts in highly technical policy areas. In order for the co-legislature to use the control powers effectively, it must create other types of monitoring bodies with sufficient technical expertise. It is well known that the EP and the Council do not have such technical knowledge and expertise.

63 P Craig, 'The role of the European Parliament under the Lisbon Treaty', in S Griller and J Ziller, *The Lisbon Treaty: EU Constitutionalism without a Constitutional Treaty?* (Springer 2008) p. 116.
64 *Ibid.*

Second, the basic act may provide for a time limit in which either the Council or the EP can object to the entry into force of the delegated act. Both institutions again are placed on an equal footing, something which shows that the EP's concerns over the last four decades have not fallen on deaf ears, but rather has led to a Treaty amendment. Therefore, the EP and the Council must create the appropriate infrastructure in order to control the tasks delegated to the Commission effectively. However, the Council and the EP need information on the acts proposed by the Commission. But which bodies will provide this kind of information and how will the public have access to draft delegated acts at an early stage?

The question that needs to be answered is whether the legislator is capable of using these control powers. In order for the control mechanism to be effective, the legislator must create monitoring bodies with technical knowledge and scientific expertise to provide the legislator with the information required to control the Commission's delegated powers.

It was argued that the removal of comitology committees under Article 290 of the TFEU would have the effect of depriving the Commission of the expertise required to regulate highly complicated issues.[65] The Commission continues to use Article 290 of the TFEU as the Member States' experts. What is different, however, is the formal withdrawal of the committees as far as delegated acts are concerned.[66] The difference with the prior Lisbon regime, regarding the delegated acts, is the abolition of the formal powers of comitology committees when their negative opinions under the previous system would have provoked an appeal to the Council to modify the Commission's draft. The adopted delegated acts show that the Commission continues to consult the Member States' experts before submitting the delegated acts to the Council and the EP. In particular, when drawing up its proposals, in most cases the Commission consulted Member States' experts and stakeholders widely, and took considerable account of the comments and objections expressed.[67] However, the Council and the EP, as has already been argued by Craig, will only exercise ex post political control, whereas under the comitology regime the committees provided more than that.

The EP pressed for further reforms, as it still considered that an act adopted under the co-decision procedure (as it was then), which provided for the comitology procedure, should provide for control to be exercised by both arms of the legislature equally. Addressing these objections, the 2006 amendments to

65 *See* Craig, op. cit. n 63 *supra*, pp. 117–118.

66 Commission Delegated Regulations 1059-1062/2010 [2010] OJ L314/1, 17, 47 and 64, and 626/2011 [2011] OJ L178/1.

67 *See* the proposals for the delegated acts, in Council documents 14246/10, 14251/10, 14253/10 and 14256/10, all 29 September 2010, and 9968/11, 11 May 2011. Two further delegated acts have been proposed and are subject to EP and Council scrutiny at the time of writing: *see* Council docs 12931/11 and 12933/11, both 14 July 2011, concerning controls of infections of pets. The only proposed delegated act which was not preceded by extensive stakeholder consultation was Council document 12931/11.

the comitology decision[68] granted more control powers to the EP by introducing the RPS, which reflected its powers as a co-legislator by giving it the power to revoke implementing measures. More specifically, the 2006 decision provides that where the basic act in question was adopted under the co-decision procedure and called for the adoption of a measure of 'general application, designed to amend non-essential elements of that instrument, *inter alia* by deleting some of those elements or by supplementing the instrument by the addition of new non-essential elements', the new RPS would apply.[69]

The legislature's control function operates ex post, meaning that it cannot influence the content of the act. Still, the legislature may be able to indicate its preferences to the Commission, which will have to comply otherwise it will face the rejection of the measure.

However, having taken this report into account it is obvious that the EP has failed in its more fundamental aim of securing a fixed date for converting all existing comitology rules, which should be covered by the delegation procedure, into that procedure. The EP asked the Commission to act *as soon as possible* (emphasis added) in order to align the measures previously dealt with under the RPS to the delegated acts procedure. The EP was quite generous with the Commission and lost a significant opportunity to push for a better text on this point.

The legislative powers of the EP in relation to the adoption of the comitology rules have significantly increased by virtue of Article 291 of the TFEU. This has resulted in the adoption of the Implementing Acts Regulation under the ordinary legislative procedure, whereas pre-Lisbon the comitology decision was adopted and amended by the Council alone, and the EP formally only needed to be consulted according to ex Article 202 of the EC Treaty.

Implementing acts

The committee structure of the comitology procedure is of course still applicable under the Treaty of Lisbon as far as implementing measures in the strict sense are concerned. Pursuant to Article 291(1) TFEU, which incorporates the well-known principle of subsidiarity, Member States are required to implement EU legislation. However, Article 291(2) TFEU provides that where uniform conditions for implementing legally binding acts are needed, implementing powers shall be conferred to the Commission. When the latter happens, control mechanisms are exercised by the Member States (Article 291(3) of the TFEU). These control mechanisms refer to comitology committees.

The Commission has proposed limiting the remit of the comitology committees known hitherto.[70] Based on the interpretation given by the Commission in its proposal for the Implementing Acts Regulation, these committees should

68 *See* Council Decision, op. cit. n 19 *supra*.
69 Article 2(2) as inserted by the 2006 amendment (*ibid.*).
70 COM (2010) 83, 9 March 2010.

mostly function as a forum for advice. Taking into account the White Paper on European Governance, where the Commission was previously supporting the idea of abolishing comitology committees,[71] this is not surprising. What is surprising, however, is that Article 291 TFEU does not provide the EP or the Council with any powers regarding the control of the Commission's draft implementing measures. However, Article 11 of the Implementing Acts Regulation provides that the *ultra vires* control mechanism is still applicable.

The Implementing Acts Regulation

Soon after the entry into force of the new Treaty, the Commission made a legislative proposal[72] for the implementation of Article 291 TFEU. Following negotiations between the EP and the Council on the Commission's proposal, these institutions reached a 'first-reading' deal, which was supported by the EP plenary in December 2010. The new Implementing Acts Regulation was formally adopted in February 2011, and the Regulation came into force on 1 March 2011.[73] The Regulation lays down the rules and general principles concerning mechanisms for control by Member States of the Commission's exercise of implementing powers. For the first time, according to Article 291 TFEU, the EP had the ability to adopt the rules governing comitology committees under the ordinary legislative procedure. One would have wished that the EP could have secured a better text as far as accountability to the public was concerned.

Article 4 of the Implementing Acts Regulation provides for the advisory procedure, which remains exactly the same as it was before.[74] The examination procedure, however, replaced the management and regulatory procedure of the 2006 comitology decision.[75] Under the examination procedure, according to Article 7 of the Regulation, in exceptional circumstances the Commission still has the powers to adopt the proposed draft measure even though the comitology committees have opposed it, provided that its 'non adoption within an imperative deadline would create a significant disruption of the markets . . . or for the financial interests of the Union'.[76] The Regulation provides for immediately applicable measures bypassing the committees' involvement (Article 8 of the Regulation). Referral to the Council has also been replaced by an appeal committee consisting of Member States' representatives in cases where a committee gives a negative opinion (Article 5 of the Regulation).

Unfortunately, the Implementing Acts Regulation does not provide for enhanced information rights at all. It is very ironic that the Commission defines

71 European Commission, 'White Paper on European governance' COM (2001) 428, p. 31.

72 COM (2010) 83, 9 March 2010.

73 *See* S Peers and M Costa, op. cit. n 1 *supra*.

74 The opinion of the Committee is not legally binding upon the Commission, which takes the utmost account of it.

75 Council Decision, op. cit. n 19 *supra*.

76 *See* S Peers and M Costa, op. cit. n 1 *supra*.

full transparency only with reference to the Council and the EP, and not the general public. By doing so, it defeats the very purpose of transparency, which is namely for the public to hold decision-makers to account.[77]

Comitology meetings continue to take place behind closed doors. The EP did not even try for open committee doors; possibilities could have been either for a select public to attend or for the broadcasting of their meetings. Currently, acting behind closed doors gives the impression that decisions of high importance are taken in these committees, whereas, in fact, most of the decisions are over issues of a routine nature. In order not to sacrifice efficiency, one possibility would be that the 'outside' experts would not attend all committee meetings, but would have to place a request to attend to the committee chair.[78] More importantly, this could enhance democratic accountability. Political control of comitology by 'alternative technical experts and a technical partial public'[79] would effectuate an 'intelligence of democracy'.[80] Moreover, these experts could liaise with MEPs in such a way as to perform a 'fire alarm' function. For the practical political process, this would imply that MEPs would be informed whenever issues of great political sensitivity came up and the EP could thus resort to its control functions under comitology.

The EP proposed solving this problem by arguing during the negotiations of the second comitology decision[81] that MEPs *themselves* should attend comitology committee meetings, rather than having to rely on external actors. This view was rejected by the Commission and the Council on the basis that enhanced information rights of the EP and the public might solve the problem,[82] but as discussed already, previous experience revealed that this is not sufficient to remedy the accountability deficit.

Concluding remarks: accountability of the committee-based system – myth or reality?

The Lisbon Treaty attempted to rectify the accountability inadequacies of the comitology committees. The drafters of the Treaty provided enough room in order for the accountability framework to take place and for the exercise of the delegated and implementing acts to comply with the accountability requirements. Notably, the EP as an accountability forum has the powers to control *ex ante* and *ex post* the delegated powers of the Commission in relation to

77 Commission Press Release IP/10/1735, 16 December 2010.

78 H Hofmann and A Toeller, 'Democracy and the reform of comitology', in A Mads and A Turk, *Delegated Legislation and the Role of Committees in the EC* (Kluwer Law International 2000).

79 *Ibid.*

80 *Ibid.*

81 *See* Council Decision, op. cit. n 18 *supra*.

82 G Schusterschitz and S Kotz, 'The comitology reform of 2006: Increasing the powers of the European Parliament without changing the Treaties' (2007) 3 *European Constitutional Law Review* 68.

delegated acts. It is regrettable, however, that the new procedures do not call for more accountability to the public through transparency. After all, the ultimate accountability forum as already explained in Chapter 1 is the general public. More democratic control through the EP is welcome and impressive in theory, but, in practice, as far the general public is concerned, little or nothing has changed. It is good to see, however, that the Commission publishes the draft delegated acts on its website. The Commission does so on its own motion whereas it would have made more sense if there were a proviso in place obliging the Commission to publish the draft delegated acts. Yet, more transparency is urgently needed for the expert groups' register. Technically, comitology committees have now ceased to exist and the Commission is using its expert groups in order to equip itself with the highly technical and scientific knowledge required for the drafting of the delegated acts. The general public needs to be aware of what is happening in order to hold the Commission and the legislature to account. More transparency is needed there.

As far as the implementing acts are concerned, it is equally regrettable that the Commission did not enhance transparency of the expert groups' register. The Regulation does not provide for an exact date for the transformation of the current RPS into the delegated acts procedure. Even more regrettably, there is no enhanced transparency for the public.

Overall, the pre-Lisbon comitology system has been fundamentally amended and is not applicable anymore in relation to the delegated acts under Article 290 of the TFEU. The delegated acts procedure has given more powers to the EP in particular – but not more transparency for the general public. The involvement of the EP, however, in the adoption of the Implementing Acts Regulation under the ordinary legislative procedure is seen to 'increase democratic legitimacy of "quasi-legislative" measures and thus contributes to a better acceptance of European legislation by citizens'.[83] Yet, comitology committees remain in relation to the implementing acts of Article 291 of the TFEU with no substantial changes in relation to accountability to the general public.

83 *Ibid.*

6 Accountability through *locus standi* and the role of the Court of Justice[1]

Introduction

Having assessed the regime for delegated and implementing acts in the previous chapter, along with examining alternatives on how to mitigate these deficits, the current chapter focuses upon the role of the Court of Justice in securing accountability. In doing so, this chapter first examines the circumstances in which EU measures can be challenged directly as well as indirectly before the Court by adversely affected private litigants. Second, the chapter focuses on whether the tendency of the Court to justify limitations of the actions of annulment and direct private plaintiffs to national courts respects basic accountability requirements, as examined in Chapter 1. In particular, it is argued here that the legal gaps of access to justice substantially affect the accountability of EU institutions. After all, without access to the Court, it is impossible for the various accountability forums to hold the actors to account. Yet, the post-Lisbon framework was very promising: the insertion of the term 'regulatory act' in Article 263(4) TFEU was seen as the solution to the problem in the area of judicial accountability. But, nevertheless, the earlier interpretation given to 'regulatory act' by the Court raises fundamental constitutional questions insofar as it does not fill the access to justice gaps identified by the legal literature as well as by the Court in *Jégo-Quéré*.[2]

This chapter starts by examining the jurisprudence in relation to direct and indirect access to justice by private plaintiffs. It does so in order to examine the consequences upon accountability in the EU. It then moves on to examine the changes introduced by the Treaty of Lisbon, in particular the concept of the term regulatory act found in Article 263(4) TFEU. The chapter concludes that the Lisbon changes, as currently interpreted by the Court, do not fill the already identified pre-Lisbon gaps in access to justice.

1 For a detailed analysis with regards to the contribution of the General Court in case T-18/10, *Inuit Tapiriit Kanatami and Others* v. *European Parliament and Council of the European Union* [2011] ECR II-5599, *see* S Peers and M Costa 'Judicial review of EU Acts after the Treaty of Lisbon' (2012) 8 *European Constitutional Law Review*, pp. 82–104.

2 Case T-177/01, *Jégo-Quéré et Cie SA* v. *Commission* [2001] ECR II-2365, para. 51.

Overview of the access to justice regime

The strictly interpreted *locus standi* requirements of the private litigants to challenge the legality of EU measures directly before the General Court have been the object of severe criticism in the legal literature for some time now. The Court of Justice, however, insists on its consistent line of case law and argues that 'the Treaty established a complete system of legal remedies and procedures designed to permit the Court of Justice to review the legality of measures adopted by the institutions'.[3] Does that line of case law respect judicial accountability, a fundamental prerequisite to the rule of law?

Strict *locus standi* requirements for private litigants constitute one of the very few areas of EU law where the legal literature is so united and almost unanimously agreed that fundamental gaps in judicial protection exist.[4] The TFEU provides two different methods of judicial control 'designed to ensure the legal exercise of power by [the Union] institutions'.[5] First, Article 263 TFEU provides for direct actions for annulment to review the legality of the EU acts brought before the EU Courts. Second, Article 267 TFEU provides for the indirect review of legality via the preliminary referencing procedure from national courts. They read as follows:

> *Article 263*
>
> The Court of Justice of the European Union shall review the legality of legislative acts, of acts of the Council, of the Commission and of the European Central Bank, other than recommendations and opinions, and of acts of the European Parliament and of the European Council intended to produce legal effects vis-à-vis third parties. It shall also review the legality of bodies, offices, or agencies of the Union intended to produce legal effects vis-à-vis third parties.

3 Case 294/83, *Parti Ecologiste 'Les Verts'* v. *European Parliament* [1986] ECR 1339, para. 23.

4 A Arnull, 'Editorial: April shower for Jégo-Quéré' (2004) *European Law Review*, p. 287; C Koch, '*Locus standi* of private applicants under the EU Constitution: Preserving gaps in the protection of individuals' right to an effective remedy' (2005) *European Law Review*, p. 511; P Craig, 'Standing, rights, and the structure of legal argument' (2003) *European Public Law*, p. 493; A Cygan, 'Protecting the interests of civil society in community decision-making: The limits of Art. 230 EC' (2003) *International and Comparative Law Quarterly*, p. 995; 'Editorial: What should replace the Constitutional Treaty?' (2007) *Common Market Law Review*, p. 561; 'Editorial: EU leaders strike deal on reform treaty' (2007) *EU Focus*, p. 213; S Enchelmaier, 'No-one slips through the net? Latest developments, and non-developments, in the European Court of Justice's jurisprudence on Art. 230(4) EC' (2005) *Yearbook of European Law*, p. 173; S Flogaitis and A Pottakis, 'Judicial protection under the Constitution' (2005) *European Constitutional Law Review*, p. 108; E Garcia De Enterria, 'The extension of jurisdiction of national administrative courts by the Community law: The judgment of the Court of Justice in Borelli and Art. 5 of the EC Treaty' (1993) *Year Book of European Law*, p. 19; C Harding, 'The impact of Art 177 of the EEC Treaty on the review of Community action' (1981) *Year Book of European Law*, p. 93; C Harlow, 'Towards a theory of access for the European Court of Justice' (1992) *Year Book of European Law*, p. 213.

5 G Bebr, 'Direct and indirect judicial control of Community Acts in practice: The relation between Arts 173 and 177 of the EEC Treaty' (1984) *Michigan Law Review*, p. 1229.

It shall for this purpose have jurisdiction in actions brought by a Member State, the European Parliament, the Council or the Commission on grounds of lack of competence, infringement of an essential procedural requirement, infringement of the Treaties, or of any rule of law relating to their application, or misuse of powers.

The Court shall have jurisdiction under the same conditions in actions brought by the Court of Auditors, by the European Central Bank, and by the Committee of the Regions for the purpose of protecting their prerogatives.

Any natural or legal person may, under the conditions laid down in the first and second paragraphs, institute proceedings against an act to that person, or which is of direct and individual concern to them, and against a regulatory act which is of direct concern to them and does not entail any implementing measures.

Acts setting up bodies, offices, and agencies of the Union may lay down specific conditions and arrangements concerning actions brought by natural or legal persons against acts of these bodies, offices, or agencies intended to produce legal effects in relation to them.

The proceeding provided for in this article shall be instituted within two months of the publication of the measure, or of its notification to the plaintiff, or, in the absence thereof, of the day on which it came to the knowledge of the latter, as the case may be.

Article 267

The Court of Justice of the European Union shall have jurisdiction to give preliminary rulings concerning:

(a) the interpretation of the Treaties;
(b) the validity and interpretation of acts of the institutions, bodies, offices, or agencies of the Union.

Where such a question is raised before any court or tribunal of a Member State, that court or tribunal may, if it considers that a decision on the question is necessary to enable it to give judgment, request the Court to give a ruling thereon.

Where any such question is raised in a case pending before a court or tribunal of a Member State against whose decisions there is no judicial remedy under national law, that court or tribunal shall bring the matter before the Court.

If such a question is raised in a case pending before a court or tribunal of a Member State with regard to a person in custody, the Court of Justice of the European Union shall act with the minimum of delay.

From the early days, private parties were entitled to bring annulment proceedings before the Court so long as they were 'directly and individually concerned' by the allegedly unlawful EU measure. The then Article 230(4) EC read as follows:

> Any natural or legal person may . . . institute proceedings against a decision addressed to that person or against a decision which, although in the form of a regulation or a decision addressed to another person, is of direct and individual concern to the former.

The Court of Justice responded to the critics by placing the burden upon the Member States for a Treaty amendment, ruling that 'it is for the Member States, if necessary . . . to reform the system currently in force'.[6] To that end, the Treaty of Lisbon amended the provision of Article 230(4) EC with Article 263(4) TFEU quoted fully above.

In particular, the insertion of the term 'regulatory act' as a third possibility of bringing proceedings had the potential of mitigating the gaps in relation to the *locus standi* of private plaintiffs, subject to acceptable interpretation by the judiciary. The recent order of the General Court[7] ruled, rather disappointingly, on the interpretation of Article 263(4) TFEU. According to the Court, the new provisions do not make it easier for private parties to challenge EU legislative measures as defined by Article 289(3) TFEU, since such acts cannot be considered to be regulatory acts. In consequence, the requirement of individual concern, as traditionally interpreted, continues to apply in full in such cases. Based on the Lisbon reforms and on the recent *Microban*[8] judgment, this line of reasoning is controversial. A broad definition of 'regulatory act' to cover legislative and non-legislative regulations would have resulted in a more liberal approach to *locus standi*, exempting private plaintiffs from the need to meet the test of individual concern, if the act concerned does not entail implementing measures.

Access to justice

The challenge of the legality of administrative as well as legislative acts should be a characteristic of every democratic society which claims to protect its members from any arbitrary and unlawful acts. Similarly:

> [n]o society can be considered truly democratic if its citizens are denied the possibility of vindicating their legal rights in judicial proceedings, whether against the oppressive acts of a powerful legislature – even a democratically elected one – or against the unlawful practices of an overweening administration.[9]

6 Case C-50/00, *Union de Pequenos Agricultores* v. *Council (UPA)* [2002] ECR I-6677, para. 45.

7 Case T-18/10, *Inuit Tapiriit Kanatami and Others* v. *European Parliament and Council of the European Union* [2011] ECR II-5599.

8 Case T-262/10, *Microban International Ltd and Microban (Europe) Ltd* v. *European Commission* [2011] ECR II-7697.

9 *See* Mancini and Keeling, Chapter 1, op. cit. n 46 *supra*.

The lack of access to an effective judicial protection creates a gap with regards to the accountability of EU institutions, bodies, offices and agencies. When citizens are denied the possibility to access the Courts, they are deprived of their right to hold decision-makers to account and therefore a substantial accountability gap is created. Consequently, effective judicial system is 'a fundamental prerequisite for effective executive accountability'[10] since the EU Courts play a crucial role in securing public accountability. They also contribute to transparency when court cases bring information to public attention:

> The fact that the citizens are aware of what the administration is doing is a guarantee that it will operate properly. Supervision by those who confer legitimacy on the public authorities encourages them to be effective in adhering to their [citizens'] initial will and can thereby inspire their confidence, which is a guarantee of public content as well as the proper functioning of the democratic system.[11]

Article 263 TFEU differentiates between privileged and non-privileged applicants. The Member States, the Commission, the Council and the European Parliament (EP) are considered to be privileged applicants. As such, they are empowered to challenge any type of binding act and there is no need to satisfy *any* standing requirements. The European Central Bank (ECB) and the European Court of Auditors (ECA) are semi-privileged applicants and can challenge any type of binding act in order to protect their prerogatives. The last type of applicants found in Article 263 TFEU refers to the non-privileged litigants (natural or legal persons) who have restricted ability with regards to the type of acts that they can challenge.

A literal interpretation of the pre-Lisbon provision indicated that private plaintiffs could, in principle, only challenge decisions, something which in effect excluded the possibility of challenging legislative acts of general application. The Court has, however, departed from the wording of the provision and interpreted that restriction broadly. By doing so, the Court has relaxed the standing requirements in relation to the type of act that could be challenged by ruling that 'an action for annulment must therefore be available in the case of all measures adopted by the institutions, whatever their nature or form, which are intended to have legal effects'.[12] Since *Codorniu*,[13] it is clear that private plaintiffs can challenge regulations so long as they are directly and individually concerned by them. In the wording of the judiciary:

> Although it is true that according to the criteria in the second paragraph of Article 173 of the Treaty the contested provision is, by nature and by virtue

10 *See* Mulgan, Chapter 1, op. cit. n 6 *supra*, p 76.

11 Case C-353/99 P, *Hautala* v. *Council* [2001] ECR I-9565, opinion of Advocate-General Leger, para. 52.

12 Case 22/70, *Commission* v. *Council (ERTA)* [1971] ECR 263, para. 42.

13 Case C-309/89, *Codorniu* v. *Council* [1994] ECR I-1853.

> of its sphere of application, of a legislative nature and in that it applies to the traders concerned in general, that does not prevent it from being of individual concern to some of them.[14]

More problematic, however, has been the issue of whether private parties fulfil the standing requirements to challenge the legality of directives before the EU Court. This is due to the fact that directives by definition leave discretion to Member States. Pursuant to settled case law, directives can only be challenged by private parties where the effects of the directive are automatic or where the Member States are expressly authorised to act in a particular manner.[15] The Court of Justice tended to direct private litigants to their national courts to raise indirectly the legality of the directive when they review its transportation into the Member State's national legal system:

> The fourth paragraph of Article 173 of the Treaty makes no provision for the benefit of individuals for a direct action before the Community judicature against directives or against decisions adopted in the form of directives. The justification for that exclusion lies in the fact that, in the case of directives, the judicial protection of individuals is duly and sufficiently assured by the national courts, which review the transposition of directives into the domestic law of the various Member States.[16]

The applicants in the *Salamander*[17] case, however, argued that not all directives leave discretion to Member States as to their substantive implementation, and that the directive in question was substantially clear, precise and unconditional and was having a legal effect on the applicants.[18] It seems clear now that directives can also be challenged directly as long as the plaintiff satisfies the requirements of direct and individual concern.[19] However, while in principle directives can be challenged directly, the problem is to meet the requirement of direct concern, since 'a directive cannot of itself impose obligations on an individual and may

14 Case C-309/89, *Codorniu* v. *Council* [1994] ECR I-1853, para. 19.

15 Joined Cases T-172/98, T-175/98 to T-177/98, *Salamander AG, Una Film 'City Revue' GmbH, Alma Media Group Advertising SA & Co. Partnership, Panel Two and Four Advertising SA, Rythmos Outdoor Advertising SA, Media Center Advertising SA, Zino Davidoff SA and Davidoff & Cie SA* v. *European Parliament and Council* [2000] ECR II-2487.

16 Case T-99/94, *Asocarne* v. *Council* [1994] ECR II-871, para. 17.

17 Joined Cases T-172/98, T-175/98 to T- 177/98, *Salamander AG, Una Film 'City Revue' GmbH, Alma Media Group Advertising SA & Co. Partnership, Panel Two and Four Advertising SA, Rythmos Outdoor Advertising SA, Media Center Advertising SA, Zino Davidoff SA and Davidoff & Cie SA* v. *European Parliament and Council* [2000] ECR II-2487.

18 In this case, the time limit for transposition had not been expired.

19 Joined Cases T-172/98, T-175/98 to T-177/98, *Salamander AG, Una Film 'City Revue' GmbH, Alma Media Group Advertising SA & Co. Partnership, Panel Two and Four Advertising SA, Rythmos Outdoor Advertising SA, Media Center Advertising SA, Zino Davidoff SA and Davidoff & Cie SA* v. *European Parliament and Council* [2000] ECR II-2487.

therefore not be relied on as much against him'.[20] The most recent approach is, however, exactly the same as the approach in *Codorniu*:[21] directives fell within the scope of Article 230(4) EC, even though they were not mentioned in that provision, provided the applicant could show direct and individual concern.

According to the cumulative criteria, the measure must directly and individually concern the legal position of the applicant, without leaving any discretion to the addressee of the measure. A private party is directly concerned when there is a direct causal link between the measure and the applicant's legal position. More specifically, the measures must be 'sufficient in themselves and require no implementing provisions'.[22] Additionally, the individual concern defined in the *Plaumann* case[23] was extremely narrow. Particularly, individuals must be affected:

> [b]y reason of certain attributes which are peculiar to them or by reason of circumstances in which they are differentiated from all other persons and by virtue of these factors distinguishes them individually just as in the case of the person addressed.[24]

Therefore, individual concern is met when plaintiffs possess 'certain attributes that are peculiar to them' or 'by reason of circumstances' that differentiate them from others and distinguishes them just as in the case of the addressee. Plaintiffs must show that they fall within a 'closed category', which is determined by a fixed membership by the time the act was adopted or entered into force, a requirement that cannot be satisfied when a membership is small and identifiable. This approach can be verified by the fact that the requirement of 'individual concern' in relation to directives and regulations has only been met in an extremely limited number of cases.[25]

The test of individual concern was criticised for being very restrictive, since it renders it impossible for an applicant to establish individual concern except in exceptional circumstances related to past events.[26] It is evident that the *Plaumann* formula sets a very difficult test that can only be satisfied in very few cases related to past events. Advocate-General Jacobs, in his opinion delivered in the *UPA* case, challenged the interpretation of individual concern and

20 *See Salamander* (*ibid.*), at para. 54.

21 *See* Joined Cases 239 and 275/82, *Allied Corporation and others* v. *Commission* [1984] ECR 1005; Case C-358/89, *Extramet* v. *Council* [1991] ECR I-2501; and Case C-308/89, *Codorniu* v. *Council* [1994] ECR I-1853.

22 Case 294/83, *Parti Ecologiste 'Les Verts'* v. *European Parliament* [1986] ECR 1339, para. 31.

23 Case 25/62, *Plaumann & Co* v. *Commission* [1963] ECR 95.

24 *Ibid.*, para. 31.

25 Case T-135/96, *UEAPME* v. *Council* [1998] ECR II-2335; Joined cases 87, 130/77, 22/83, 9 and 10/84, *Salerno* v. *Commission and Council* [1985] ECR 2523.

26 A Ward, *Judicial Review and the Rights of Private Parties in EU Law* (Oxford University Press 2007).

suggested that individual concern is met when 'the measure has, or is liable to have, a substantial adverse effect on [the applicant's] interest'.[27]

Shortly after the delivery of that opinion, the Court of First Instance, now the General Court, delivered a judgment highly influenced by the opinion of the Advocate-General in *UPA*. The Court ruled that individual concern is met 'if the measure in question affects his legal position, in a manner which is both definite and immediate, by restricting his rights or by imposing obligations on him'.[28] The Court of Justice, however, refused to relax the strict standing criteria and in *UPA* reaffirmed its unsatisfactory restrictive case law leaving the burden on the Member States 'to establish a system of legal remedies and procedures . . . [and require national courts] to interpret and apply national procedural rules governing the exercise of action in a way that enables natural and legal persons to challenge the legality of any decision'.[29] The same approach was confirmed in the *Jégo-Quéré* appeal.[30]

As already explained, the Court has repeatedly responded to the criticism by stating that the Treaty guarantees judicial review of the Union acts by establishing a complete system of judicial remedies that consist of the direct actions for annulment and of indirect review through the preliminary ruling procedure.[31] By doing so, the Court indicates that it considers indirect challenges to be sufficiently effective. This approach, however, appears to be problematic mainly for two reasons. First, it has been rightly pointed out by Advocate-General Jacobs in his opinion delivered in the *UPA* case, that national judges have no power to rule that EU measures are invalid.[32] This is a power that can be exercised only by the EU Courts. Instead, national courts can issue provisional measures as well as refer the case via the preliminary ruling procedure if they are of the opinion that the impugned measure may be invalid. Private litigants at this stage can only argue for the invalidity of the measure, but the decision to refer the case is exclusively taken by the national judge. In consequence, clearly private parties cannot initiate proceedings concerning the invalidity of EU law via Article 267 TFEU as a matter of legal right. The only possibility for private parties adversely affected by a Union act is to initiate legal proceedings before their national Court against the authority which enforces the measure, by pleading that the parent EU legislation is not legal. Second, there can be cases where the indirect challenge is not

27 Case C-50/00, *Union de Pequenos Agricultores* v. *Council (UPA)* [2002] ECR I-6677, opinion of Advocate-General Jacobs, para. 60.

28 Case T-177/01, *Jégo-Quéré et Cie SA* v. *Commission* [2001] ECR II-2365, para. 51.

29 Case C-50/00, *Union de Pequenos Agricultores* v. *Council (UPA)* [2002] ECR I-6677, paras 41–45.

30 Case C-263/02 P, *Jégo-Quéré et Cie SA* v. *Commission* [2004] ECR I-3425, paras 33, 34.

31 Case 294/83, *Parti Ecologiste 'Les Verts'* v. *European Parliament* [1986] ECR 1339; Case C-321/95 P, *Greenpeace and others* v. *Commission* [1998] ECR I-1651; Case C-50/00, *Union de Pequenos Agricultores* v. *Council (UPA)* [2002] ECR I-6677; Case C-263/02 P, *Jégo-Quéré et Cie SA* v. *Commission* [2004] ECR I-3425.

32 Case 314/85, *Firma Foto-Frost* v. *Hauptzollant Lübeck-Ost* [1987] ECR 4199 where the Court of Justice based its reasoning on the need to safeguard the uniformity of EU law.

available because there is no national act to challenge. This is where substantial gaps in judicial protection occur, which cannot be tolerated in a democratic society based on the rule of law. These gaps cannot, under any circumstances, be ignored by the Court.[33] To the extent that these gaps are not in compliance with the Treaty of Lisbon as well as with the Charter of Fundamental Rights of the European Union, a more relaxed interpretation of the standing of private parties is necessary because the Charter protects the right to an effective remedy.

Locus standi post Lisbon: the contribution of the Court

The General Court ruled in *Inuit Tapiriit Kanatami*[34] on the interpretation of the term *regulatory act*. It was made clear that the term covers all measures of general application except legislative acts. It is suggested, however, with great respect to the order, that to be in line with the Lisbon reforms as well as with the recent *Microban*[35] judgment, the term could have been interpreted more broadly to cover at least some legislative regulations. That broader interpretation would have closed the accountability gap with regards to access to justice. Nevertheless, the Court of Justice confirmed on appeal[36] the unsatisfactory meaning, in terms of accountability, given to 'regulatory act' by the General Court.

In the *Inuit Tapiriit Kanatami and others* case, a group of entities consisting of Inuit seal hunters and trappers and other organisations representing the interests of Inuit as well as individuals and companies involved in the processing of seal products sought the annulment of Regulation 1007/2009, adopted pursuant to the former co-decision procedure, on the prohibition of the marketing of seal products.[37] The applicants sought for the annulment of the Commission regulation implementing Regulation 1007/2009,[38] arguing against the validity of the parent measure on the basis of the exception of illegality pursuant to Article 277 TFEU and that, as a subsidiary argument, the Commission misused the powers conferred upon it by the basic Regulation.

In *Microban*, the dispute concerned the decision of the Commission to withdraw from the list of additives a material, triclosan, which is used in the manufacture of plastic materials intended to come into contact with foodstuffs.

33 Case T-177/01, *Jégo-Quéré et Cie SA* v. *Commission* [2001] ECR II-2365. The CFI referred in paras 45 and 29 to the opinion of the Advocate-General Jacobs in Case C-50/00, *Union de Pequenos Agricultores* v. *Council (UPA)* [2002] ECR I-6677, who suggested a more relaxed definition of the notion of individual concern in order to mitigate the gaps in judicial protection.

34 Case T-18/10, *Inuit Tapiriit Kanatami and Others* v. *European Parliament and Council of the European Union* [2011] ECR II-5599.

35 Case T-262/10, *Microban International Ltd and Microban (Europe) Ltd* v. *European Commission* [2011] ECR II-7697.

36 Case C-583/11 P, *Inuit Tapiriit Kanatami and Others* v. *European Parliament and Council of the European Union* [2013] ECLI:EU:C:2013:625.

37 Regulation 1007/2009 [2009] OJ L286/36.

38 Case T-18/10, *Inuit Tapiriit Kanatami and Others* v. *European Parliament and Council of the European Union* [2011] ECR II-5599.

The applicants were engaged in the production and marketing of those materials. The removal of that material from the list resulted in the exclusion of the marketing of triclosan in the Union, and therefore the applicants sought for the annulment of the contested decision. The Court ruled that the decision of the Commission to withdraw triclosan from the list was a 'regulatory act' for the purposes of Article 263(4) TFEU. The Court emphasised that the contested decision was: (i) adopted by the Commission in the exercise of its implementing powers, (ii) of general application as long as it applies objectively to categories of persons in general and abstract manner and (iii) does not leave any discretion to the addresses of the measures who are entrusted with the task of implementing it.[39] The contribution of *Microban* in relation to the *locus standi* of non-privileged parties is of ultimate significance. The Court made it clear that Article 263(4) and particularly the inclusion of the term regulatory act 'pursues an objective of opening up the conditions for bringing direct actions'.[40] This approach is fully compatible with the vast majority of legal literature in this area and also with the opinion of the former Advocate-General Jacobs in *UPA*[41] and *Jégo-Quéré*.[42] Therefore, the General Court explicitly accepted that the reason for incorporating the regulatory act in Article 263(4) was to enhance direct access before the EU Courts, something which implicitly accepts that indirect challenges through Article 267 TFEU offer a lesser quality of justice. The *Microban*[43] case illustrates that Article 263(4) TFEU now grants more access to justice directly before the EU Courts.

Comments and analysis of the *Inuit* case

The General Court dismissed the action as inadmissible. The Court started by analysing the *locus standi* requirements for private parties after the Treaty of Lisbon. In particular, the Court provided an overview of Article 263(4) TFEU, which permits a natural and legal person to challenge: (i) the validity of any type of act addressed to that person, (ii) the validity of (implicitly) a legislative or a regulatory act that is of direct and individual concern to them and (iii) the validity of a regulatory act which is of direct concern to them provided that it does not entail any implementing measures. The Court went on to provide a definition of 'regulatory act'. According to the General Court 'the meaning of "regulatory act" for the purposes of the fourth paragraph of Article 263

39 Case T-262/10, *Microban International Ltd and Microban (Europe) Ltd* v. *European Commission* [2011] ECR II-7697, paras 28–38.

40 *Ibid.*, para. 32.

41 Case C-50/00, *Union de Pequenos Agricultores* v. *Council (UPA)* [2002] ECR I-6677, opinion of Advocate-General Jacobs.

42 Case C-263/02 P, *Jégo-Quéré et Cie SA* v. *Commission* [2004] ECR I-3425, opinion of Advocate-General Jacobs.

43 Case T-262/10, *Microban International Ltd and Microban (Europe) Ltd* v. *European Commission* [2011] ECR II-7697.

TFEU must be understood as covering all acts of general application apart from legislative acts'.

However, with all due respect, it seems that the Court, in relation to the meaning of the term 'regulatory act', has failed to consider the distinction between directives and regulations. In particular, the exclusion of directives from the concept of the regulatory act as a general rule seems to fit well with the requirements of Article 263(4) TFEU for two principal reasons. First, directives normally entail implementing measures because they require Member States to achieve the directives' objectives through the Member States' national laws.[44] Second, the direct concern requirement would normally rule out the admissibility of annulment actions in relation to directives, because it is unlikely that a private party could prove that a directive includes 'a complete set of rules which are sufficient in themselves and which require no implementing provisions'.[45] Having said that, it is important to note that where there are cases where national law has already complied with the directive and the applicant has run out of time to challenge it, then the individual will not be allowed to challenge the validity of the directive in proceedings before national courts, where the private party 'without any doubt' was entitled to bring a direct action for annulment but has failed to bring such an action within the time limit prescribed by Article 263 (5).[46]

In relation to the temporal application of Article 263(4) TFEU, the General Court ruled that the question of admissibility of an application for annulment brought before it is resolved by the rules in force on the day on which the application for annulment is submitted. Therefore, proceedings brought before the entry into force of the Treaty of Lisbon do not benefit from the more flexible rules.[47] This approach, however, is not consistent with the case law of the Court of Justice regarding the extension of the Court's jurisdiction over immigration, asylum and civil cases pursuant to the Treaty of Lisbon, which repealed Article 68(1) EC, which had previously restricted its jurisdiction pursuant to Article 234

44 S Balthasar, '*Locus standi* rules for challenges to regulatory acts by private applicants: The New Art. 263(4) TFEU' (2010) *European Law Review*, p. 542.

45 Joined Cases T-172/98, T-175/98 to T-177/98 *Salamander AG, Una Film 'City Revue' GmbH, Alma Media Group Advertising SA & Co. Partnership, Panel Two and Four Advertising SA, Rythmos Outdoor Advertising SA, Media Center Advertising SA, Zino Davidoff SA and Davidoff & Cie SA* v. *European Parliament and Council* [2000] ECR II-2487; Case T-135/96, *UEAPME* v. *Council* [1998] ECR II-2335; Case T-223/01, *Japan Tobacco Inc* v. *Parliament* [2002] ECR II-3259; *See* A. Albors-Llorens, 'The standing of private parties to challenge Community measures: Has the European Court missed the boat?' (2003) *Cambridge Law Journal* 72; Case 294/83, *Parti Ecologiste 'Les Verts'* v. *European Parliament* [1986] ECR 1339, para. 31.

46 Case C-188/92, *TWD Textilwerke Deggendorf* v. *Germany* [1994] ECR I-833, paras 24–26. This approach applies to any legal act, not just directives, and is also applicable to privileged applicants: Case C-241/01, *National Farmers' Union* v. *Secrétariat general du gouvernement* [2002] ECR I-9079.

47 Case T-539/08, *Etimine SA and Ab Etiproducts Oy* v. *European Commission* [2010] ECR II-4017, para. 76.

EC to final courts only. That case law establishes that the Court's wider jurisdiction must be extended to cases which were referred to it from national courts before the Treaty of Lisbon came into force.[48]

The Court concluded that the contested Regulation is not a legislative act since 'its categorisation as a legislative act or a regulatory act according to the TFEU is based on the criterion of the procedure, legislative or not, which led to its adoption'.[49] Consequently, the Court ruled that since the contested Regulation is not a regulatory act, the pre-Lisbon framework of direct and individual concern needs to be established and therefore examined whether the criterion of 'individual concern' was satisfied. Unsurprisingly, the interpretation of this criterion has not changed at all. In the words of the judiciary, 'the contested regulation directly affects only the legal situation of those of the applicants who are active in the placing on the market of the European Union of seal products'.[50]

Has the Treaty of Lisbon solved or postponed the accountability problem?

The Treaty of Lisbon has amended substantially the wording of the ex Article 230 EC Treaty. The new provision provides that whatever the type of act (directive, decision and regulation), it can be challenged directly. This is a very welcome amendment since it incorporates the pre-Lisbon case law and also clarifies at a Treaty level that private parties can challenge any type of act: legislative or non-legislative. Therefore, post Lisbon, the Treaty has clarified that the type of acts that can be challenged by private litigants are of a historical use only if they can challenge any type of act that affects them directly as well as individually and a regulatory act that affects them directly and does not entail any implementing measures.

The most significant amendment in relation to the Lisbon Treaty concerns the ability of private plaintiffs to directly challenge regulatory acts. Post Lisbon, private litigants can only challenge regulatory acts that concern them directly. Nevertheless, there is an additional requirement; the regulatory act must not entail any implementing measures. Consequently, the third possibility inserted in Article 263(4) TFEU rectifies the pre-Lisbon cases where individuals were left without a remedy, since there were no implementing measures to challenge before the national courts. It was seen above that the main problem in *UPA*[51] and *Jégo-Quéré*[52] was that indirect review was not possible. The impugned measures were regulations which did not require any domestic implementing measure and

48 Case C-283/09, *Artur Wery ski* v. *Mediatel 4B spółka z o.o* [2011] ECR I-601, para. 28 followed in Case C-396/09, *Interedil Srl, in liquidation* v. *Fallimento Interedil Srl and Intesa Gestione Crediti SpA* [2011] ECR I-9915, para. 20.

49 Case T-18/10, *Inuit Tapiriit Kanatami and Others* v. *European Parliament and Council of the European Union* [2011] ECR II-5599, para. 65.

50 *Ibid.*, para. 75.

51 Case C-50/00, *Union de Pequenos Agricultores* v. *Council (UPA)* [2002] ECR I-6677.

52 Case C-263/02 P, *Jégo-Quéré et Cie SA* v. *Commission* [2004] ECR I-3425.

therefore there was nothing in the national legal system to review. Therefore, the Treaty of Lisbon, with the insertion of the term regulatory act, seems to cover the access to justice gaps identified in *UPA*[53] and *Jégo-Quéré*.[54]

The term regulatory act has not been defined in the Treaty, and this is regrettable. To this extent, the Treaty of Lisbon represents a missed opportunity to resolve the uncertainty covering the standing of private parties in EU law and provide a coherent and uncontroversial set of rules governing access to judicial review. The *travaux preparatoire* of the Constitutional Treaty referred to *non-legislative acts* of general application. In order to understand the content of the term regulatory act, it is necessary to examine the distinction drawn by the Treaty between legislative and non-legislative acts. Legislative acts can be challenged by private litigants only when they are directly and individually concerned. In terms of these measures, the applicants still have to fulfil the same strict standing criteria as under the EC Treaty.

The concept of a 'legislative procedure' is now officially defined in the Treaties, following the entry into force of the Treaty of Lisbon. Article 289 TFEU specifies that there are two types of legislative procedure: the ordinary legislative procedure and the special legislative procedure. Any EU measure adopted by means of a legislative procedure is a legislative act (Article 289(3) TFEU). The obvious implication is that any EU measure *not* adopted by a legislative procedure is *not* a legislative act. Additionally, there are several different types of non-legislative acts. First, there are non-legislative acts based on the Treaties, i.e. for which the legal base is provided for in the Treaty on European Union (TEU) or TFEU. For instance, Article 81(3) TFEU (second sub-paragraph) states that the Council may adopt a decision changing the decision-making procedure relating to family law legislation. Since the Treaty does not specify that this decision would be adopted by a legislative procedure, it would therefore be a non-legislative act. The General Court in the *Inuit* order has aligned the concept of regulatory act on this definition.

The Court of Justice considers the preliminary reference procedure as 'part of a system of remedies' available under EU law.[55] It has ruled that where the principal avenue of direct access is closed, then private plaintiffs are able to challenge the impugned measure indirectly via the preliminary ruling procedure.[56] The Court of Justice, while acknowledging that the principle of effective judicial protection ranks amongst the general principles of EU law, 'stemming from the constitutional traditions common to the Member States',[57] insists that the

53 *Ibid.*

54 *Ibid.*

55 Case 294/83, *Parti Ecologiste 'Les Verts'* v. *European Parliament* [1986] ECR 1339. Case C-321/95 P, *Greenpeace and others* v. *Commission* [1998] ECR I-1651; Case C-50/00, *Union de Pequenos Agricultores* v. *Council (UPA)* [2002] ECR I-6677; Case C-263/02 P, *Jégo-Quéré et Cie SA* v. *Commission* [2004] ECR I-3425.

56 Case C-263/02 P, *Jégo-Quéré et Cie SA* v. *Commission* [2004] ECR I-3425.

57 Case C-50/00, *Union de Pequenos Agricultores* v. *Council (UPA)* [2002] ECR I-6677, para. 39.

Treaty has established 'a complete system of legal remedies' to ensure judicial review of EU acts.[58] However, the Court of Justice has accepted implicitly that 'instances of lack of effective judicial protection might arise in the [EU] legal order'.[59] According to the Court, it is for the Member States and their national courts to establish a system of legal remedies and procedures to entitle individuals to bring proceedings before a national court, challenging the legality of a national measure, based on an allegedly illegal EU act.[60]

As already explained above, the then Advocate-General Jacobs in his opinion delivered in *UPA*[61] challenged the Court's propositions on the ground that proceedings via Article 234, now Article 267, do not comply fully with the principle of effective judicial protection.[62] Yet, the General Court in *Inuit Tapiriit Kanatami*,[63] with the exclusion of legislative acts from the definition of regulatory act, disregards, it seems, the cases in which the alternative route of indirect review is closed, simply because no implementing measures were taken, and there is no national act to challenge before domestic courts.[64] At the same time, the current version of Article 19.1 TEU could be interpreted as providing a general right to challenge EU measures before national courts, even in the absence of national measures, subject to the general principles of equality and effectiveness, interpreted by analogy with the case law on national remedies for enforcement of EU law. The General Court and the Court of Justice should clarify the usefulness of Article 19.1 TEU at the earliest opportunity. Opinion 1/2009 of the Court refers to the significance of national courts pursuant to Article 19.1 TEU, even though national courts are not expressly mentioned within that provision. There is, however, no other reference to this Article in case law yet.

The General Court in *Inuit Tapiriit Kanatami*[65] ignored the access to justice gaps identified in *UPA*[66] and *Jégo-Quéré*,[67] which could be remedied if the

58 Case C-50/00, *Union de Pequenos Agricultores* v. *Council (UPA)* [2002] ECR I-6677; Case C-263/02P, *Jégo-Quéré et Cie SA* v. *Commission* [2004] ECR I-3425.

59 *See* Albors-Llorens, op. cit. n 45 *supra*, p. 87.

60 Case C-50/00, *Union de Pequenos Agricultores* v. *Council (UPA)* [2002] ECR I-6677, paras 41, 42.

61 Case C-50/00, *Union de Pequenos Agricultores* v. *Council (UPA)* [2002] ECR I-6677, opinion of Advocate-General Jacobs.

62 Case C-50/00, *Union de Pequenos Agricultores* v. *Council (UPA)* [2002] ECR I-6677, opinion of Advocate-General Jacobs.

63 Case T-18/10, *Inuit Tapiriit Kanatami and Others* v. *European Parliament and Council of the European Union* [2011] ECR II-5599.

64 Although the Court of Justice has ruled in Case C-491/01, *British American Tobacco (Investments) and Imperial Tobacco* [2002] ECR I-11453 that the challenge of the validity of an EU measure before national courts and via the preliminary reference procedure can be made even where implementing measures have not been adopted, it shall not be ignored that this could only be possible where the national law confers a remedy to the private party.

65 Case T-18/10, *Inuit Tapiriit Kanatami and Others* v. *European Parliament and Council of the European Union* [2011] ECR II-5599.

66 Case C-50/00, *Union de Pequenos Agricultores* v. *Council (UPA)* [2002] ECR I-6677.

67 Case C-263/02 P, *Jégo-Quéré et Cie SA* v. *Commission* [2004] ECR I-3425.

term regulatory act was interpreted to cover both legislative and non-legislative acts. Therefore, even post Lisbon, there are applicants left without any right to an effective remedy provided by Articles 6 and 13 of the European Convention on Human Rights (ECHR)[68] and by Article 47 of the Charter of Fundamental Rights of the European Union.[69] The fact that the applicant can access the Court by breaking the law in order to challenge the validity of the parent EU law measure in subsequent national proceedings, cannot, in any case, constitute a means of redress. As Advocate-General Jacobs has stressed in *UPA*, 'individuals cannot be required to breach the law in order to gain access to justice'.[70] These gaps are regrettable.

Concluding remarks

This chapter examined the strict interpretation of the *locus standi* requirements for private plaintiffs under EU law and the relationship with accountability. In the light of the restrictive jurisprudence concerning the rules on the standing of private parties seeking judicial review, this chapter examined the appropriateness of the preliminary reference procedure as an alternative route for private parties seeking to challenge the validity of EU measures. Although the insertion of the term regulatory act post Lisbon has improved the position of private litigants, there are still fundamental gaps in judicial protection particularly with reference to legislative regulations.

There are sound reasons to justify the Court's order in *Inuit Tapiriit Katami*, both as regards the argument that legislative acts in several jurisdictions deserve some degree of immunity from judicial review,[71] and as regards the fact that the intention of the drafters of the Treaty was to exclude legislative acts from the term 'regulatory act'. But the detailed reasoning is controversial, since it ignores the risk that some litigants will face a complete denial of justice, something which can be avoided either by a different interpretation of the concept of regulatory act or by strengthening the Article 267 TFEU process for challenging the validity of EU acts in the light of Article19 (1) TEU. Given the importance of these issues for the rights of private parties in EU law, the term should be reassessed at the earliest opportunity.

68 Case 222/84, *Johnston* v. *Chief Constable of the Royal Ulster Constabulary* [1986] ECR 1651. This approach, however, contradicts ECHR case law, which confirms that article 6 TEU does not give the right to challenge legislative acts.

69 Case C-263/02 P, *Jégo-Quéré et Cie SA* v. *Commission* [2004] ECR I-3425, para. 42.

70 Case C-50/00, *Union de Pequenos Agricultores* v. *Council (UPA)* [2002] ECR I-6677, opinion of Advocate-General Jacobs.

71 This relates to the constitutional principle of the division of powers, which provides for greater checks and balances and therefore grants the legislature greater legitimacy.

7 Concluding remarks

What is the future for accountability in the EU?

The topic of accountability in the EU is a subject of great interest to scholars. They are largely in agreement that the accountability deficits in the EU are constantly growing and, as a result, they compromise the EU's legitimacy in the eyes of the people. There is therefore a pressing need to consider whether it is constitutionally feasible to establish an alternative model of governance at the EU level. In this regard, this book has identified areas for improvement. At the same time, this book has provided sufficient evidence that accountability has largely been improved. In particular, if one takes into account the allegations of fraud, maladministration and chronic mismanagement that led to the fall of the Santer Commission in 1999, examined in Chapter 2, as well as the difficulties that occurred during the process of ratification of the Maastricht Treaty, the non-ratification of the Constitutional Treaty and the main problems that the Union faced in relation to the ratification of the Lisbon Treaty, it is clear that progress has been made in terms of accountability.

In practice, in order to assess the accountability regime in the EU, there needs to be a common understanding of the term by reference to the EU legal order. Clearly, accountability in the EU does not necessarily mean moving to an elected government. Constitutionally, that is not feasible. Yet, there are alternative ways that accountability can be secured within the EU level of governance. In this regard, an essential prerequisite of EU accountability is to strengthen the access to documents rules so that citizens can become closer to the EU and feel that they have a say on how laws and policies are made and implemented. But how open can the Union's decision-making be, and what is the role of the Court of Justice in securing accountability through transparency? Had the Regulation 1049/2001 been interpreted in a more liberal way by the EU Courts, the EU could have been more accountable and more legitimate. But, nevertheless, the contribution of the judiciary, to a greater or a lesser extent, has been significant. At the moment, there are cases that have shaped and developed the access to documents right. For instance, the Court of Justice, in the *Turco* appeal, held that the Court of First Instance erred in law by finding that the *raison d'être* of the legal advice exception is not to fuel doubts over the legality of EU legislation. In fact, the Court of Justice has ruled that preventing the disclosure of legal advice can lead to the contrary and raise doubts in citizens' minds over the legality and democratic aspect of the EU decision-making process as a whole. This finding rightly equates the access to documents rules with the principle of democracy and civil participation in the decision-making process, and, consequently, brings the EU closer to its citizens by reducing the accountability gap.

The Access Info Europe[1] is another example which contributed to the development of the access right. The judgment reinforces the dynamic of the access right and ensures that citizens can participate in the decision-making process. Nevertheless, the case law on access to documents does not provide us with clear guidance as to the outcome of future cases. This is problematic since the fine balancing exercised by the Court, in favour or against openness, can go either way.

At the same time, the EU as we know it today would not have been able to function without the regulatory contribution provided by the so-called independent agencies established and active at the EU level of governance. Nevertheless, it was seen (Chapter 4) that EU agencies suffered from fundamental accountability problems, which could not continue to be ignored on the basis of scientific legitimacy. Delegation of tasks entailing the exercise of wide discretionary powers is, of course, not compatible with the institutional balance provided by the Treaties. In this regard, the Court of Justice in *ESMA* has rather tactfully and carefully confirmed that the EP and the Council are empowered to control the acts drafted by agencies. Nevertheless, with all due respect, it seems the Court ignored that ESMA's control powers were indeed drafted by ESMA, and therefore in order to comply with the accountability requirements explained above (Chapter 1), they demanded more intensive control. After all, judicial review can only be effective if it is addressed to the actual body undertaking the decision under review.

Finally, the agencies' accountability regime needs to be revised in order to balance political neutrality with the requirements of accountability. Currently, the structure of EU governance depends on a variety of actors and, in reality, it would be wrong for just one of those actors to be held accountable. There is, therefore, a pressing need to ensure that everyone is being held accountable for their wrongdoings. It is, however, very early at this stage to say with certainty that the development of the Common Approach will secure accountability in this area. The Common Approach has the potential to enhance the accountability mechanisms by requiring all decentralised agencies to be adopted and function under the same rules. Nevertheless, the initial indication is that the institutions lack the political will to ensure that agencies are actually reformed in accordance with the same standard rules.

Chapter 5 assessed the accountability regime of delegated and implementing acts, pre-Lisbon, known as the comitology regime. The Lisbon Treaty attempted to rectify the accountability inadequacies of the comitology committees by replacing them with a two-part framework with conceptually different types of

1 Case T-233/09, *Access Info Europe* v. *Council of the European Union* [2011] ECR II-1073.

control procedures. The Treaty provides for sufficient possibilities in Articles 290 and 291 TFEU to establish an adequate accountability framework as regards the exercise of the delegated and implementing acts. Notably, the EP and the Council have the powers to control *ex ante* and *ex post* the delegated powers of the Commission in relation to delegated measures, while the Member States in practice retain most of their previous powers as regards implementing acts.

It is regrettable, however, that the new procedures are not sufficiently transparent to ensure accountability to the public. In particular, the opportunity to increase transparency standards as regards implementing acts has been missed and the standards in relation to delegated acts are lower than those which previously applied under the RPS, taking into account the absence of binding rules and the opaqueness of the Commission's expert groups. After all, the ultimate accountability forum is the general public. Greater democratic control through the EP is welcome and, though impressive in theory, as far as the general public is concerned, little if any has changed in practice. Citizens need to be aware of what is happening in order to hold the Commission and the legislature to account.

Chapter 6 dealt with the various deficits in the field of access to justice, which I term 'legal accountability'. In the light of the restrictive jurisprudence with regards to the *locus standi* requirements, we examined the appropriateness of the preliminary reference procedure as an alternative route for private parties seeking to challenge the validity of EU measures. Although the position of private parties seeking to challenge EU measures is better than the one usually presented, there are still fundamental gaps in judicial protection. Post Lisbon, the insertion of the term 'regulatory act' as a third possibility of bringing proceedings has the potential of mitigating the gaps in relation to the *locus standi* of private plaintiffs, subject to acceptable interpretation by the judiciary. Nevertheless, the Court is not willing to relax the draconian requirements.

Overall, it is necessary to answer the question of whether the Lisbon Treaty has mitigated the overall accountability inadequacies identified in the pre-Lisbon regime. It is the view of the author that the Lisbon Treaty clearly attempted to rectify the accountability deficits identified by the legal literature previously. The Treaty provides for sufficient possibilities in Articles 290 and 291 TFEU to establish an adequate accountability framework as regards the exercise of the delegated and implementing acts.

The final point that needs to be addressed here and is crucial to our understanding in relation to the issue of whether the EU is on the right track to move towards a more transparent and more accountable era, is the current negotiation procedure to amend Regulation 1049/2001. It is clear from the proposed amendments and from the Danish EU presidency mandate that the EU is willing to move in the opposite direction: towards secrecy. It is deeply unsatisfactory that the level of openness, which has taken more than two decades to build, is about to be destroyed. Even the *Turco* appeal would not be good law if the Council's position is adopted. There would be a new presumption against access to legal advice, and the principles underlying the Regulation would not constitute sufficient grounds for disclosure. Similarly, the definition of what constitutes a document would be significantly amended from any document *possessed* by the institution to a document that is *formally transmitted or otherwise registered*. Therefore, the proposed amendments would significantly reduce the current accountability standards. It is very likely that the institutions can refuse to formally register or transmit documents in order to exclude the application of the freedom of information rules. These proposed amendments illustrate that the EU is contemplating reducing the current standards in favour of more secrecy than transparency, something which is of serious concern to the advocates of transparency. Luckily, the negotiation procedure is still on-going and the EP is in a position to exercise political pressure in order for the current transparency standards to be retained as well as improved.

Appendix I

EU DECENTRALIZED AGENCIES

The EU budgetary procedure applies in the following agencies

Agency for the Cooperation of Energy Regulators (ACER)
Body of European Regulators for Electronic Communications (BEREC)
European Centre for the Development of vocational Training (CEDEFOP)
European Police College (CEPOL)
Community Plant Variety Office (CPVO)
European Aviation Safety Agency (EASA)
European Asylum Support Office (EASO)
European Banking Authority (EBA)
European Centre for Disease Prevention and Control (ECDC)
European Chemicals Agency (ECHA)
European Environment Agency (EEA)
European Fisheries Control Agency (EFCA)
European Food Safety Authority (EFSA)
European Institute for Gender Equality (EIGE)
European Insurance and Occupational Pensions Authority (EIOPA)
European Medicines Agency (EMA)
European Monitoring Centre for Drugs and Drug Addiction (EMCDDA)
European Maritime Safety Agency (EMSA)
European Network and Information Security Agency (ENISA)
European Railway Agency (ERA)
European Securities and Markets Authority (ESMA)
European Training Foundation (EFT)
European Agency for Safety and Health at Work (EU-OSHA)
European Foundation for the Improvement of Living and working Conditions (EUROFOUND)
European Union's Judicial Cooperation Unit (EUROJUST)

European Police Office (Europol)

European Fundamental Rights Agency (FRA)

European Agency for the Management of Operational Cooperation at the External Borders of the Member States of the European Union (FRONTEX)

European GNSS Supervisory Authority (GSA)

European Agency for the operational management of large-scale IT systems in the area of freedom, security and justice (EU-LISA)

Involvement of the European Parliament in the appointment of the director of the agency applies inter alia in the following agencies

---

European Agency for the operational management of large-scale IT systems in the area of freedom, security and justice (EU LISA), Art. 18 (2) of Reg. (EU) No 1077/2011

European Asylum Support Office (EASO), Art. 30 (1) of Reg. (EU) No 439/2010

European Aviation Security Agency (EASA), Art. 39 (1) of Reg. (EC) No 216/2008

European Banking Authority (EBA), Art. 51 (2) of Reg. (EU) No 1093/2010

European Centre for Disease Prevention and Control (ECDC), Art. 17 (2) of Reg. Art. 84 (1) of Reg. (EC) No 1907/2006

European Chemicals Agency (ECHA), Art. 84 (1) of Reg. (EC) No 1907/2006

European Food Safety Authority, Art. 26 (1) of Reg. (EC) No 178/2002

European Fundamental Rights Agency (FRA), Art. 15(2) of Reg. (EC) No 168/2007

European Institute for Gender Equality (EIGE), Art. 12(1) of Reg. (EC) No 1922/2006

European Insurance and Occupational Pensions Authority (EIOPA), Art. 51(2) of Reg. (EU) No 1094/2010

European Maritime Safety Agency (EMSA), Art. 16 (1) of Reg. (EC) No 1406/2002, as amended by Reg. (EU) No 100/2013

European Medicines Agency (EMA), Art. 64 (1) of Reg. (EC) No 726/2004

European Monitoring Centre for Drugs and Drug Addiction, Art. 11(2) of Reg. (EC) No 1920/2006

European Network and Information Security Agency (ENISA), Art. 24 (2) of Reg. (EU) No 526/2013

European Securities and Markets Authority (ESMA), Art. 51 (2) of Reg. (EU) No 1095/2010

Involvement of the European Parliament in nominating the Members of the Management Boards applies inter alia in the following agencies

---

European Centre for Disease Prevention and Control (ECDC), Art. 14 (1) of Reg. Art. 84 (1) of Reg. (EC) No 1907/2006

European Environment Agency, Art. 8 of Regulation (EC) No 401/2009

European Monitoring Centre for Drugs and Drug Addiction, Art. 9(1) of Reg. (EC) No 1920/2006
European Food Safety Authority, Art. 25 (1) of Reg. (EC) No 178/2002
European Medicines Agency (EMA), Art. 65 (1) of Reg. (EC) No 726/2004
European GNSS Supervisory Authority (GSA), Art. 5(2) of Reg. (EU) No 912/2010
European Environment Agency (EEA), Art. 8(1) of Reg. (EC) No 401/2009
European Chemicals Agency, (ECHA), Art. 79(1) of Reg. (EC) No 1907/2006

Appendix II

Joint Statement of the European Parliament, the Council of the EU and the European Commission on decentralised agencies

As in many Member States, EU decentralised agencies have become an established part of the way the EU operates. In 2011, thirty one decentralised agencies perform a wide range of important tasks, using a significant amount of resources: they contribute to the implementation of important Union policies, thus helping all the institutions, in particular the Commission, to concentrate on core policy-making tasks. Agencies also have a role in supporting the decision-making process by pooling the technical or specialist expertise available at European and national level and thereby help enhance the cooperation between Member States and the EU in important policy areas. Moreover, the spread of agencies beyond Brussels and Luxembourg adds to the visibility of the Union in the different Member States.

The establishment of agencies was done on a case by case basis and has not been accompanied by an overall vision of their role and place in the Union. Following the Commission Communication entitled "European agencies: the way forward"[1], addressed to the European Parliament and to the Council in March 2008, the three Institutions have recognised the important role of decentralised agencies in implementing the policies of the EU as independent legal entities and the need to make them a more effective tool in this respect. With a view to assessing the existing situation, specifically the coherence, effectiveness, accountability and transparency of these agencies, and finding common ground on how to improve their work, the European Parliament, the Council of the European Union and the European Commission have agreed to launch an inter-institutional dialogue on decentralised agencies leading to the creation of an Inter-Institutional Working Group (IIWG) in March 2009.

The IIWG has addressed a number of key issues put forward by the participating institutions, including the role and position of the agencies in the EU's institutional landscape, the creation, structure and operation of these agencies, together with funding, budgetary, supervision and management issues.

1 See COM(2008) 135.

The Common Approach in the annex is based on the conclusions reached by the IIWG on decentralised agencies. This Common Approach relates neither to agencies operating in the field of Foreign and Security Policy, nor to executive agencies.

The European Parliament, the Council of the European Union and the European Commission will refer to the Common Approach set out in the annex to this document. While fully acknowledging the legally non-binding character of this Joint Statement and of the Common Approach in its annex, and without prejudice to their attributions in the legislative and annual budgetary procedures, the institutions will take this Common Approach into account in the context of all their future decisions concerning EU decentralised agencies, following a case by case analysis.

In a political and economic context that is driven by the concern for efficiency gains, the three institutions urge decentralised agencies to pursue their efforts to streamline their activities and increase their performance by implementing those principles set out in the Common Approach which are within their remit.

Member States are also invited to create the conditions for decentralised agencies to operate as efficiently as possible by taking into account the elements of the Common Approach that relate to them.

Taking into account the specificities of each agency, the Commission should present a roadmap on the follow-up to the Common Approach with concrete timetables for the planned initiatives by the end of 2012 at the latest. The implementation of the roadmap should be done in cooperation with agencies whenever relevant. The Commission should inform the European Parliament and the Council regularly, and for the first time by the end of 2013, about progress on the implementation of the roadmap.

For the European Parliament:

Martin Schulz,
President of the European Parliament

For the Council of the EU:

Andreas D. Mavroyiannis,
Deputy Minister for European Affairs

For the European Commission:

Maroš Šefčovič,
Vice-President of the European Commission

1 9 JUIL. 2012

Common Approach

I. Role and position of agencies in the EU's institutional landscape

Definition and classification of agencies

1. To avoid confusion among citizens and stakeholders:

    - a standard term should be used for future agencies, "European Union agency for . . . "
    - aligning the names of existing agencies should be explored; however the costs that this would entail and the already established image of the agency should be taken into account.

Establishment and ending of agencies

2. The decision to create a new agency should be based on objective impact assessments of all relevant options. Models for standard provisions to be used in any founding act could be developed by the Commission in order to streamline the process.
3. It is important to manage in the best possible way the start-up phase of agencies, for which the Commission is responsible. To this end, the Commission should be empowered to take management measures, including the appointment, for a limited period, of seconded staff and of the interim Director (in principle a Commission official, although justified exceptions can be made).
4. Agencies' founding acts should contain either a sunset or a review clause. Whether a sunset clause or a review clause is the better solution should be decided on a case-by-case basis, taking into account the specificities of each agency. Any sunset clause must be accompanied by the concomitant provisions for disbanding the agency, addressing in particular issues related to staff contracts and budget arrangements.
5. Common and objective criteria should be used to assess both the opportunity to disband agencies or the possibility to merge them:

    - merging agencies should be considered in cases where their respective tasks are overlapping, where synergies can be contemplated or when agencies would be more efficient if inserted in a bigger structure.
    - closing down an agency could be a solution for dealing with underperforming agencies unless the agency is still the most relevant policy option, in which case the Agency should be reformed.

Agencies' seat and role of the host country

6. Without prejudice to the political decision on an agency's seat taken by common agreement between the representatives of the Member States meeting at Head of State or government level or by the Council, to the desirability of geographical spread, and to the objective set in December 2003 by the representatives of the Member States, meeting at head of State or government level (when deciding the seat of new agencies, priority should be given to new Member States):

    - the decision on the agency's seat should be taken before the end of the legislative process, in order to allow the agency to be set up directly in the location of its seat.
    - objective criteria to be taken into account in order to contribute to the decision making process for choosing an agency's seat may include:
        - the assurance that the agency can be set up on site upon the entry into force of its founding act,
        - the accessibility of the location,
        - the existence of adequate education facilities for the children of staff members,
        - appropriate access to the labour market, social security and medical care for both children and spouses,
    - Member States should address those criteria in a transparent way when presenting their offers to host an agency. The Commission is available to help assess the offers of the Member States, if necessary.

7. Concerning the specific criteria of accessibility:

    - Member States currently hosting an agency could consider if and how accessibility can be improved in order to increase agencies' overall efficiency and ensure an even better interaction with stakeholders
    - during agencies' regular evaluations, the accessibility to the agency could also be assessed.

8. The host State should make a formal commitment at the time of the adoption of the agency's founding act to ensure that all conditions necessary for the operation of the agency are in place by the time the agency starts its operational phase. In addition, it should commit itself to continue to respond to the agency's needs and provide the necessary conditions for the smooth operation of the agency, also after the latter has been set up.

9. All agencies should have headquarters agreements, which should be concluded before the agency starts its operational phase. Agencies still

lacking headquarters agreement and the host country in question should reach an agreement in accordance with the legal order of the relevant Member State. The Commission will put together a set of provisions on the basis of existing best practices, to serve as a good orientation tool for future headquarters agreements.

II. Structure and governance of agencies

Management Board

10. To improve the performance of agencies' boards and reinforce their capacity to supervise the administrative, operational and budgetary management of agencies, while guaranteeing full participation of the Member States and of the Commission:

- the composition of the board should be:
  - one representative from each Member State,
  - two representatives from the Commission without prejudice to the relevant arrangements for existing agencies,
  - where appropriate, one member designated by the European Parliament, without prejudice to the relevant arrangements for existing agencies,
  - where appropriate, a fairly limited number of stakeholders' representatives.
- members of the boards should be appointed in light of their knowledge of the agency's core business, taking into account relevant managerial, administrative and budgetary skills.
- the duration of the term of office of board members should be four years (renewable); all parties should increase efforts to limit turnover of their representatives in the boards, in order to ensure continuity of the boards' work.
- in order to streamline the decision making process in the agency and contribute to enhancing efficiency and effectiveness, a two-level governance structure should be introduced, when this promises more efficiency: in addition to the Management Board, giving general orientations for the agency's activities, a small-sized Executive Board, with the presence of a Commission representative, should operate and be more closely involved in the monitoring of the agency's activities, with a view to reinforcing supervision of administrative and budgetary management, in particular on audit matters.

11. A coherent policy on preventing and managing conflict of interests concerning members of the Management Board, whether or not they sit in personal capacity, should be developed and applied in all agencies.

12. In order to align it with the situation within the Institutions, the agency's Management Board should be given the powers of the Appointing Authority, not only for the Director but also for the rest of the staff. Except for the appointment of the Director, these competences should, however, be delegated to the Director and the board should only become involved on a case by case basis in exceptional circumstances.

13. For the sake of consistency, agencies' boards should in principle take decisions with the same voting rules:

    - absolute majority voting for current business matters
    - 2/3 majority for the appointment and dismissal of the director, the designation of the chairperson of the board, adoption of the annual budget and of the work programme. Exceptions to this approach can be foreseen, if justified in specific cases.

Director

14. Given the wide tasks attributed to Agencies' Directors by agencies' constituent acts, their role is crucial for agencies' governance, notably as regards the overall agencies' management and relationship towards EU institutions. They are responsible for the administrative management of the agencies, and for the implementation of the duties assigned to the agencies. In this framework, they are in particular in charge of the implementation of work programmes, budget and decisions taken by the Management Board and are a full management power concerning financial and staff matters. They are the legal representatives of the agencies.

15. Agencies' Directors are, first and foremost, accountable to their Management Board, to which they submit an annual report, including accounts. They are also accountable to the European Parliament and the Council for the use of the EU contribution through the annual discharge procedure. However, the discharge procedure focuses on accountability and regulatory compliance, rather than on performance per se. This is due, inter alia, to the lack of performance indicators. Agencies' Directors should therefore be more clearly accountable for performance. To this end, tailored performance indicators should be introduced allowing for effective assessment of the results achieved in terms of objectives.

16. To respect the autonomy of the agencies, it is up to the Management Board to appoint Directors on the basis of a shortlist drawn up by the Commission following an open and transparent selection procedure that guarantees a rigorous evaluation of candidates and a high level of independence. Exceptions to this approach can be foreseen if justified in specific cases.

17. Directors' terms of office are defined in Agencies' constituent acts. In those cases where the Director has performed well, the Management Board, acting as appointing authority, may decide to extend once his/her mandate. The opportunity is assessed against the evaluation of the Director's first mandate which takes into account both annual appraisal reports and foreseen requirements of the Agency for the next years. A director whose term of office has been extended should not participate in another selection procedure for the same post at the end of the overall period.

18. A coherent policy on preventing and managing conflict of interests concerning the Director should be developed and applied in all agencies. The Commission should examine, together with the agencies, whether there is scope for a harmonised approach.

19. A procedure should be foreseen for dismissing the Director in the event of misconduct, unsatisfactory performance or recurring/serious irregularities; it should mirror the appointment procedure.

Other internal bodies:

20. The functioning of scientific committees should be improved:

    - Agencies should exchange information on their experience with scientific committees and possibly contribute to developing a coordinated approach to common problems in this area. The Commission will provide support, as appropriate.

    - Selection procedures should be periodically reviewed, notably in the context of the agency's evaluations. The following elements should be assessed: their degree of transparency, their cost-effectiveness, and their suitability to ensure independence and competence of members of scientific committees and to prevent conflicts of interests.

    - The independence of the scientific experts should be fully ensured, inter alia by promoting the highest standards, setting sound selection criteria and promoting best practices. The Commission will provide guidelines on standards, criteria and best practice, including on how EU agencies' national counterparts should be involved. In addition, this issue should also be covered by the regular external evaluations of the agencies.

21. For Boards of appeal, the same measures as for scientific committees, notably in terms of exchange of best practice and assessment of selection procedures, should apply. The impartiality and independence of their members should continue to be guaranteed, on the basis of transparent and objectively verifiable criteria to be defined by agencies. In this context, recruitment of Board of Appeal's members from among the staff of the agency and/or the agency's Management Board should be taken with great care and should not put into question the above-mentioned principles of impartiality and independence.

22. Taking into account the importance of their contributions to the work of agencies' internal bodies, it is advisable that Member States regularly review the adequacy of resources/staff they assign for this purpose and take appropriate actions to remedy possible weaknesses. In addition, it is important that they ensure information flows between the different authorities concerned at national level in relation to agencies' activities, inter alia by appointing contact points in their national administrations for relations with the given agency. This contact point should be in principle the representative of the Member State sitting in the management board.

III. <u>Operation of agencies</u>

23. In order to deliver the administrative support that agencies need to operate in the most efficient manner, the following three options can be envisaged:

- improving or extending the services provided by the Commission
- merging smaller agencies to achieve economies of scale based on an impact assessment
- sharing services between agencies, either by proximity of locations or by policy area.

24. Concerning the creation or handling of EU classified information, agencies should apply a level of protection equivalent to that afforded by the security rules of the Council or the Commission, as appropriate:

- relevant provisions should be introduced in the founding acts. For existing agencies, agencies' Management Boards should adopt appropriate decisions as soon as possible, even before the founding acts are formally amended.
- the introduction of any new provisions on classified information should not be detrimental to the European Parliament's current right of access to agencies' information, nor imply the multiplication of bilateral agreements between the EP and EU bodies and agencies

25. Agencies' international relations should be streamlined:

- Agencies whose mandate or work programme foresees cooperation with third countries and/or international organisations should have a clear strategy for those activities. This strategy should, in principle, be embedded in the annual and/or multi-annual work programme(s), with a specification of associated resources, and should lay down a number of principles and modalities for international cooperation.
- This strategy and appropriate working arrangements with partner DGs in the Commission should ensure that the agencies operate within their mandate and the existing institutional framework, and that they are not seen as representing the EU position to an outside audience or as committing the EU to international obligations.
- The strategy and specific initiatives with an international dimension (e.g. administrative arrangements with third countries) should be subject to approval by the Management Board.
- An early exchange of information should take place on respective international activities between agencies, the Commission and the relevant EU Delegations, to ensure the consistency of EU policy.

26. Agencies should be entitled to engage in communication activities, within the following framework:

- the content and implementation of an agency's communication strategy should be coherent, relevant and coordinated with the strategies and activities of the Commission and the other institutions in order to take into consideration the broader EU image.
- ground rules for agencies' communication strategies will be developed by the Commission, in cooperation with the agencies.
- Communication activities should not be detrimental to agencies' core tasks.
- Agencies' access to central communication tools and coordination structures should be facilitated. Agencies should also be able to make use of Commission's framework contracts.

IV. Programming of activities and resources

Annual and multiannual work programmes

27. As far as possible, annual work programmes could be based on a template, in order to ease comparisons.

28. In addition to annual work programmes, agencies should draw up multiannual strategic programmes or guidelines, tailored to the specificities of their activities. Such multiannual activity planning should be linked with multiannual resource planning (budget and staff in particular).

29. The Commission should always be consulted and issue a formal advice on both documents. The European Parliament should be consulted on the multiannual work programmes of agencies, provided that the purpose of the consultations is an exchange of views and the outcome is not binding on the agency. For the annual work programme, the actual practice of the agency's Director presenting it to the relevant EP committee should continue.

30. Multi-annual work programmes should include the actions necessary to respond to the outcome of overall evaluations.

31. Key performance indicators should be developed by the agencies and the Commission and be adapted to agencies' specificities. Furthermore, the link between financial and human resources and each specific action to be carried out should be reinforced and become systematic. The link between successive annual work programmes and the multiannual programme should be enhanced.

32. The Director should report to the Management Board on the agency's progress in implementing the multiannual work programme. This reporting should take place prior to setting the objectives of the following annual work programme and be integrated in the reporting cycle on the annual work programme.

Human resources

33. While fully guaranteeing the respect of the principles of accountability and transparency, an effort should be made to simplify Agencies' human resources procedures and to better take into account their specificities in this field, to the extent necessary for ensuring their smooth functioning.

34. Agencies' Staff Policy Plans (SPP) should provide a full picture of their staff needs and therefore include comprehensive and detailed information on the number of all types of external staff, including interim staff and service providers; information on promotions, as well as gender and geographical balance should continue to be reflected. The smallest agencies should not be requested to provide the number of estimated promotions per grade, but only an overall figure, so as to avoid the early identification of individual promotions. The Commission, in cooperation with agencies, should make the necessary adjustments to the SPP template and consider potential other improvements to the SPP format.

35. Agencies' human resources programming as presented in the SPP and the preparation of the Draft Budget of the Union need to be consistent. The respective calendars of the presentation of the establishment plans and SPPs should therefore be aligned. The agencies should submit their draft SPPs and establishment plans to the Commission (and for information to the Management Board) by 31 January. Taking into account the Commission's reasoned opinion on the draft SPPs, agencies should adopt their final SPPs and submit them to the budgetary authority and the Commission by end May. For transparency purposes, agencies need to provide adequate explanations if they decide not to fully take into account the Commission's opinion on their draft SPP.

Funding, management of budgetary resources and budgetary procedure

36. Agencies should improve their internal planning and general revenue forecasting in order to reduce their high carry over and cancellation rates. The Commission will provide guidance in this regard. In addition, agencies should improve their management of commitments in order to align them with real needs.

37. For agencies fully financed from the EU budget, the surplus should continue to be recovered in the usual manner, i.e. unused funds from year n are deducted from the EU subsidy for year n+2, after recovery in year n+1.

38. For self-financed agencies, fees should be set at a realistic level to avoid the accumulation of significant surpluses.

39. For partially self-financed agencies, the clients should pay for the full cost of the services provided to them by those agencies, including the employer's prorata contribution to the pension scheme. Concerning the issue of how to deal with a possible shortfall against forecast of fee revenue from the clients and the need to ensure the availability of necessary funding to agencies, the Commission will investigate the necessity and possible modalities of creating a limited ring-fenced reserve fund to be operated in a transparent way.

40. All agencies should apply, more systematically than at present, a system of activity based budgeting/activity based management (ABB/ABM). The available ABB/ABM tools (i.e. to plan, monitor, report and evaluate activities) should be adapted to the reality of agencies. In this context, agencies should be encouraged to exchange best practice and their idea to develop an ABB/ABM toolbox is to be welcomed. The Commission will provide assistance in this regard, for instance by giving a general ABB training to agencies.

41. In order to avoid automatisms, all relevant actors should respect their duty, within the budgetary procedure, to provide adequate justification for their requests with regard to each agency's budget (initial budget request, increases, decreases).

42. In order to justify the need for additional (financial and/or human) resources in the case of agencies being in their "start-up phase" or agencies being entrusted with new tasks, a legislative financial statement should be presented to the legislative and budgetary authorities.

43. Should the legislative authority decide to assign additional tasks to agencies as compared to the initial Commission proposal, the reprioritization of their activities should always be considered as an alternative besides granting additional resources. In the latter case, the Commission will update previous legislative financial statements, so as to clarify the additional resources required by the agency in question to carry out such additional tasks. Subsequently, the revised legislative financial statement would be presented to a budgetary trilogue. The same procedure should apply to new agency's tasks which do not derive from a modification of the basic act of the agency.

44. Any modification to agencies' budgets which does not require the budget authority's approval should be communicated to the latter, together with adequate justification.

45. While respecting the principles of transparency, accountability and sound financial management, an effort should be made to simplify the implementation of the Financial Regulation rules by the Agencies, to the extent necessary for ensuring their smooth functioning.

V. Accountability, controls and transparency and relations with stakeholders

Reporting requirements

46. Agencies reporting obligations need to be streamlined and harmonized. In principle, agencies should produce one single Annual Report; exceptions should however be possible.

47. The single Annual Report should include information on the implementation of their annual work programme, budget and staff policy plan, management and internal control systems, internal/external audit findings, the follow-up to the audit recommendations and to the discharge recommendation, as well as the statement of assurance of the Executive Director. The single Annual Report could also include the information

resulting from the Financial Statements and from the report on budgetary and financial management foreseen in the context of the discharge procedure, provided the time constraints of the preparation of the EU annual consolidated accounts are respected.

48. As far as possible, the structure of the single Annual Report should include a number of common elements based on best practice across agencies, with a view to easing comparison. The Commission should develop an indicative template in cooperation with agencies.

49. This single Annual Report should be drawn by the agency's Director, who should present it to the agency's Management Board for assessment. The Director or the Board itself should then transmit the Report and the assessment of the Management Board to the Court of Auditors, to the Parliament and Council and to the Commission by 1 July.

Internal audit

50. The costs of basic Internal Audit Service (IAS) work should remain to be covered by the Commission. As basic audit work, IAS will undertake a risk assessment to maximise its coverage of major risks over a three-year cycle, maintaining, as far as possible, the current practice of one audit per year in each agency.

51. Internal audits have a clear added value and agencies need to accept the burden associated to them. To facilitate this acceptance, IAS should discuss its audit planning with agencies' management, in order to avoid an overlap of audit topics or calendar with audits from the Internal Audit Capabilities (IACs), when they exist, or from the European Court of Auditors (ECA).

52. The internal auditor shall continue to report to the executive director and to the management board. The appropriate follow-up of IAS audit conclusions should be organised at board level, possibly by the Executive Board if there is one. This should not increase administrative expenses.

53. Concerning the internal audit architecture of agencies, agencies should have the possibility to set up internal audit services to complement the work of the IAS. Therefore, Agencies (Executive Directors and Boards) may decide to set up an Internal Audit Capability (IAC) that follows internationally recognised standards of internal auditing and coordinate audit work and exchange information with IAS. If this is not cost-effective or possible, agencies may decide to contribute resources and share a full-fledged IAC with another agency. IACs should also be required to coordinate audit plans with the IAS.

External audit

54. Without prejudice to the competences of the European Court of Auditors (ECA), private sector auditors might have to be involved in the external audit of agencies accounts in order to remedy the lack of resources of the ECA. Should this be the case, the appointment of those private sector auditors should be done in conformity with the applicable rules and appropriate control mechanisms should be put in place, in order to ensure that work on the legality and regularity of revenue and expenditure and the reliability of an agency's accounts is carried out in accordance with the required standards. All aspects of such outsourced external audits, including the reported audit findings, remain under the full responsibility of the ECA, which manages all administrative and procurement procedures required and finances these, as well as any other costs associated with outsourced external audits, from its own budget.

55. Cooperation should continue to be promoted between all audit bodies involved, bearing in mind their respective mandate, purposes as well as their legal or regulatory bases.

Discharge

56. Agencies should systematically inform their partner Directorate General and the Directorate General for the Budget within the Commission of the results of the audit of the European Court of Auditors (at the earliest stage possible), as well as of the measures taken to meet the recommendations of the discharge authority and those of the Court.

57. A more rigorous differentiation between the responsibilities of the Commission and those of the agencies would be appropriate in discharge decisions and resolutions. Council's recommendations on the discharge of each agency should be fully taken into consideration.

58. The possibilities for securing democratic accountability for fully self-financed agencies (i.e. financed by their clients) should be explored, as they are Union bodies in charge of implementing EU policies but not subject to a discharge within the meaning of the TFUE. A possibility could be that the agencies in question, submit to the European Parliament, to the Council and to the Commission an annual report on the execution of their budget and consider requests or recommendations issued by the Parliament and Council.

Alert/warning system

59. An alert/warning system will be activated by the Commission if it has serious reasons for concern that an agency's Management Board is about to take decisions which may not comply with the mandate of the agency, may violate EU law or be in manifest contradiction with EU policy objectives. In these cases, the Commission will raise formally the question in the Management Board and request it to refrain from adopting the relevant decision. Should the Management Board set aside the request, the Commission will formally inform the European Parliament and the Council, with a view to allow the three institutions to react quickly. The Commission may request the Management Board to refrain from implementing the contentious decision while the representatives of the three institutions are still discussing the issue.

Evaluation of the agencies

60. Each agency's founding act should provide for a periodic overall evaluation, to be commissioned by the Commission. The first evaluation should take place five years after the agency has started its operational phase. Subsequent evaluations should be conducted every five years and on the occasion of every second evaluation the sunset/review clause should be applied. Evaluations should be conducted in a manner that provides solid grounds for a decision to continue or discontinue the agency's mandate. The feasibility of a common template for agencies' evaluation should be explored.

61. Ex-ante evaluation of agencies' activities/programmes should be either made mandatory for programmes/activities of a significant budget, or done at the request of the Management board or the executive board, if deemed necessary. Ex-post evaluation should be mandatory for all programmes/activities.

62. Agencies should prepare a roadmap with a follow-up action plan regarding the conclusions of retrospective evaluations, and report on progress bi-annually to the Commission. Follow-up to evaluations should be a task of the Management Board, and of the Executive Board if there is one.

63. In addition to the performance information presented in agencies' annual reports, the Commission should provide Parliament and Council with any other information on the evaluation of agencies if requested.

Transparency and relations with stakeholders

64. Agencies' websites should be made as multilingual as possible, in order to facilitate their consultation by citizens of all Member States. Agencies should provide, via their websites, information necessary to ensure transparency, including financial transparency.

65. Agencies' relations with stakeholders should be coherent with their mandate, the institutional division of tasks in international relations, EU policies and priorities and Commission's actions. Agencies should exercise their functions in coordination with the different actors charged with the definition and implementation of the given policy. Agencies should also clarify the sharing of roles between them and their national counterparts. When relevant stakeholders are not represented in management boards, they should be involved in agencies' internal bodies and/or advisory groups/working groups, if appropriate.

Prevention, detection and investigation of fraud, corruption, irregularities and other illegal activities

66. OLAF's role vis-à-vis agencies should be formalised, enhanced and made more visible. In order to preserve evidence and/or to avoid inadvertently alerting persons concerned, agencies should refrain from carrying out investigations on facts liable to lead to an investigation by OLAF, in conformity with relevant EU legislation. In addition, agencies should be more active in relation to fraud prevention and should also better communicate on those activities.

Appendix III

COUNCIL OF THE EUROPEAN UNION

Brussels, 4 April 2011

8640/11

PE-L 40
INST 192

COVER NOTE

from:	Mr. Jerzy BUZEK, President of the European Parliament
date of receipt:	4 April 2011
to:	Mr. János MARTONYI, President of the Council of the European Union
Subject:	Common Understanding on delegated acts

Delegations will find attached a letter from the President of the European Parliament on the subject.

Encl.: Letter

ЕВРОПЕЙСКИ ПАРЛАМЕНТ PARLAMENTO EUROPEO EVROPSKÝ PARLAMENT EUROPA-PARLAMENTET
EUROPÄISCHES PARLAMENT EUROOPA PARLAMENT ΕΥΡΩΠΑΪΚΟ ΚΟΙΝΟΒΟΥΛΙΟ EUROPEAN PARLIAMENT
PARLEMENT EUROPÉEN PARLAIMINT NA hEORPA PARLAMENTO EUROPEO EIROPAS PARLAMENTS
EUROPOS PARLAMENTAS EURÓPAI PARLAMENT IL-PARLAMENT EWROPEW EUROPEES PARLEMENT
PARLAMENT EUROPEJSKI PARLAMENTO EUROPEU PARLAMENTUL EUROPEAN
EURÓPSKY PARLAMENT EVROPSKI PARLAMENT EUROOPAN PARLAMENTTI EUROPAPARLAMENTET

The President
Mr János MARTONYI
President-in-Office
Council of the European Union
Rue de la Loi 175 305623 30.03.2011

B-1049 BRUSSELS

Dear President, *Dear János,*

As you are aware, Article 290(1) of the Treaty on the Functioning of the European Union (TFEU) confers upon the Commission the power to adopt non-legislative acts of general application to supplement or amend certain non-essential elements of a legislative act if this is explicitly defined in the latter.

After consultations between the Parliament, the Council and the Commission, the Conference of Presidents of the European Parliament approved the attached Common Understanding on practical arrangements for the use of delegated acts at its meeting on 3 March 2011. For the Parliament, the Common Understanding sets out the practical arrangements and agreed clarifications and preferences applicable to delegations of legislative power under Article 290 of the TFEU, with the main objective to offer a flexible framework offering minimum standards without limiting in any way the prerogatives of the co-legislators.

The Conference of Presidents also decided that an evaluation should be carried out of the Common Understanding after one year of operation, in order to monitor its functioning and, if deemed necessary, to initiate a revision of it with the Commission and the Council.

I look forward to receiving further information on the conclusion of your internal procedures for the approval of the Common Understanding so as to ensure that these practical arrangements can be introduced without undue delay.

Please note that I am sending a similar letter to Mr Jose Manuel BARROSO, President of the European Commission

Yours sincerely,

Jerzy Buzek

Encl.: Common Understanding on delegated acts

Common Understanding

I. Scope and general principles

1. Taking into account the commitments mentioned by the Commission in the communication of 9 December 2009, this Common Understanding builds further on that communication and streamlines the practice established thereafter by the European Parliament and the Council. It sets out the practical arrangements and agreed clarifications and preferences applicable to delegations of legislative power under Article 290 of the Treaty on the Functioning of the European Union (TFEU), in accordance with the objectives, content, scope and duration of a delegation must be expressly defined in each legislative act making a delegation (hereinafter "the basic act").
2. In exercising their powers and in compliance with the procedures laid down in the TFEU, the three Institutions shall cooperate throughout the procedure with a view to a smooth exercise of delegated power and an effective control of this power by the European Parliament and the Council. To this effect, appropriate contacts at administrative level shall be established.
3. The Institutions concerned, depending on the procedure for the adoption of the basic act, undertake to refer as far as possible to the standard clauses annexed to this Common Understanding when proposing or making delegations of power under Article 290 TFEU.

II. Consultations in the preparation and drawing-up of delegated acts

4. The Commission, when preparing and drawing up delegated acts, will ensure a simultaneous, timely and appropriate transmission of relevant documents to the European Parliament and the Council and carry out appropriate and transparent consultations well in advance, including at expert level. The European Parliament and the Council shall indicate to the Commission their respective functional mailboxes to be used for the transmission of documents relating to these consultations.

III. Arrangements for the transmission of documents and computation of time periods

5. By way of an appropriate mechanism, the Commission shall officially transmit the delegated acts to the European Parliament and the Council. Classified documents shall be processed in accordance with internal administrative procedures drawn up by each institution with a view to providing all the requisite guarantees.

6. In order to ensure that the European Parliament and the Council are able to exercise the rights provided for in Article 290 TFEU within the time limits laid down in each basic act, the Commission shall not transmit any delegated acts during the following periods:

   - From 22 December until 6 January.
   - From 15 July until 20 August.

   These periods shall only apply when the period of objection is based on paragraph 10.

   These periods shall not apply for delegated acts adopted under the urgency procedure, as set out in part VI of this Common Understanding. In the event that a delegated act is adopted under the urgency procedure during these periods, the time limit for objection provided for in the basic act shall start to run only when this period is finished.

   The three institutions shall agree by 1 October 2013 on an arrangement for the notification of delegated acts during the European Elections in 2014.

7. The period for expressing objections shall start when all official language versions of the delegated act have been received by the European Parliament and the Council.

IV. Duration of the delegation

8. The basic act may empower the Commission to adopt delegated acts for an undetermined or determined period of time.
9. Where a determined period of time is provided, the basic act should in principle provide for the delegation of power to be tacitly extended for periods of an identical duration, unless the European Parliament or the Council opposes the extension not later than three months before the end of each period. The Commission shall draw up a report in respect of the delegated power not later than nine months before the end of each period. This paragraph does not affect the European Parliament or the Council's right of revocation.

V. Periods for objection by the European Parliament and Council

10. Without prejudice to the urgency procedure, the period for objection defined on a case-by-case basis in each basic act should in principle be of two months, and not less than that, extendable by two months at the initiative of the European Parliament or the Council.
11. However, the delegated act may be published in the *Official Journal of the European Union* and enter into force before the expiry of that period if the European Parliament and the Council have both informed the Commission that they will not object.

VI. Urgency procedure

12. An urgency procedure should be reserved for exceptional cases, such as security and safety matters, the protection of health and safety, or external relations, including humanitarian crises. The European Parliament and the Council should justify the choice of an urgency procedure in the basic act. The basic act shall specify the cases in which the urgency procedure shall be used.
13. The Commission undertakes to keep the European Parliament and the Council fully informed about the possibility of a delegated act being adopted under the urgency procedure. As soon as the Commission services foresee such a possibility, they shall informally forewarn the secretariats of the European Parliament and the Council via the functional mailboxes mentioned in point 4.
14. A delegated act adopted under the urgency procedure shall enter into force without delay and apply as long as no objection is expressed within the period provided for in the basic act. If an objection is expressed, the Commission shall repeal the act without delay following the notification by the European Parliament or the Council of the decision to object.
15. When notifying a delegated act under the urgency procedure to Parliament and the Council, the Commission shall state the reasons for its use.

VII. Publication in the Official Journal

16. Delegated acts shall be published in the L series of the *Official Journal of the European Union* only after the expiry of the period for objection, with the exception of paragraph 11 above. Delegated acts adopted under the urgency procedure shall be published without delay.
17. Without prejudice to Article 297 TFEU, decisions by the European Parliament or Council to revoke a delegation, to object to a delegated act adopted under the urgency procedure or to oppose the tacit renewal of a delegation of power shall also be published in the L series of the *Official Journal of the European, Union*. A decision to revoke shall enter into force the day following its publication of the decision in the *Official Journal of the European Union*.
18. The Commission shall also publish in the *Official Journal of the European Union* the decisions repealing delegated acts adopted under the urgency procedure.

VIII. Mutual exchange of information, in particular in the event of a revocation

19. When exercising their rights in applying the conditions laid down in the basic act, the European Parliament and the Council will inform each other and the Commission.

20. When either the European Parliament or the Council initiates a procedure which could lead to the revocation of a delegation, it will inform the other two institutions at the latest one month before taking the decision to revoke.

Annex: standard clauses

Recital:

In order to [objective], the power to adopt acts in accordance with Article 290 of the Treaty on the Functioning of the European Union should be delegated to the Conimission in respect of [content and scope]. It is of particular importance that the Commission carry out appropriate consultations during its preparatory work, including at expert level.

The Commission, when preparing and drawing-up delegated acts, should ensure a simultaneous, timely and appropriate transmission of relevant documents to the European Parliament and Council.

Article(s) delegating power

The Commission shall be empowered to adopt delegated acts in accordance with Article a concerning *[content and scope].*

Supplementary paragraph to be added where urgency procedure applies:

Where, in the case of *[content and scope],* imperative grounds of urgency so require, the procedure provided for in Article b shall apply to delegated acts adopted pursuant to this Article.

Article a
Exercise of filelegation

1. The power to adopt delegated acts is conferred on the Commission subject to the conditions laid down in this Article.
2. *[duration]*

   Option 1:
   The delegation of power referred to in Article[s] shall be conferred on the Commission for an indeterminate period of time from the (*)

   Option 2:
   The delegation of power referred to in Article[s] . . . shall be conferred on the Commission for a period of X years from the (*). The Commission shall draw up a report in respect of the delegation of power not later

than nine months before the end of the X-year period. The delegation of power shall be tacitly extended for periods of an identical duration, unless the European Parliament or the Council opposes such extension not later than three months before the end of each period.

Option 3:
The delegation of power referred to in Article[s] . . . shall be conferred on the Commission for a period of X years from the (*)

(*) date of entry into force of the basic legislative act or from any other date set by the legislator.

3. The delegation of power referred to in Article[s] . . . may be revoked at any time by the European Parliament or by the Council. A decision of revocation shall put an end to the delegation of the power specified in that decision. It shall take effect the day following the publication of the decision in the *Official Journal of the European Union* or at a later date specified therein. It shall not affect the validity of any delegated acts already in force.
4. As soon as it adopts a delegated act, the Commission shall notify it simultaneously to the European Parliament and to the Council.
5. A delegated act adopted pursuant to Article[s] . . . shall enter into force only if no objection has been expressed either by the European Parliament or the Council within a period of [2 months] of notification of that act to the European Parliament and the Council or if before the expiry of that period, the European Parliament and the Council have both informed the Commission that they will not object. That period shall be extended by [2 months] at the initiative of the European Parliament or the Council.

Supplementary article to be added where urgency procedure applies:

Article b
Urgency procedure

1. Delegated acts adopted under this Article shall enter into force without delay and shall apply as long as no objection is expressed in accordance with paragraph 2. The notification of a delegated act to the European Parliament and to the Council shall state the reasons for the use of the urgency procedure.
2. Either the European Parliament or the Council may object to a delegated act in accordance with the procedure referred to in Article a (5). In such a case, the Commission shall repeal the act without delay following the notification of the decision to object by the European Parliament or the Council.

Bibliography

Adamski D, 'How wide is "the widest possible"'? Judicial interpretation of the exceptions to the right of access to official documents revisited' (2009) 46 (2) *Common Market Law Review*, pp. 521–549.

Albors-Llorens A, 'The standing of private parties to challenge Community measures: Has the European Court missed the boat?' (2003) 62 (1) *Cambridge Law Journal*, pp. 72–92.

Alemanno A and Meuwese A, 'Impact assessment of EU non-legislative rulemaking: The missing link in "new comitology"' (2013) 19 (1) *European Law Journal*, pp. 76–92.

Alfe M, 'Institutional tensions in the evolution of the comitology system', in Christiansen T and Oettel TJ and Vaccari B, *21st Century Comitology: The Role of Implementing Committees in the Wider European Union* (European Institute of Public Administration 2009), pp. 52–70.

Arnull A, 'Introduction: The EU's accountability and legitimacy deficit', in Arnull A and Wincott D, *Accountability and Legitimacy in the EU* (Oxford University Press 2003).

Arnull A, 'Editorial: April shower for Jégo-Quéré' (2004) 29 (3) *European Law Review*, pp. 287–288.

Balthasar S, 'Locus standi rules for challenges to regulatory acts by private applicants: The new art. 263(4) TFEU' (2010) 35 (4) *European Law Review*, pp. 542–550.

Bast J, 'New categories of acts after the Lisbon reform: Dynamics of parliamentarization in EU law' (2012) 49 (3) *Common Market Law Review*, pp. 885–928.

Bebr G, 'Direct and indirect judicial control of Community acts in practice: The relation between Arts 173 and 177 of the EEC Treaty' (1984) 82 (5, 6) *Michigan Law Review*, pp. 1229–1249.

Behn R, *Rethinking Democratic Accountability* (Brooking Institution Press 2001).

Benz A, 'Special issue: Accountability in EU multilevel governance' (2007) 13 (4) *European Law Journal*, pp. 505–522.

Bergström CF, *Comitology: Delegation of Powers in the European Union and the Committee System* (Oxford University Press 2005).

Best E, 'Transparency and European governance: Clearly not a simple matter', in Deckmyn V, *Increasing Transparency in the European Union* (European Institute of Public Administration 2002), pp. 91–118.

Blom-Hansen J, 'The EU comitology system: Taking stock before the new Lisbon regime' (2011) 18 (4) *Journal of European Public Policy*, pp. 607–617.

Blom-Hansen J, *The EU Comitology System in Theory and Practice: Keeping an Eye on the Commission?* (Palgrave Macmillan 2011).

Blom-Hansen J, 'Legislative control of powers delegated to the Executive: The case of the EU' (2013) 26 (3) *Governance*, pp. 425–488.

Blom-Hansen J and Brandsma GJ, 'The EU comitology system: Intergovernmental bargaining *and* deliberative supranationalism?' (2009) 47 (4) *Journal of Common Market Studies*, pp. 719–740.

Böhling K, 'Sidelined member states: Commission-learning from experts in the face of comitology' (2014) 36 (2) *Journal of European Integration*, pp. 117–134.

Borras S, Koutalakis C and Wendler F, 'European agencies and input legitimacy: EFSA, EMEA and EPO in the post-delegation phase' (2007) 29 (5) *Journal of European Public Policy*, pp. 583–600.

Bovens M, 'Analysing and assessing accountability: A conceptual framework' (2007) 13 (4) *European Law Journal*, pp. 447–468.

Bovens M, Curtin D and Hart P, *The Real World of EU Accountability, What Deficit?* (Oxford University Press 2010).

Brandsma GJ, 'Accountability deficits in European "comitology" decision-making' (2011) 11 (4) *European Integration Online Papers*, pp. 1–15.

Brandsma GJ, 'The effect of information on oversight: The European Parliament's response to increasing information on comitology decision-making' (2012) 78 (1) *International Review of the Administrative Sciences*, pp. 74–92.

Brandsma GJ, *Controlling Comitology: Accountability in a Multi-Level System* (Palgrave Macmillan 2013).

Brandsma GJ, 'Comitology: Over 50 years of institutional reforms and emerging practices', in Bauer M and Trondal J (eds), *The Palgrave Handbook on the European Administrative System* (Palgrave MacMillan 2015), pp. 419–431.

Brandsma GJ, 'Holding the European Commission to account: The promise of delegated acts' (2015) Published online, International Review of the Administrative Sciences.

Brandsma GJ and Blom-Hansen J, 'Negotiating the post-Lisbon comitology system: Institutional battles over delegated decision-making' (2012) 50 (6) *Journal of Common Market Studies*, pp. 939–957.

Brandsma GJ and Blom-Hansen J, 'Controlling delegated powers in the post-Lisbon European Union' (2015) 23 (4) *Journal of European Public Policy*, pp. 531–549.

Brandsma GJ, Curtin D and Meijer A, 'How transparent are EU "comitology" committees in practice?' (2008) 14 (6) *European Law Journal*, pp. 819–838.

Bromberg M, 'Access to documents: A general principle of Community law' (2002) 27 (2) *European Law Review*, pp. 194–205.

Brunmayr H, 'The Council's policy on transparency', in Deckmyn V and Thomson I, *Openness and Transparency in the European Union* (European Institute of public Administration 1998).

Bunyan T, *Secrecy and Openness in the European Union* (Kogan Page 1999).

Bunyan T, 'Secrecy and openness in the European Union: The ongoing struggle for freedom of information', available at www.statewatch.org/secret/freeinfo/index.html, accessed 28 January 2016.

Busuioc M, 'Accountability, control and independence: The case of European agencies' (2009) 15 (5) *European Law Journal*, pp. 599–615.

Busuioc M, Curtin D and Groenleer M, 'Agency growth between autonomy and accountability: The European police office as a "living institution"' (2011) 18 (6) *Journal of European Public Policy*, pp. 848–867.

Cabral P, 'Access to Member State documents in EC law' (2006) 31 (3) *European Law Review*, pp. 378–389.

Chiti E, 'The emergence of a community administration: The case of European agencies' (2000) 37 (2) *Common Market Law Review*, pp. 309–343.

Christiansen T and Dobbels M, 'Non-legislative rule making after the Lisbon Treaty: Implementing the new system of comitology and delegated acts' (2013) 19 (1) *European Law Journal*, pp. 42–56.

Christiansen T, Oettel JM and Vaccari B (eds), *21st Century Comitology. Implementing Committees in the Enlarged European Union* (The European Institute of Public Administration 2009).

Committee of Independent Experts, *First Report on Allegations regarding Fraud, Mismanagement and Nepotism in the European Commission* (1999).

Committee of Independent Experts, *Second Report on Reform of the Commission: Analysis of Current Practice and Proposals for Tackling Mismanagement, Irregularities and Fraud* (1999).

Corona D, 'The adoption of secondary legislation through comitology in the EU: Some reflections on the Regulation (EU) 182/2011 in comparison with the pre-Lisbon reform' (2014) 2 (1) *The Theory and Practice of Legislation*, pp. 85–107.

Costa M and Peers S, 'Beware of courts bearing gifts' (2016) 91 (16) *Nederlands Juristenblad*, pp. 1107–1116.

Craig P, 'Democracy and rulemaking within the EC: An empirical and normative assessment' (1997) 3 (2) *European Law Journal*, pp. 105–130.

Craig P, 'Standing, rights, and the structure of legal argument' (2003) 9 (4) *European Public Law*, pp. 493–508.

Craig P, 'The constitutionalization of community administration' (2003) New York University School of Law, Jean Monnet Working Paper 3/03, available at www.jeanmonnetprogram.org/papers/03/030301.pdf, accessed 10 May 2010.

Craig P, *EU Administrative Law* (Oxford University Press 2006).

Craig P, 'The role of the European Parliament under the Lisbon Treaty', in Griller S and Ziller J (eds), *The Lisbon Treaty: EU Constitutionalism without a Constitutional Treaty?* (Springer 2008), pp. 109–134.

Craig P, *The Lisbon Treaty: Law Politics and Treaty Reform* (Oxford University Press 2010).

Craig P, 'Integration, democracy and legitimacy', in Craig P and De Burca G (eds), *The Evolution of EU Law* (2nd edn, Oxford University Press 2011).

Craig P, 'Delegated acts, implementing acts and the new comitology regulation' (2011) 36 (5) *European Law Review*, pp. 671–687.

Craig P, 'Comitology, rulemaking and the Lisbon settlement: Tensions and strains', in Bergström CF and Ritleng D (eds), *Rulemaking by the Commission: The New System* (Oxford University Press 2016), pp. 173–204.

Curtin D, 'Betwixt and between: Democracy and transparency in the governance of the European Union', in De Witte B et al., *Reforming the Treaty on European Union: The Legal Debate* (Brill 1996), pp. 95–130.

Curtin D, 'The fundamental principle of open decision-making and EU (political) citizenship', in O'Keeffe D and Twomey P, *Legal Issues of the Amsterdam Treaty* (Hart Publishing 1999), pp. 71–92.

Curtin D, 'Citizens' fundamental right of access to EU information: An evolving digital passepartout?' (2000) 37 (1) *Common Market Law Review*, pp. 7–41.

Curtin D, 'Delegation to EU non-majoritarian agencies and emerging practices of public accountability', in Gerardin et al., *Regulation through Agencies in the EU: A New Paradigm of European Governance* (Edward Elgar 2005), pp. 88–119.

Curtin D and Meijers H, 'The principle of open government in Schengen and the European Union: Democratic retrogression?' (1995) 32 (2) *Common Market Law Review*, pp. 391–442.

Curtin D and Nollkaemper A, 'Conceptualizing accountability in international and European law' (2005) 36 *Netherlands Yearbook of International Law*, pp. 3–20.

Cygan A, 'Democracy and accountability in the European Union: The view from the House of Commons' (2003) 66 (3) *Modern Law Review*, pp. 384–401.

Cygan A, 'Protecting the interests of civil society in Community decision-making: The limits of Art. 230 EC' (2003) 52 (4) *International and Comparative Law Quarterly*, pp. 995–1012.

Davies A, *Accountability: A Public Law Analysis of Government by Contract* (Oxford University Press 2001).

Davis RW, 'Public access to community documents: A fundamental human right?' (1999) 3 *European Integration Online Papers*, pp. 1–14.

Davis RW, 'The Court of Justice and the right of public access to Community-held documents' (2000) 25 (3) *European Law Review*, pp. 303–309.

Dehousse R, Pasarin AF and Plaza J, 'How consensual is comitology? (2014) 21 (6) *Journal of European Public Policy*, pp. 842–859.

Dehousse R, 'Delegation of powers in the European Union: The need for a multi-principals model' Centre d' etudes européennes de sciences Po, available at chairemadp.sciences-po.fr/pdf/seminaires/2007/Contribution_Renaud_DEHOUSSE.pdf, accessed 13 May 2010.

De Leeuw M, 'The regulation on public access to EP, Council and Commission Documents in the European Union: Are citizens better off?' (2003) 28 (3) *European Law Review*, pp. 324–348.

De Witte B, 'Legal instruments and law-making in the Lisbon Treaty', in Griller S and Ziller J (eds), *The Lisbon Treaty: EU Constitutionalism without a Constitutional Treaty* (Springer 2008), pp. 79–108.

Diamandouros N, 'Contribution of the European Ombudsman to the public hearing on the revision of Regulation 1049/2001 on public access to documents', speech delivered in the EP on 2 June 2008.

Dordi C and Forganni A, 'The comitology reform in the EU: Potential effects on trade defence instruments' (2013) 47 (2) *Journal of World Trade*, pp. 359–389.

Driessen B, 'Access to Member State documents in EC law: A comment' (2006) 31 (6) *European Law Review*, pp. 906–911.

Driessen B, 'Delegated legislation after the Treaty of Lisbon: An analysis of Article 290 TFEU' (2010) 35 (6) *European Law Review*, pp. 837–848.

Dubnick M, 'Seeking salvation for accountability' (2002) Paper presented at the annual meeting of the American Political Science Association, Boston Marriott Copley Place, Sheraton Boston & Hynes Convention Centre, Boston, MA.

Dyrberg P, 'Current issues in the public debate on access to documents' (1999) 24 (2) *European Law Review*, pp. 157–170.

ec.europa.eu/transparencyregister/public/, accessed 29 January 2016.

ec.europa.eu/transparency/regexpert/, accessed 1 February 2016.

Editorial: 'EU leaders strike deal on reform treaty' (2007) *EU Focus*.

Editorial Comments, 'What should replace the Constitutional Treaty?' (2007) 44 (3) *Common Market Law Review*, pp. 561–566.

Enchelmaier S, 'No-one slips through the net? Latest developments, and non-developments, in the European Court of Justice's jurisprudence on Art. 230(4) EC' (2005) 24 (1) *Yearbook of European Law*, pp. 173–221.

EP resolution (INI/2010/2021) of 5 May 2010.

europa.eu/legislation_summaries/glossary/comitology_en.htm, accessed 10 August 2015.

European Parliament Press Release, available at: www.europarl.europa.eu/sides/getDoc.do?language=EN&type=IMPRESS&reference=20100406STO72095, accessed 30 January 2016.

Everson M, 'Independent agencies: Hierarchy beaters?' (1995) 1 (2) *European Law Journal*, pp. 180–204.

Everson M et al., 'European agencies within the treaties of the European Union', in Majone G, *The Role of the Specialised Agencies in Decentralising EU Governance* (Report presented to the Commission 1999).

Fisher E, 'The EU in the age of accountability' (2004) 24 (3) *Oxford of Journal Legal Studies*, pp. 495–515.

Flanagan A, 'EU freedom of information: Determining where the interest lies' (2007) 13 (4) *European Public Law*, pp. 595–730.

Flinders M, 'Distributed public governance in the European Union' (2004) 11 (3) *Journal of European Public Policy*, pp. 520–544.

Flogaitis S and Pottakis A, 'Judicial protection under the Constitution' (2005) 1 (1) *European Constitutional Law Review*, pp. 108–111.

Frost A, 'Restoring faith in government: Transparency reform in the United States and the EU' (2003) 9 (1) *European Public Law*, pp. 87–104.

Garcia De Enterria E, 'The extension of jurisdiction of national administrative courts by the Community law: The judgment of the Court of Justice in Borelli and Art. 5 of the EC Treaty' (1993) 13 (1) *Year Book of European Law*, pp. 19–37.

Georgiev V, 'Too much executive power? Delegated lawmaking and comitology in perspective' (2013) 20 (4) *Journal of European Public Policy*, pp. 535–551.

Gerardin D and Petit N, 'The development of agencies at EU and national levels: Conceptual analysis and proposal for reform' (2004) Jean Monnet Working Paper 01/04, available at centers.law.nyu.edu/jeanmonnet/papers/04/040101.pdf, accessed 15 June 2010.

Grant RW and Keohane RO, 'Accountability and abuses of power in world politics' (2005) 99 (1) *American Political Science Review*, pp. 29–43.

Guggenbuhl A, 'A miracle formula or an old powder in new packaging? Transparency and openness after Amsterdam', in Deckmyn V and Thomson I (eds), *Openness and Transparency in the European Union* (European Institute of Public Administration 1998), pp. 9–38.

Harden I, 'Citizenship and information' (2001) 7 (2) *European Public Law*, pp. 165–193.

Harding C, 'The impact of Art 177 of the EEC Treaty on the review of Community action' (1981) 1 (1) *Year Book of European Law*, pp. 93–113.

Harlow C, 'Towards a theory of access for the European Court of Justice' (1992) 12 (1) *Year Book of European Law*, pp. 213–248.

Harlow C, *Accountability in the European Union* (Oxford University Press 2002).

Harlow C, 'European governance and accountability', in Bamforth N and Leyland P (eds), *Public Law in a Multi-layered Constitution* (Hart 2003).

Harlow C and Rawlings R, 'Promoting accountability in multilevel governance: A network approach' (2007) 13 (4) *European Law Journal*, pp. 542–562.

Heliskoski J and Leino P, 'Darkness at the break of noon: The case law on Regulation No. 1049/2001 on access to documents' (2006) 43 (3) *Common Market Law Review*, pp. 735–781.

Heritier A, Moury C, Bischoff C and Bergstrom CF, *Changing Rules of Delegation: A Contest for Power in Comitology* (Oxford University Press 2012).

Hofmann H, 'Legislation delegation and implementation under the Treaty of Lisbon: Typology meets reality' (2009) 15 (4) *European Law Journal*, pp. 482–505.

Hofmann H and Toeller A, 'Democracy and the reform of comitology', in Mads A and Turk A, *Delegated Legislation and the Role of Committees in the EC* (Kluwer Law International 2000).

House of Lords, Select committee on the European Communities, *Delegation of Powers to the Commission: Reforming Comitology* (2 February 1999), 3rd Report. 2 February 1999, available at www.google.co.uk/url?sa=t&rct=j&q=&esrc=s&source=web&cd=1&ved=0ahUKEwjgltyM7cbNAhWJKMAKHWYvDaEQFggcMAA&url=http%3A%2F%2Fwww.publications.parliament.uk%2Fpa%2Fld199899%2Fldselect%2Fldeucom%2F23%2F2302.htm&usg=AFQjCNEl2Jb9Lcw7PCMQNk_-bTTzw9alAA&sig2=k8iBav08feEsnBGk4LZ5cQ, accessed 30 June 2016.

Joerges C and Neyer J, 'Transforming strategic interaction into deliberative problem-solving: European comitology in the food stuff sector' (1997) 4 (4) *Journal of European Public Policy*, pp. 609–625.

Joerges C and Vos E, *EU Committees: Social Regulation, Law and Politics* (Hart 1999).

Kaeding M and Hardacre A, 'The European Parliament and the future of comitology after Lisbon' (2013) 19 (3) *European Law Journal*, pp. 382–403.

Kaeding M and Stack KM, 'Legislative scrutiny? The political economy and practice of legislative vetoes in the European Union' (2015) 53 (6) *Journal of Common Market Studies*, pp. 1268–1284.

Kierkegaard S, 'Open access to public documents: More secrecy, less transparency!' (2009) 25 (1) *Computer Law and Security Report*, pp. 3–27.

Kiewiet R and McCubbins M, *The Logic of Delegation, Congressional Parties and the Appropriation Process* (University of Chicago Press 1991).

Koch C, 'Locus standi of private applicants under the EU Constitution: Preserving gaps in the protection of individuals' right to an effective remedy' (2005) 30 (4) *European Law Review*, pp. 511–527.

Kranenborg H, 'Is it time to revise the European regulation on public access to documents?' (2006) 12 (2) *European Public Law*, pp. 251–274.

Kranenborg H, 'Access to documents and data protection in the European Union: On the public nature of personal data' (2008) 45 (4) *Common Market Law Review*, pp. 1079–1114.

Kranenborg H and Voermans W, *Access to Information in the European Union: A Comparative Analysis of EC and Member State Legislation* (Europa Law Publishing 2005).

Kreher A, 'Agencies in the European Community: A step towards administrative integration in Europe' (1997) 4 (2) *Journal of European Public Policy*, pp. 225–245.

Larsson T, *Precooking in the European Union – The World of Expert Groups* (Fritzes Offentliga Publikationer 2003).

Leino P, 'Just a little sunshine in the rain: The 2010 case law of the European Court of Justice on access to documents' (2011) 48 (4) *Common Market Law Review*, pp. 1215–1252.

Lenaerts K, 'Regulating the regulatory process: "Delegation of powers" in the European Community' (1993) 18(1) *European Law Review*, pp. 23–49.

Lord C, 'The hidden public sector: The "Quangocratization" of the world', in Kaufmann G, Majone G and Ostrom V, *Guidance, Control and Evaluation in the Public Sector* (de Gruyter 1986).

Lord C, *Democracy in the European Union* (Sheffield Academic Press 1998).

Mack R, 'Lobbying effectively in Brussels and Washington: Getting the right result' (2005) 9 (4) *Journal of Communication Management*, pp. 339–347.

Majone G, 'The new European agencies: Regulation by information' (1997) 4 (2) *Journal of European Public Policy*, pp. 262–275.

Majone G, 'The agency model: The growth of regulation and regulatory institutions in the European Union' (1997) 3 (1) *Eiascope, Journal of the European Institute for Public Administration*, pp. 6–14.

Majone G, 'The new European agencies: Regulation by information' (1997) 4 (2) *Journal of European Public Policy*, pp. 262–275.

Majone G, 'Functional interests: European agencies', in Shackleton M, *The Institutions of the European Union* (Oxford University Press 2002), pp. 299–325.

Mancini F and Keeling D, 'Democracy and the European Court of Justice' (1994) 57 (2) *Modern Law Review*, pp. 175–190.

Mendes J, 'Delegated and implementing rule making: Proceduralisation and constitutional design' (2013) 19 (1) *European Law Journal*, pp. 22–41.

Moe T, 'Interests, institutions and positive theory: The politics of NLRB' (1987) 2 (1) *Studies in American Development*, pp. 236–299.

Moncrieffe JM, 'Accountability: Ideals, ideas, constraints' (2001) 8 (3) *Democratization*, pp. 26–50.

Moore M and Gates M, *Inspectors-General: Junkyard Dogs or Man's Best Friend?* (Russel Sage Foundation 1986).

Mulgan R, 'Accountability: An ever-expanding concept?' (2000) 78 (3) *Public Administration*, pp. 555–573.

Mulgan R, *Holding Power to Account, Accountability in Modern Democracies* (Palgrave Macmillan 2003).

Neuhold C, 'Taming the "Trojan horse" of comitology? Accountability issues of comitology and the role of the European Parliament' (2008) 12 (1) *European Integration Online Papers*, pp. 1–16.

No 10 Bulletin of the European Communities (1993).

Norgaard RW, Nedergaard P and Blom-Hansen J, 'Lobbying in the EU comitology system' (2014) 36 (5) *Journal of European Integration*, pp. 491–507.

Normanton E, *The Accountability and Audit of Governments: A Comparative Study* (Manchester University Press 1996).

Oberg U, 'Public access to documents after the entry into force of the Amsterdam Treaty: Much ado about nothing?' (1998) 2 (8) *European Integration Online Papers*, pp. 1–27.

Oberg U, 'The EU citizens' right to know: The improbable adoption of a European Freedom of Information Act' (1999) 2 (1) *Cambridge Yearbook of European Legal Studies*, pp. 303–328.

Oliver D, *Government in the United Kingdom: The Search for Accountability, Effectiveness and Citizenship* (Open University Press 1991).

Osborne D and Gaebler T, *Reinventing Government: How the Entrepreneurial Spirit is Transforming the Public Sector* (Plume 1992).

Osterdahl I, 'Openness v. secrecy: Public access to documents in Sweden and the European Union' (1998) 23 (4) *European Law Review*, pp. 336–356.

Peers S, 'The new regulation on access to documents: A critical analysis' (2001) 21 (1) *Yearbook of European Law*, pp. 385–442.

Peers S, 'From Maastricht to Laeken: The political agenda of openness and transparency in the EU', in Deckmyn V, *Increasing Transparency in the European Union* (European Institute of Public Administration 2002).

Peers S and Costa M, 'Accountability for delegated and implementing acts after the Treaty of Lisbon' (2012) 18 (3) *European Law Journal*, pp. 427–460.
Peers S and Costa M, 'Judicial review of EU Acts after the Treaty of Lisbon' (2012) 8 (1) *European Constitutional Law Review*, pp. 82–104.
Peers S and Costa M, 'Accountability for EU decentralized agencies: Mind the independence gap' (forthcoming) *European Public Law*.
Penny L, 'News: How accessible is it? An examination of the public's right to access information in the European Union' (2007) 18 (1) *Entertainment Law Review*, pp. 1–6.
Ponzano P, '"Executive" and "Delegated" Acts: The situation after the Lisbon Treaty', in Griller S and Ziller J (eds), *The Lisbon Treaty: EU Constitutionalism without a Constitutional Treaty?* (Springer 2008).
Power M, *The Audit Society, Rituals of Verification* (Oxford University Press 1997).
Puntscher Riekmann S, 'In search of lost norms: Is accountability the solution to the legitimacy problems in the European Union?' (2007) 5 (1) *Comparative European Politics*, pp. 121–137.
Ragnemalm H, 'The Community courts and openness within the European Union' (1999) 2 *Cambridge Yearbook of European Legal Studies*, pp. 19–30.
Rambøll Management, Euréval and Matrix, 'Evaluation of the EU decentralised agencies in 2009' (2009) *Final Report*: Volume I, Volume II, Volume III, Volume IV.
Roche D, *Accountability in Restorative Justice* (Oxford University Press 2003).
Schedler A, 'Conceptualizing accountability', in Schedler A, *The Self-Restraining State: Power and Accountability in New Democracies* (Lynne Rienner Publishers 1997).
Schusterschitz G and Kotz S, 'The comitology reform of 2006: Increasing the powers of the European Parliament without changing the Treaties' (2007) 3 (1) *European Constitutional Law Review*, pp. 68–90.
Schütze R, '"Delegated" legislation in the (new) European Union: A constitutional analysis' (2011) 74 (5) *Modern Law Review*, pp. 661–693.
Scott C, 'Accountability in the regulatory state' (2000) 27 (1) *Journal of Legal Studies*, pp. 38–60.
Shapiro M, 'The problems of independent agencies in the United States and the European Union' (1997) 4 (2) *Journal of European Public Policy*, pp. 276–277.
Slaughter AM, 'The accountability of government networks' (2001) 8 (2) *Indiana Journal of Global Legal Studies*, pp. 347–367.
Soderman J, 'The role and impact of the European Ombudsman in access to documentation and transparency of decision-making', in Deckmyn V and Thomson I, *Openness and Transparency in the European Union* (European Institute of Public Administration 1998).
Stack KM, 'The irony of oversight: Delegated acts and the political economy of the European Union's legislative veto under the Treaty of Lisbon' (2014) 2 (1) *The Theory and Practice of Legislation*, pp. 61–84.
The Report (616/PUHAB/F/IHJ), available on the website of the European Ombudsman, www.euro-ombudsman.eu.int, accessed 1 February 2016.
Tomkins A, 'Transparency and the emergence of a European administrative law' (1999) 19 (1) *Yearbook of European Law*, pp. 217–256.
Treaty of Nice, *Declaration on the Future of the Union* No 23.
Türk A, 'Transparency and comitology', in Demmke C and Engel C, *Continuity and Change in the European Integration Process* (European Institute of Public Administration 2003).
Van Ballaert B and Delreux T, 'Preparing comitology in commission expert groups: Reducing duration or minimizing contestation?' (2015) Unpublished working paper available through researchgate.net, accessed 20 February 2016.

Van Gerven W, 'Which form of accountable government for the EU?' (2005) 36 (3) *Netherlands Yearbook of International Law*, pp. 227–258.

Van Ooik R, 'The growing importance of agencies in the EU: Shifting governance and the institutional balance', in Curtin D et al., *Good Governance and the European Union. Reflections on Concepts, Institutions and Substance* (Intersentia 2005).

Vesterdorf B, 'Transparency: Not just a vague word' (1999) 22 (3) *Fordham International Law Journal*, pp. 902–929.

Voermans W, Hartmann JM and Kaeding M, 'The quest for legitimacy in EU secondary legislation' (2014) 2 (1) *The Theory and Practice of Legislation*, pp. 5–32.

Vos E, 'The rise of committees' (1997) 3 (3) *European Law Journal*, pp. 210–229.

Vos E, 'Reforming the European Commission: What role to play for EU agencies?' (2000) 37 (5) *Common Market Law Review*, pp. 1113–1134.

Ward A, *Judicial Review and the Rights of Private Parties in EU Law* (Oxford University Press 2007).

Wessels W, 'Comitology: Fusion in action. Politico-administrative trends in the EU system' (1998) 5 (2) *Journal of European Public Policy*, pp. 209–234.

Wincott D, 'Looking forward or harking back? The Commission and the reform of governance in the European Union' (2001) 39 (5) *Journal of Common Market Studies*, pp. 897–911.

Yataganas X, 'Delegation of regulatory authority in the EU: The relevance of the American model of independent agencies' (2004) Jean Monnet Working Paper 3/01, available at www.jeanmonnetprogram.org.paper/01/010301.html, accessed 20 July 2010.

Zilioli C, 'Accountability and independence: Irreconcilable values or complementary instruments for democracy? The specific case of the European Central Bank' in Vandersanden G, *Melanges en hommage a Jean-Victor Louis* (Editions de I'Université de 2003).

Index

Only cases and regulations discussed within the body of the book have been included in the index. They have been indexed so that the entry term matches the way that the text refers to them.
Page numbers followed by 'n' and 'app' refer to notes and appendix entries respectively.

For Product Safety Concerns and Information please contact our EU representative GPSR@taylorandfrancis.com
Taylor & Francis Verlag GmbH, Kaufingerstraße 24, 80331 München, Germany

www.ingramcontent.com/pod-product-compliance
Ingram Content Group UK Ltd.
Pitfield, Milton Keynes, MK11 3LW, UK
UKHW011016180926
475701UK00004B/779

9780367595944